The
Fastest Bicycle Rider in the World

The True Story of America's First Black World Champion

Major Taylor

Foreword by Ayesha McGowan

Introduction by Adonia E. Lugo, PhD

Microcosm Publishing
Portland, OR

The Fastest Bicycle Rider in the World: The True Story of America's First Black World Champion

© Ayesha McGowan, 2023
© Adonia Lugo PhD, 2023
This Edition © Microcosm Publishing 2023
This Edition First Published January 10, 2023

ISBN 9781648411328
This is Microcosm #504
Cover by Matt Gauck
Book design by Joe Biel

To join the ranks of high-class stores that feature Microcosm titles, talk to your local rep: In the U.S. COMO (Atlantic), FUJII (Midwest), BOOK TRAVELERS WEST (Pacific), TURNAROUND (Europe), UTP/MANDA (Canada), NEW SOUTH (Australia/New Zealand), GPS in Asia, Africa, India, South America, and other countries, or FAIRE in the gift trade.

For a catalog, write or visit:
Microcosm Publishing
2752 N Williams Ave.
Portland, OR 97227
www.Microcosm.Pub/FastestBicycle

Microcosm Publishing is Portland's most diversified publishing house and distributor with a focus on the colorful, authentic, and empowering. Our books and zines have put your power in your hands since 1996, equipping readers to make positive changes in their lives and in the world around them. Microcosm emphasizes skill-building, showing hidden histories, and fostering creativity through challenging conventional publishing wisdom with books and bookettes about DIY skills, food, bicycling, gender, self-care, and social justice. What was once a distro and record label started by Joe Biel in a drafty bedroom, was determined to be Publisher's Weekly's fastest growing publisher of 2022 and has become among the oldest independent publishing houses in Portland, OR and Cleveland, OH. We are a politically moderate, centrist publisher in a world that has inched to the right for the past 80 years.

Did you know that you can buy our books directly from us at sliding scale rates? Support a small, independent publisher and pay less than Amazon's price at www.Microcosm.Pub

This book was originally self-published in 1928 as a 460 page edition. Chapters 13, 21-26, 30-32, 34, 43, 50-56, 61-63, 66-69, and 71-89 from the original have been removed and simplified to increase cohesion and readability.

Global labor conditions are bad, and our roots in industrial Cleveland in the 70s and 80s made us appreciate the need to treat workers right. Therefore, our books are MADE IN THE USA.

Library of Congress Cataloging-in-Publication Data
Names: Taylor, Major, 1878-1932, author.
Title: The fastest bicycle rider in the world : a Black boy's indomitable
   courage and success against great odds / by Marshall W. Taylor (author)
   ; foreword by Adonia E. Lugo
Description: New Edition. | [Portland] : Microcosm Publishing, [2023] |
   Summary: "Born in 1878, bicycle racer Marshall "Major" Taylor became the
   first Black sports star to become a global celebrity when he won the
   world cycling championship in 1899. Throughout his bike-racing career,
   he won awards and set records on and off the track. But in his native
   United States, he faced racist discrimination and violence at every
   turn, causing him to spend most of his time in Europe where fans saw his
   vale. After he retired from racing, he wrote and published his
   autobiography and traveled the world promoting it. Written in the 1920s,
   his story feels fresh, contemporary, and readable. His life was too
   short, but his legacy lives on in the many organizations and clubs that
   bear his name, and generations of new cyclists who look up to him. His
   intelligence, good humor, and global perspective shine through on every
   page in this candid account of a remarkable life. This new edition
   features a foreword by bicycle advocate Adonia Lugo, author of Bicycle /
   Race"-- Provided by publisher.
Identifiers: LCCN 2022013926 | ISBN 9781648411328 (Trade Paperback)
Subjects: LCSH: Taylor, Major, 1878-1932. | Cyclists--United
   States--Biography. | African American athletes--United
   States--Biography. | Bicycle racing--History. | Discrimination in
   sports--United States.
Classification: LCC GV1051.T3 A3 2023 | DDC 796.6092 [B]--dc23/eng/20220825
LC record available at https://lccn.loc.gov/2022013926

Foreword to the 2023 Edition

There are so many folks in this world with the potential to do great things, but only a small percentage of people find themselves in the right circumstances to achieve the highest levels of success. Much like Major Taylor, "a freak of fate" set me on a path that I could not deny was for me, and the instant gratification of early successes lit a fire in me that has yet to be extinguished.

It all started when I was living in Brooklyn and finally coming around the idea of getting into road racing. I was trying to find the necessary gear, but I didn't have a ton of money. I saw a Facebook post for free cycling shoes and in the process made the acquaintance of William Montgomery, a prominent Black cyclist and experienced road racer in New York City. Beyond hooking me up with a free pair of shoes, Montgomery saw how excited I was about getting into road racing, offered to coach me, and helped me find a road bike. Although I'd barely done any road racing, he convinced me to show up to the state championships because he thought I would have fun. He also told me if I won, I'd get a free shirt! Without his enthusiasm and support, I would never have gone to that race, won that championship jersey, or set my sights on the Women's World Tour—achieving my goal of becoming the first African American woman professional road cyclist.

Since that race, it was an incredibly long journey to my first World Tour contract. One thing that really struck me when I first started racing was the lack of representation for women of color in the peloton. I was determined to forge a path not just for myself but for other women of color who might stumble into the sport. After my first season of racing, I was struggling to figure out what direction to go in when I learned about a mentorship program started by professional bike racer, Amber Pierce. She was partnering aspiring professional athletes with current professional athletes. Amber has been an incredible resource of knowledge and information for me over the years, and it was through her that I met several professional cyclists that I could trust to help guide me when I found myself lost.

I was also fortunate to befriend Randy Locklair, another NYC local who was determined to support women's racing. I pitched the idea of traveling and racing around the US in the summer of 2016. Not only did he help fund the entire thing, he helped me design the beginnings of the A Quick Brown Fox brand and assisted me in finding equipment sponsors. He supported me with his money, his time, and his word, which gave me legitimacy in the eyes of sponsors I wouldn't have had on my own. I would continue to race anywhere and everywhere I could for about six years until I found myself in the right circles with the right people. Gradually, with the right combination of results and networking, I made it to the WorldTour in 2022 as a rider for Liv Racing Xstra.

Major Taylor also benefited from having a supportive inner circle of co-conspirators that encouraged him early on and told him what he needed to hear in order for him to set and achieve big goals. These folks had his back in ways that allowed him to navigate obstacles with both the resources necessary to compete and in finding the connections and opportunities that allowed him to keep progressing.

I appreciate that Taylor also saw the necessity in always being a good sport yet managed to maintain a set of non-negotiable principles. I feel this deeply in my soul in that there are just some things that cannot be compromised. By being unwilling to accept punishment for choosing not to be bullied by racist competitors, racist promoters, and other racist community members, he set a foundation for folks like me to build upon for the next generation. Oftentimes, Black people are taught to stay in our place and accept responsibility for some fictional inherent inferiority that comes with being Black. Taylor knew this was ridiculous over a century ago, and I'm glad he did.

We both faced many challenges and transgressions in our careers, some because of our race and some not. Without a close network of folks who truly believed in us, neither of us would have made it as far as we were able to.

Most important, in my opinion, is that Taylor understood the value in paying it forward and sharing his wisdom and knowledge with aspiring up-and-comers. If there is anything I hope folks take away from this story, it is that it was a fairly consistent stream of support and opportunity that kept him going.

Taylor's talent and hard work are a given, and inspiring to read about, but what's essential for all of us to remember is that none of our stories can, or do, happen in a vacuum. We must cultivate and contribute to communities of support, mentorship, and allyship—how else will we ever show the world what we can do?

—Ayesha Rosena Anna McGowan,
Professional Road Racing Cyclist, Activist, and Advocate

Introduction: Major Taylor's Centuries

The movie opens with the sounds of cheering and a black screen. A caption appears: Madison Square Garden, Winter 1896. Then the picture begins, and we see the wooden ellipse of a bicycle track laid out around the perimeter of the show floor. Seating climbs the walls, and naked bulbs line the soaring rafters. Pennants, flags, and ads for bicycle businesses hang overhead. People in fine clothes fill the stands. A young man, racing clothes hugging a physique molded by years of relentless training, enters the track on his wheel. It's the half-mile handicap race. Our protagonist is eighteen years old and a well-known rider in this era when bicycle racing is a serious spectator sport in the United States. He is a five-year veteran of the amateur racing circuit, which is wired against him. Not because he lacks skill, dedication, or spirit but because Major Taylor is a Black man. Jealousy and contempt from white riders and their backers chase him in every race—but they do not keep him from the two hundred dollar prize today. He wires the money home to his mother in Indianapolis.

Scenes like this are just made for cinema, aren't they? Yet the racism that shaped our twentieth-century media machines limited the kinds of stories that could be told in widely-distributed books and movies, instead giving us truckloads of narratives following white men on quests to satisfy their egos or libidos. There is a surplus of all the Others' stories—and then there are those stories that were recorded but shamefully ignored and those that can only be recovered through research. Major Taylor's story is in the former category: he knew his story was worth telling, so he wrote it down.

When Taylor's memoir was ready to share in 1928, either no publisher was interested or he chose not to seek one, and he self published the book. It has languished for nearly a century, mostly circulated among cycling enthusiasts. Taylor's sport had long been out of the spotlight in the U.S. by 1928. Velodromes and racing tracks had disappeared, and this country's obsession with the automobile made the bicycle a lot more accessible—but decidedly second-class. But there's no griping about the loss of cheering audiences in his book. Instead, he shares an American tale about a boy from a working family in Indianapolis. Hardscrabble roots? Check. Unexpected boost from a wealthy protector? Check. Finding a passion and working his tail off to succeed against the odds? Yup. Yet because he was a Black man, Taylor faced challenges that the white readers of Horatio Alger and other writers of bootstraps stories would have been conditioned to ignore.

His wealthy protectors were the parents of a white child who effectively rented little Marshall as a playmate for their son. This arrangement introduced the bicycle, considered a gentleman's toy, into a Black boy's late nineteenth-century story. The odds against Taylor were stacked by white people who first mocked him for riding a bicycle and then for being better at it than every other racer. There was nothing fair or sportsmanlike about the menacing threat of physical harm that snapped at Taylor's heels. To Taylor, his story "proves to the world...that there are positively no mental, physical, moral or other attainments too lofty for a Negro to accomplish if granted a fair and equal opportunity." He used his exceptional talent to argue for the ordinary humanity of his maligned people. Bicycle racing happened to be the medium through which Taylor argued that any Black person has similar potential for excellence.

I learned about Major Taylor around 2011, a pivotal year for my own thinking about bicycles and race (my specialty). By then, bicycles had made a resurgence for some of us: the wheel was decades into being a symbol of a human-scaled future, an antidote to the poison of myriad industrial complexes. It was the fun machine that messengers use to dance through traffic in alleycat races and the center of Critical Mass rides across the world. In my city, Los Angeles, the bicycle was at the center of city night rides bringing together all kinds of people for what academics like me call flânerie (urban exploration). The bicycle, in 2011, was also a poor man's vehicle, with frames and parts piled up next to makeshift homes under freeway overpasses, though its image was already undergoing gentrification by this time. I'd been participating in bicycle projects as an anthropologist for three years by then, and I was starting to grasp how bicycle movements tend to express racial and class segregation more than they disrupt it.

Then, in the winter of 2011, I moved to the Pacific Northwest, and in the dark, rainy days, I grasped that those we don't see in our present are absent from the past we imagine and the future we plan. I missed the Latinx vibe that had been part of L.A.'s multiracial bike scenes, since it shapes so much public space in Southern California. Up north, I felt out of place as a mixed-race woman whose Indigenous Mexican genes show up more clearly than the European ones. On nostalgic bike rides, white people dressed for Major Taylor's glory days, reinventing the 1890s as a golden age of bicycling before the auto industry destroyed egalitarian streets, never mind the racism that lived and breathed in the era of separate but equal. Taylor writes about the fear that rode alongside him as he pedaled a lonely stretch of race road, suddenly aware of his vulnerability. He couldn't count on the protection of racing institutions such as the League of American Wheelmen, which barred Black members in 1896. This was cycling in the 1890s.

I started writing online about the contradictions I saw and learned that some white cycling enthusiasts felt compelled to silence people of color who spoke about the racism they encountered on bikes and in bike spaces. In Seattle and Portland, I found established bicycle cultures whose practitioners were deeply invested in proselytizing bicycle gospel to the whole country but who had little interest in hearing truth that contradicted their white worldviews. I was obsessed with shifting our transportation habits, too, but they told me I was a troublemaker for narrating the relationships I saw between how we move and our racialized power divides. Without recognizing the toll it took on me, I started to feel embattled.

The anxiety was instructive, though. Away from the multiracial Chicano and Asian-Am culture of Southern California, it was easier for me to witness the exclusion of Black communities from white spaces. Black bicycle realities get distorted through a white savior lens; middle-class Black individuals' reluctance to ride bicycles, exposed, through whitening neighborhoods policed by white supremacist cops, is pathologized as something white planners could and should fix through pressuring transportation agencies and elected officials to adopt Northern European street designs such as separated bike lanes. The utility of these infrastructure designs get obscured when they become symbols of white cluelessness, of willful denial of all the other factors that put white people on top in public space. Many white people are trained not to see the work they demand of non-whites to hold them up; even the ones who go to planning school to study infrastructure ignore the segregationist underpinnings to their city ideals.

In 2013, Hamzat Sani and Carolyn Szczepanski brought me into contact with the League of American Bicyclists, the successor organization to the League of American Wheelmen that figured into Taylor's 1890s story. White supporters had considered this organization important enough to revive multiple times over the twentieth century, so that it brought its racist legacy into the twenty-first. They lifted the color bar officially in 1999, more than a century after their membership voted to put it in place. The organization felt too hostile, so I moved away from it with others and created a space for mobility justice, focusing on the unsafeties such as what Taylor experienced, as a man treated like a subhuman by white supremacists. These unsafeties plague all kinds of mobilities, not just bicycling; the immobility of non-white refugees forced from home by war and hunger; the immobility of so, so many Black and brown bodies held in cages; the forced mobility of families who cannot remain in place as gentrification puts their neighborhoods into the hands of people who benefited from the racialized wealth gap that white supremacy created and still upholds.

I got to tell my story in a 2018 book, *Bicycle / Race*, and I have been invited to speak on these topics in many cities. I feel like my space to speak as a witness should get smaller so that the space for others to speak from experience can expand. Case in point: I don't navigate the world in a Black body. I've mapped Taylor's early separation from his own family and placement in a wealthy white child's nursery onto my own mestizaje, guessing at some of the complicated ways he must have felt. When I read Taylor's memoir, analytical words like "gaslighting" and "codeswitching" come to mind. His experiences of being desired yet disrespected provoke mental outrage emojis. Like in 1898 at Cape Girardeau, Missouri, where a hotelier and race organizer lured him under false promises of equal treatment. When Taylor was barred from staying at the hotel lodging the white racers, he decided to leave town. The race organizers stopped him on a train platform and threatened to get him thrown out of racing if he did not compete in their event. (Taylor got on the train anyway.) Or how in that same year, the *Cycling Gazette* noted that, "It is, of course, a degradation for a white man to contest any point with a Negro. It is even worse than that, and becomes an absolute grief and social disaster when the Negro persistently wins out in the competitions." I relate to Taylor's memoir as an example of a phenomenon I have witnessed and narrated, not as my own story and scars. I think the time has come, though, that we should all be able to recognize the hostilities he navigated as a Black human being, whether we have faced them or not. As fellow travelers or allies, let's make visible the hate flung his way and appreciate that Taylor still won the day.

The Fastest Bicycle Rider in the World should have been a victory lap, but no matter how fast he rode, Major Taylor couldn't escape what he called "that color business." Because of this, the memoir often sounds like a quest to prove that he really did win all those races, that he really was that great. I don't know what path the movie would take through Major Taylor's life, because this would need to be a Black-written, Black-directed, Black-produced film. Lived experience matters in creating a sensitive representation of tragedy and triumph. I just know that it's time to affirm what Taylor experienced. Until 2024, we're in what the U.N. named the International Decade for People of Black Descent. Decade, heck— let's go for a Black century.

—Adonia Lugo, Urban Anthropologist and Mobility Justice Strategist

Foreword

These reminiscences, covering the most colorful chapter in all the history of bicycle racing, among other remarkable facts, brings out very clearly many of the outstanding qualities characteristic of my race, such as perseverance, courage, and that marvelous spirit of forgiveness.

It also proves to the world literally, that there are positively no mental, physical, moral or other attainments too lofty for a Negro to accomplish if granted a fair and equal opportunity. The records and success that I achieved in my chosen line of athletic sports, certainly the greatest of all if played fair, and the brilliant performances of other colored athletes in various branches of the sports where permitted to compete will verify this somewhat emphatic assertion.

The primary object of this narrative, however, is not for any personal glory, or self praise but rather to perpetuate my achievements on the bicycle tracks of the world, for the benefit of all youths aspiring to an athletic career, and especially boys of my own group as they strive for fame and glory in the athletic world.

A perusal of the following autobiography and chronologically arranged news clippings will reveal many of the secrets of my great success, notwithstanding the tremendous odds and almost tragic hardships that I was forced to do extra battle against owing to color prejudice and jealousy of the bitterest form. With the aid of the press, however, the strict application to the rules of training, and the help of God, I was able to overcome that bitter intensity of feeling to some extent, or sufficiently at least to accomplish my life's greatest objective, namely, "The Fastest Bicycle Rider in the World."

Judging by the manner in which colored athletes have repeatedly demonstrated their skill and prowess in the athletic world, it is quite obvious what might well be accomplished on a whole as a race in other pursuits of life if granted a square deal and a fair field. We ask no special favor or advantage over other groups in the great game of life; we only ask for an even break.

I am writing my memoirs, however, in the spirit calculated to solicit simple justice, equal rights, and a square deal for the posterity of my down-trodden but brave people, not only in athletic games and sports, but in every honorable game of human endeavor.

How I Started Riding

(1891)

A freak of fate started me on what was destined to be my racing career which was climaxed by my becoming champion of the world when I was only twenty-two years of age. Born in Indianapolis, November 26, 1878, I was one of eight children, five girls and three boys. When I was eight years old my father was employed by a wealthy family in that city named Southard, as a coachman. Occasionally my father would take me to work with him when the horses needed exercising, and in time I became acquainted with the rich young son Daniel, who was just my age.

We soon became the best of friends, so much so in fact, that I was eventually employed as his playmate and companion. My clothing was furnished and we were kept dressed just alike all the time. "Dan" had a wonderful play room stacked with every kind of toy imaginable, but his work shop was to me the one best room in the whole house, and when there I was the happiest boy in the world.

The rest of "Dan's" playmates were of wealthy families too, and I was not in the neighborhood long before I learned to ride a bicycle just as they did. All the boys owned bicycles excepting myself, but "Dan" saw to it that I had one too. I soon became a big favorite among them, perhaps because of my ability to hold up my end in all the different games we played, such as baseball, tennis, football, roller-skating, running and cycling, trick riding, and all the rest.

There was only one thing, though, that I could not beat them at, and that was when we went down to the Young Men's Christian Association gymnasium. It was there that I was first introduced to that dreadful monster prejudice, which became my bitterest foe from that very same day, and one which I have never as yet been able to defeat. Owing to my color, I was not allowed to join the Y. M. C. A., and in consequence was not permitted to go on the gymnasium floor with my companions. The boys protested to their parents about it, but they, even with their powerful influence, were unable to do anything about it, consequently I could only watch the other boys from the gallery go through their callisthenics, and how my poor little heart would ache to think that I was denied an opportunity to exercise and develop my muscles in the same manner as they, and for really no reason that I was responsible for. However, I made the best of matters knowing that I could beat them on the campus.

Some time later the Southard family moved to Chicago, and because my mother could not bear the idea of parting with me, I dropped from the happy life of a "millionaire kid" to that of a common errand boy, all within a few weeks.

Not satisfied with having this bicycle all to myself I decided to become a trick rider. It will be well to remember at this point that in those days bicycles held the same relative position that the automobile occupied a generation ago. That meant that in reality I was a pioneer in this trick-riding field, and had to teach myself. However, the same perseverance that later played such a prominent part in my successful career on the bicycle track evidenced itself while I was a barefoot boy. After long hours practicing I became a pretty fair trick rider and to my skill along this line I attribute my initial appearance in a bicycle race when I was thirteen years old.

It came about in this way. I went to the bicycle store owned by Hay & Willits in Indianapolis, to get a minor repair made on my machine. After the repair had been made I made a fancy mount on my bicycle in the middle of the store and immediately drew the attention of Mr. Hay. He asked me who taught me that trick, and when I replied myself he smiled doubtfully. I told Mr. Hay that that was one of my easiest tricks and that I had a number of others that I would like to show him if he was interested. He was, and he ordered the store cleared to a certain extent and I did a number of my homemade tricks for him and his guests of the occasion that made them fairly gasp. In fact the exhibition was so good that Mr. Hay, his mind ever alert for good advertising for his store, invited me to repeat them in the street in front of his place of business. In a short time there was so much congestion on the spot that the police were called to open it up for traffic.

Going into the store later on Mr. Hay's invitation he asked me how I would like to go to work for the firm. I told him I was peddling a paper route and earning $5.00 a week at it, and that, of course, I would expect a little more for my services if my mother would allow me to work for him. My eyes nearly popped out of my head when he said, "I will give you that $35.00 bicycle and $6.00 a week if you will come to work for me. I told him I would consult my mother and let him know shortly. I went to work for him in the course of a few days.

My first duty in the store every morning was to sweep and dust, but every afternoon at four I was booked to give an exhibition of trick and fancy riding in my nice new uniform out in the street in front of the store. At the time there was a gold medal on exhibition in one of our show windows, the first prize for the annual ten-mile road race which was promoted by my employers, and which was one of the outstanding sporting events of Indianapolis. I spent more time daily fondling that medal than I did wielding the duster. It seemed to me like that would probably be the only chance that I would have to be near such a valuable prize. I recall clearly being so bold one day as to pin the medal on the lapel of my coat and strut with it for five minutes in front of the mirror.

However, it was in the books that within a comparatively short time that medal was to be all my own—the reward of my first victory in a bicycle race. My entry into this event was an accident pure and simple. I had gone out to witness the event, which attracted the cream of the amateur riders of Indiana, and had taken a vantage point near the start when Mr. Hay spotted me. Thinking to inject a laugh into the race for the benefit of the thousands that lined the course, Mr. Hay insisted that I take my place on the starting line. I rebelled, but he fairly dragged me and my bicycle across the road saying, "Come on here, young man, you have got to start in this race." I was badly scared at the thought as one may well imagine since I had never seen a bicycle race before.

Although the band was playing a lively tune and the crowd was cheering wildly I was crying. When Mr. Hay saw that he started to lift me from my wheel, but stopped and whispered in my ear, "I know you can't go the full distance, but just ride up the road a little way, it will please the crowd, and you can come back as soon as you get tired."

Crack! went the pistol, and with tears in my eyes I was off with a fifteen minute handicap on the scratch man. There were hundreds of cyclists stretched along the route, and it seemed to be a friendly sort of cheer and one that encouraged me and inspired me to keep on going even after I had begun to feel very tired. Those words telling me that I could turn back after going a short distance inspired me on when it seemed like fatigue was about to overtake me. They made me all the more determined to show my employer that I could go the distance. As I pedalled along the seemingly endless route I felt sure my knees had been torn out of their sockets by my pedals, but I was determined to cover the entire distance no matter how long it took.

After I had ridden some distance I noticed a group of riders coming to meet me. As they drew closer I recognized Mr. Hay among them. He had the gold medal that was hung up for first prize and dangled it in front of my eyes as we rode along. As he did so he informed me that I was a mile ahead of the field and had half of the distance left to go. The thought flashed through my mind that I had a chance to own that medal which I had so many times pinned on myself in the store. The sight of it seemed to give me a fresh start, and I felt as though I had only just begun the race. The thought of that gold medal becoming my property spurred me on to my greatest efforts.

The act on Mr. Hay's part was the psychological turning point of the race for me. From then on I rode like mad and wobbled across the tape more dead than alive in first place about six seconds ahead of the scratch man, Walter Marmon. Incidentally this same Walter Marmon is president of the Marmon Automobile Co. today.

Once across the finishing line I collapsed and fell in a heap in the roadway. Kind hands revived me shortly and I recall clearly that the first thing I saw on regaining consciousness was that big gold medal pinned on my chest. I had been through a nerve-racking, heart-breaking race, my legs pained me terribly, but I felt amply repaid for my efforts as I scanned that medal. My first thought was to take it home and show it to my mother. Fast as I had ridden that race I rode with greater speed to my home. My mother laughed and cried in turn as I related the incident of my first race. And one may well imagine my enthusiasm as I told her about the race, as I was but thirteen years old at the time.

When Fear Paced Me to Victory

(1893)

My next race was in Peoria, Illinois, in the summer of 1892, an event for boys under sixteen. I was fourteen at the time. Although I did not win the race, I was third, but the kindly manner of the public toward me created a lasting impression in my mind. Little did I imagine then that the next time I appeared on this track that I would be greeted as the Champion of America and it is a safe bet that nobody else imagined so. Thanks to the encouragement given me on that occasion I continued striving towards championship honors, and was elated several years later to be able to return to Peoria as champion sprinter of America.

Peoria was the Mecca of bicycle racing in those days. On its historical track all of the fastest riders in the world struggled for fame and glory. Among the most noted of them were: Zimmerman, Windle, Van Sicklen, Lumsden, Munger, Spooner, Githens, Stone, Temple, Davis, Thorne, Dernberger, Barrett, Kinsley and Hollinsworth, in fact that galaxy of stars participated in the feature event of the program which included the race for boys under sixteen in which I rode.

I clearly recall seeing one of the racers in that meet, William Laurie, participating on his racing machine which was equipped with the first pneumatic tires ever ridden in a bicycle race in this country. Hitherto all racers had their wheels equipped with solid rubber tires as pneumatics had not been perfected up to that time. Hoots and jeers greeted Laurie throughout the afternoon as he blazed the trail for the use of pneumatic tires, which revolutionized bicycle racing, and the manufacture of bicycles simultaneously. Shortly came the cushion tires and soon thereafter the self same pneumatic tires that Laurie demonstrated so well that day came into common use on the bicycle tracks in the country.

The following spring I went to work for H. T. Hearsey, a bicycle dealer in Indianapolis. My principle occupation was giving bicycle lessons, although I also did general work about the store.

While in the employ of Mr. Hearsey I won a number of races, the most important one being a 75-mile road race from Indianapolis to Matthews, Indiana. It was promoted by Mr. George Catterson, a very wealthy sportsman who made his home in Indianapolis. Because of a growing feeling against me on the part of the crack bicycle riders of the day, due wholly to the fact that I was colored, the greatest secrecy surrounded the arrangements for this big event.

It may be well at this time for me to outline just how this race prejudice feeling against me came to a head. A few months before the 75-mile road race was held, Walter Sanger, one of the greatest bicycle riders of the day, made an attempt to establish a new track record for 1-mile on the Capital City race track in Indianapolis. Before an immense throng he established a mark of 2.18 and was paid a handsome bonus for his stunt.

A number of my friends secretly arranged to have me make an attempt on Sanger's record shortly after he left the track. Because of the color prejudice that my previous success had earned for me I had to be taken into a dressing room secretly. Hardly had the cheers of the immense throng which greeted the announcement of Sanger's time died away before I made my appearance on the track ready to endeavor to lower Sanger's record. Quickly the news flashed through the crowd that I was to make an attack on his recently established mark, and the crowd held their seats as I took a few preliminary trips around the track, which measured one-fifth of a mile to a lap.

One could hear a pin fall as I made my way up the track for a flying start against Sanger's record. I was paced by a number of my friends who were mounted on tandems. The first one paced me on the first three laps, and a second tandem took me over the balance of the distance going as fast as the track would permit. Those pacemakers were spurred on in their efforts by the thought that they were fighting for a principle as well as for my personal success. They were all white men, and had stacked their all in the belief that I was capable of breaking Sanger's newly established record. Because of the feeling that was stirred up against me among the bicycle riders in general simply because of my color, my pacemakers stood a chance of being scoffed at had I failed to break his record.

I made my last great effort and pulled up alongside the tandem in the last fifty yards, beating them about two lengths across the tape, and finishing the mile in 2:11, seven seconds under the highly paid Sanger.

Just to show what I could do, I came out on the track later in the evening and did a fifth of a mile unpaced. I rode around the track twice to get going properly, and then took the word. The crowd grew enthusiastic, for it was seen that the way I was riding I would come close to the fifth of a mile record on a five-lap track. The time-keepers compared watches, and I was surprised to learn that I had made a record of :23 3/5, beating the record made in Europe that spring by Macdonald, on the famous Paris track 2/5 of a second.

When the time for my ride was announced I received one of my most flattering ovations. The white riders attracted by the cheering of the spectators, crowded on to the track to see what was going on.

As I passed through them to my dressing room I heard several threatening remarks aimed at me. They were not only angry at me for having broken the records, but also at the track manager as well for having allowed me to race on the track, even though I had no white men opposing me. Incidentally my track records stood as long as the track remained.

My friends had put over a clever little trick in smuggling me on the track for my record-breaking ride, but in so doing they incurred the enmity of a group of narrow-minded people. I received no pay for my record-breaking mile, other than the satisfaction that it gave me, that feeling being enjoyed also by my good friends who were pleased that they had a part in my demonstration to the public of my riding ability provided I got a square deal. Down in my heart I felt that if I could get an even break I could make good as a sprinter on the bicycle tracks of the country. That was ample pay for me.

Thereafter I was barred from ever competing again on any track in Indianapolis. However, my being debarred from those tracks fortunately paved the way for one of the greatest races I ever participated in.

Several weeks after I had established the record for the Capital City track in Indianapolis, the See-Saw Circle Club which was composed of more than 100 colored riders, held a ten-mile road race. It was announced in advance of the event that the rider who won from scratch would represent the club in a big ten-mile road race in Chicago, all expenses being paid for by the club, including a trainer. This event was open only to Negro riders, and they came from all parts of the country.

Henry Stewart, who was known the country over as the "St. Louis Flyer," was easily the outstanding star of the event. Just before the race started one of the club officials accompanied Stewart into my tent and introduced him to me. Stewart and I were the scratch men of the occasion. He was a man of powerful physique, having well-developed legs and muscular arms and shoulders. He smiled at me cynically, being evidently bent on unnerving me. For a time it had the desired effect on me as I grew weak and nervous. It was the first time in my life that I had experienced such a reaction. As I lay trembling on my cot I heard Stewart talking, evidently for my benefit just outside. He ridiculed me and requested the secretary of the race to give me the limit handicap, as he said he felt I looked as though I needed it. His sarcastic remarks proved to be his undoing, however, as they stirred me as I never had been stirred before. Instantly all my fighting spirit rushed back to me, and I jumped into my racing togs determined to beat Stewart at any cost.

As he strutted to the starting line in his bright bath robe, I became more determined than ever to defeat him. He got a wonderful re-

ception from the immense gathering, but I don't recall whether there
was any applause for me or not—that's how worked up I was.

When the starter sent us away Stewart promptly jumped into the
front and started to sprint right from the very outset, riding as if he
was in a quarter of a mile race instead of a ten-mile grind. He set a
heartbreaking pace in an effort to shake me off in the first half-mile,
but finding me right up even with him he decided that he had better
settle down and let me do a share of the pacemaking. However, I
had an advantage over him as his big frame served as a fine windshield for me while I was so small that he did not get a similar
advantage while riding at my rear wheel.

After alternating in the pacemaking positions for several miles, and
with half the distance gone Stewart's rear tire blew out. Another
rider turned his wheel over to Stewart and the latter promptly took
up the race again. As soon as I saw Stewart in trouble I slowed down.
Soon we were at our task again, and I noticed after we had reeled
off several very hot miles that the grind was beginning to have its
effect on Stewart. My first thought was that it was a ruse on
Stewart's part to save himself for the final dash to the tape, as I knew
him to be a very tricky rider. Shortly, however, with less than a mile
to go, I could plainly see that Stewart was in distress. I held my
sprint for the last quarter of a mile, and then bolted for the tape.
Stewart fought gamely as I passed him, but I led him over the line
by ten lengths.

I was carried about on the shoulders of a number of Indianapolis
men and received a flattering ovation from the packed stands.

Stewart claimed that he lost the race to me through having to use
a strange bicycle. He challenged me to a match race for five miles,
and I promptly accepted. We raced at Rushville, Indiana, and again
I made Stewart trail me over the line. Thereafter I won three other
races on the same program.

Upon my return to Indianapolis I was accorded a splendid reception,
but I honestly believe that the greatest benefit that came out of my
victory over Stewart was the fact that it gave me confidence and assurance. After I had disposed of Stewart in those two races I felt
very certain that no rider, regardless of his size or physique could
ever shake me off his rear wheel, and no man ever did.

I wound up that very colorful racing season by winning three races,
quarter, half and mile, that were held at the Lexington, Kentucky
Fair in that city, under the auspices of the colored citizens. Those
were the only bicycle races on the program, but they attracted the
fastest riders from Louisville, St. Louis, Chicago and Cincinnati.

As word spread about my being barred from the tracks in Indianapolis, because of color, Mr. George Catterson gave me a chance to again demonstrate my ability as a bicycle rider. He decided that from Indianapolis to the town of Matthews would be the course. Keeping the fact that I was to be a competitor secret Mr. Catterson offered prizes that were sufficiently attractive to interest the best bicycle riders in the state. Had they known I was to start, none of them would have entered. However, they did not share Mr. Catterson's secret, and all of them were on hand when the starter took up his position.

Shortly after his pistol shot sent the bunch away on the 75-mile grind, I jumped from my hiding place and started in hot pursuit of the fifty-odd riders who were pedalling for all they were worth down the roadway. I trailed along in the rear for several miles and was resting up in good shape before they were aware that I was in the race. They made things disagreeable for me by calling me vile names, and trying to put me down, and they even threatened to do me bodily harm if I did not turn back. I decided that if my time had come I might just as well die trying to keep ahead of the bunch of riders, so I jumped through the first opening and went out front, never to be overtaken in the feverish dash for the finish line.

When I took the lead we had covered about half the distance and were on a weird stretch of road that was thinly inhabited, with weeping willows on one side and a cemetery opposite. The thought ran through my mind that this would make an ideal spot for my competitors to carry out their dire threats. Spurred on by such thoughts I opened up the distance between my wheel and the balance of the field to make doubly sure that none of them caught up to me and got a chance to do me bodily injury.

As we neared Marion, Indiana, I noticed a number of local riders waiting for us to pace the leaders through that city. At first I was afraid they were out to do harm and rode cautiously towards them. I was agreeably surprised, however, when I found out they were friendly to me and very anxious to pace me the final twenty miles of the race. I finished fairly fresh, considering that the last 25-miles were ridden in a hard rainstorm. I finished more than an hour ahead of the second man and happy as I was over my victory, Mr. Catterson was even more pleased. He had proven that with a square deal I was one of the fastest riders in the state.

First prize was a house lot which was located in the center of the town of Matthews, Indiana. As soon as I had tucked the deed therefor into my pocket I rushed home, and presented it to my mother, explaining how it had come into my possession. I had not previously told her of my plans to enter the race because I felt she would worry about me until I returned home. Of course she was elated over my success, but she made me promise that I would never ride such a long race again. I was only sixteen years old at the time.

LOUIS D. "BIRDIE" MUNGER

Becoming a Great Rider's Protégé
(1894)

Shortly after this I entered the employ of Louis D. (Birdie) Munger, one of the greatest riders that ever sat in a saddle and who had but recently retired from the track to engage in the manufacture of bicycles in Indianapolis. I was employed in practically every department of his plant.

Mr. Munger's bachelor quarters in Indianapolis had long since become famous among the bicycle racers and bicycle salesmen throughout the country. Many of them made their home with Mr. Munger while in the city on business. When I was not tied up with tasks in the factory I served as a helper around the house. In this capacity I came to know all of the leading bicycle racers of the country, but what is more I won the admiration of Mr. Munger and he became one of my staunchest supporters and advisers.

I clearly recall meeting Arthur A. Zimmerman, the champion bicycle rider of America, on one occasion that he came to Indianapolis to race. It had been arranged that he would be the guest of Mr. Munger and I was delegated to meet Mr. Zimmerman and conduct him to the Munger home. I recognized my hero from pictures of him that had been printed in the newspapers. While hundreds surged about the train to welcome Mr. Zimmerman to Indianapolis where he was a prime favorite, and a brass band rent the air, while a welcoming committee stood by, I worked my way to the great cyclist's side. Quickly I gave him my message and Zimmerman smiled as he grasped my hand and asked me my name. He insisted that I ride in the carriage with him to Mr. Munger's home and he talked with me continuously en route.

His attention centered on the gold medal that I had won in my first race—the ten-mile road race in Indianapolis when I was thirteen years old. He was surprised when I told him of that feat, and even more so as I told him of many other boys' races since winning that gold medal.

Once in Mr. Munger's home, Mr. Zimmerman asked his host about me. Shortly Mr. Munger confirmed all that I had told Mr. Zimmerman about my races and a lot besides. "I am going to make a champion out of that boy some day," said Mr. Munger. At Mr. Zimmerman's request I sat down to the dinner table with them—a great honor indeed.

While on my way out to the race track on an errand the next day I found myself sitting alongside one of the other big champions of

11

the day, Willie Windle of Millbury, Mass. That gold medal of mine arrested his attention and Mr. Windle inquired as to its history. I was the proudest boy in the world as it became noised about that I had shaken the hand of the two outstanding bicycle greats of the bicycle circles of the country—Zimmerman and Windle. I was

A. A. ZIMMERMAN—Champion of the World, 1893–1894

especially impressed with the friendliness of the two of them, especially towards me, a colored boy. In my youthful mind the thought flashed that men can be champions and still be broad-minded in strange contrast with the young would-be champions that I had met in and about Indianapolis. There was no race prejudice in the make-ups of Zimmerman and Windle,—they were too big for that. And that expression has been fresh in my mind ever since that day.

Strangely enough I was destined not only to equal the best performances of Zimmerman and Windle, but to actually exceed them. Meantime I remembered their sterling qualities and did my best to live up to them, endeavoring to measure up to the high standards or sportsmanship set by them. I take no little pride in the fact that throughout my racing career covering sixteen years I was never charged with an unsportsmanlike action.

Meanwhile Mr. Munger became closer and closer attached to me as time went on. Had I been his own son he could not have acted more kindly toward me. One day a member of the firm asked Mr. Munger why he bothered with that little darkey, meaning myself. He answered that I was an unusual boy and that he felt sure I had in me the makings of a champion bicycle rider. "I am going to make him the fastest bicycle rider in the world," said Mr. Munger. "He has fine habits, is quick to learn, is as game a youngster as I have ever seen, and can be relied upon to do whatever he is told. He has excellent judgment and has a remarkably cool head. Although he is only sixteen he can beat any boy in the city right now. He is improving every day, I notice it every time I go out with him."

That I might get the maximum speed in my races Mr. Munger built me the very lightest and best bicycle that could be produced. It weighed only fourteen pounds.

In those days high school and college games featured bicycle races on every athletic program they conducted. Just prior to many of the meets a number of athletes would borrow racing wheels from Mr. Munger for the games and I was assigned to instruct them on the track. Before I started to instruct the youths Mr. Munger would inform them that he would permit every one of them who led me over the tape to use the racing wheels in the meet. The young athletes realized they had little or no chance of beating me, and some of them tried to bribe me to let them nose me out. After their training preparations Mr. Munger would ask me to name the athletes who were in my opinion the best riders. They got the use of the wheels.

Incidentally, the weekly workouts with the high school boys helped mightily into rounding me into championship form. I am firmly convinced that the best way to gain experience in racing tactics is by actual participation with the various riders.

But there was a dark lining to my silver cloud. Members of the firm objected strenuously to Mr. Munger's befriending me simply because of my color, and I was inadvertently the cause of Mr. Munger's severing relations with the firm and his decision to establish a bicycle factory in Worcester, Massachusetts. At Mr. Munger's proposal I came with him and have since made my home in that city. Before our train pulled out of Indianapolis Mr. Munger informed a group of his friends that some day I would return to that city as champion bicycle rider of America.

Training in Worcester
(1895)

I was in Worcester only a very short time before I realized that there was no such race prejudice existing among the bicycle riders there as I had experienced in Indianapolis. When I realized I would have a fair chance to compete against them in races I took on a new lease of life, and when I learned that I could join the Y. M. C. A. in Worcester, I was pleased beyond expression. I recall that as a small boy I tried to join the Y. M. C. A. in Indianapolis, but was turned down on account of color, despite all the influence that some of the most influential families of the city could exert on my behalf.

It did not take me very long to get acquainted in Worcester, especially when its riders discovered that I owned a fine, light, racing wheel on which I could ride with the best of them. I shall always be grateful to Worcester as I am firmly convinced that I would shortly have dropped riding, owing to the disagreeable incidents that befell my lot while riding in and around Indianapolis, were it not for the cordial manner in which the people received me. Incidentally I was striving my utmost to make good on Mr. Munger's promise to his Indianapolis friends to have me a champion when I returned to their city. Three years later I did return a full-fledged champion, and I cannot say whether Mr. Munger or myself was the happiest, since I had previously been excluded from all racing in that city because of my color.

I wish to pay my respects at this time to Mr. Edward W. Wilder, director of Athletics in Worcester schools, who was then physical director of the Worcester Y. M. C. A. when I arrived in that city. Not long after I arrived Mr. Munger took me to the Y. M. C. A. After examining me carefully, Mr. Wilder outlined some exercises that he felt would keep me in trim throughout the winter season. He found my legs quite naturally well-developed while the upper portions of my body were sorely in need of exercise. Following his instructions to the letter I succeeded in building the upper part of my body in excellent physical form, but not until I had put in two or three winter's work in a gymnasium.

I used light dumb-bells, indian clubs and a Whitley exerciser in my room regularly, even while travelling, and became an adept at deep breathing through long and patient practice. At the height of my racing career many expert trainers declared that I was the best developed rider on the bicycle track.

There was a saying at that time that any bicyclist who could climb George Street hill, one of the steepest inclines in Worcester, had the makings of a high grade bicycle racer. Appraised of that tradition I decided to try my skill on the hill. There was a big crowd on hand to see me make my initial attempt. It was a tough assignment that I had wished on myself, but I made it on the first attempt and within fifteen minutes I repeated the stunt riding down on both occasions. That was the first time a bicycle rider ever turned this trick—and very few have accomplished it in the intervening thirty-two years.

My Last Amateur Races
(1895)

In the fall of 1895 I rode my first bicycle race in Worcester, Mass. I had joined the Albion Cycle Club which was composed of colored riders. Later I was one of the club's team selected to ride in the annual ten-mile road race that attracted hundreds of entries. My old hero, Willie Windle of Millbury, Mass., was the donor of the trophy offered the winner of first place. I won this event and repeated it the following year that I might obtain permanent possession of the cup.

When Mr. Munger's factory moved to Middletown, Conn., the following year, I had my first real test against the best amateur sprinters in the East. I went along with the firm elated at the prospect of being able to compete against the pick of the amateur bicycle sprinters of the East.

I made my début at a State meet sanctioned by The League of American Wheelmen at New Haven, Conn. I decided to start in the one-mile open race, the feature event of the day. Having qualified in the preliminary heats I lined up at the tape with eleven of the fastest amateurs in this part of the country. Naturally I was nervous in this, my first tryout, but was all primed to go. However, instead of jumping out front at the crack of the pistol I was obliged to change my tactics and rode in last place until we were three-eighths of a mile from the tape. At that point I made my spurt and passed the entire group, gaining six lengths on them before they realized what had happened. I won by six lengths and received a wonderful ovation and a gold watch which I promptly presented to my friend Mr. Munger in appreciation for some of the many kindnesses he had extended to me.

Shortly afterwards I participated in the half-mile open race at Meriden, Conn. This time I was unable to come out of a very bad pocket which I found myself in half way down the home stretch and I had to content myself with second place. The winner leading me home by a matter of inches. My prize, a beautiful dinner set, I shipped to my mother for a birthday present.

Then came one of the greatest tests of my racing ability—the famous Irvington-Milbourne, N. J., 25-mile road race. Oscar Hedstrom and I trained for a couple of weeks over the course, under the watchful eye of Robert Ellingham. As the starting hour arrived I was in excellent fettle to measure speed with over 140 of the best road racers of America. In this classic were some of the most coveted distinctions in the bicycle world.

Monte Scott, the best road-race rider in the country at the time and myself were the scratch men. Throughout the race I was never off his rear wheel, and we were having a beautiful duel until we came to within one-half mile of the tape, then somebody threw a pail full of ice water in my face, and before I recovered from the shock Scott had crossed the line a winner, while I was forced to take second place. I might say that the water throwing episode was due to accident rather than design as many of the riders arranged for such a stunt, and some trainer evidently miscalculated when he showered the ice water on me.

Itching for an opportunity to show my speed as a road-race rider, I jumped at the opportunity to enter the Tatum 25-mile road race which was scheduled to be held at Jamaica, L. I. Two other riders and myself were the scratch men, there being about 60 in the field. The other scratch men framed it up against me with the two one-minute men to have the latter stall along until the scratch men came up, and within a certain distance of them, the two scratch men were to suddenly jump away from me, catch the two minute-men, and by alternating pace make it physically impossible for me to overtake them alone. However, their plan failed. They used every trick in the calendar against me but without success.

Five miles from the finishing line I decided to try one of my own tricks to throw off my rivals. I pretended to be exhausted and made difficult work of holding on to the leaders. The field fell for my stall and immediately dropped their foul riding tactics and set sail for the tape. In reality they were playing right into my hands when they were doing that, and I held my sprint in reserve until we only had a half-mile to go. Then I shot past the bunch and won out by six lengths, George Hicks second, Wallie Owens third, and Bill Loosie fourth.

Since this was my first victory in a race of this distance I was overjoyed at winning, and particularly since I was able to overcome the foul tactics of the strong combination that was lined up against me throughout the event.

I Become a Professional
(1896–97)

Shortly after my success in the Tatum road race I decided to cast my fortunes with the professional riders. It was in the books that I was to make my professional bow on the historic Madison Square Garden track in the winter of 1896. I entered the half-mile open handicap race which was the curtain raiser for the annual six-day bicycle race that has long been staged at that famous track.

In the half-mile handicap race I started from the 35-yard mark with such stars as Eddie (Cannon) Bald, Tom Cooper, Earl Kiser, and Arthur Gardiner, as scratch men. At the crack of the pistol I shot out for the lead and gained the front position in the first three laps. Not satisfied with this I continued my wild sprint, and almost lapped the field when I won the event, and the $200 that was hung up for first prize. The Garden which was taxed to capacity on that Saturday night went wild when they noticed that I had failed to hear the bell for the last lap, and continued tearing off lap after lap until I had ridden three laps more than the required distance. I immediately wired the $200 to my mother. This was my first money prize.

A few hours later I took my place at the starting line for the six-day race. Upwards of fifty of the greatest long distance riders in the world took to the gun at one minute past midnight Sunday morning in the long grind. This was my first attempt at such a long distance and I was very anxious for the test, as I felt that if I could stay up near the front I could certainly give a good account of myself when the final sprint came. In those days this event was run off under different conditions than apply today. It was commonly termed a go-as-you-please affair. Being an individual race, each man having to ride single-handed, no partners, and with no restrictions as to when a rider could leave the track to eat, sleep, bathe or for any other purpose. Time lost in dismounting was strictly up to him.

Being the only sprinter in the race, I had no difficulty in regaining many of the laps lost in leaving the track. My greatest difficulty being to keep awake. I found the older riders, who were fully matured and thoroughly developed, could stand the strain of loss of sleep better than I. However, I managed to stick to my wheel for a stretch of eighteen hours of continuous riding, much to their amazement. I was only eighteen years old at the time.

About three o'clock one morning I complained to my trainers that I was sleepy, hungry, thirsty and fatigued, and begged them to allow

18

me to dismount. However, they urged me to continue riding just a few more laps until the doctor arrived. Later I found this was only a ruse to keep me going. I rode for three miles and four laps more, and then stepped off my wheel and went to my dressing room to eat, bathe and sleep. My nap was of short duration as I was rushed out on to the track after fifteen minutes, my trainers explaining that I had slept fifteen minutes over my schedule. On the way to the track one of my trainers gave me a glass of water into which he had dumped a powder which he claimed cost $65.00 an ounce, and which would allow me to ride without any sleep until the race was over. This was only the third day of the race. Later I found out also that this powder was nothing more than bicarbonate of soda, but it kept me going for the next eighteen hours without a wink of sleep.

Somehow or other I stuck in the race and finished in eighth place with 1,787 miles to my credit. The race was won by Teddy Hale, an Englishman.

My trainers and many of the star bicycle racers declared that this long distance race would kill my fine sprint. I returned to Worcester immediately after the race and spent the winter in the Y. M. C. A. preparing myself for the next season, determined to show the experts that the six-day grind had not put an end to my sprinting ability.

The following spring I competed in the League of American Wheelmen's opening race meet at the Charles River track, Boston, against some of the leading professional riders of the country. Among them were Tom, Nat and Frank Butler, who were widely known in racing circles as the famous Butler brothers. I won the feature event, the one-mile open race and proved to myself, at least, that the six-day grind had not killed off my sprinting ability, defeating the Butlers, Watson Coleman, Eddie McDuffee and others.

My next success was at the Providence, R. I., meet which was also staged by the League of American Wheelmen, and I ran away with the one-mile open, the feature race of that program, again defeating the famous Butler brothers and a field of the greatest professional riders. Flushed with that victory I competed in the half-mile open and was beaten for first prize by Orlando Stevens.

In those days the three Butler boys were looked upon in the bicycle world as practically invincible. When word reached the western riding circles in the spring that I had taken their measure at the Charles River Meet there was much nodding of heads. Included among the starters at the Providence Meet were Floyd MacFarland, Orlando Stevens and other star western riders. Here again I demonstrated my superiority over the Butler brothers, Stevens and MacFarland, and even the experts thereupon agreed that my experience in the six-day race had not finished my career as a sprinter, but enhanced it instead.

Despite the fact that I was at the top of my form that summer I was not able to make a fight for the championship that season because the circuit extended into the South and my entry had been refused by all southern promoters. They claimed it would be folly for me to compete with white riders in that section of the country.

I found that the color prejudice was not confined to the South entirely, in fact it had asserted itself against me even in and around Boston. It would be difficult for me to narrate all the unpleasant experiences which I underwent in my long racing career, and also to call to mind all the vicious attempts that were made in vain to eliminate me from bicycle racing. I was the only colored rider ever permitted to compete in the professional class, and one may well surmise the obstacles I had to overcome against prejudiced and narrow-minded opponents. Incidentally, there were a few stars who matched skill with me that never tried to do an underhanded trick to me whether on or off the track.

But to get back to the unpleasant experiences I had in Boston. So apparent was the ill-will of the white riders against me that the press of the city took them to task and demanded that I receive a square deal in all future races. A deliberate foul on me at Waltham on Memorial Day when I was pushed off the track, and another foul committed against me at the Charles River track were the beginning of my racing difficulties. The officials and members of the press were unanimous in their demand that I be accorded the same treatment given the white riders.

One of the Boston newspapers carried a story the day after one of my races in which it took a rider named W. E. Becker to task for choking me into a state of insensibility. This incident followed the close of the one-mile open event which was won by Tom Butler with myself second, and Becker third.

Just after we had crossed the tape Becker wheeled up and hurled me to the ground. He then started to choke me, but the police interfered. It was fifteen minutes before I regained consciousness. The crowd threatened Becker who claimed that I had crowded him into the fence. However, the judges disqualified Becker, and ordered the race re-run, but I was too badly injured to start.

I quote the following from a clipping in the Boston *Post:* "At the opening of the Southern Circuit last fall Taylor's entry was refused at Louisville, Ky., and throughout the South, on account of his color, and opposition against him has become so marked that he was compelled to give up the circuit. The League of American Wheelmen, which professes to control bicycle racing, draws the color line, and only white riders are allowed to compete in professional races. This is a violation of good sense, but if the L. A. W. permits Major Taylor to start in professional races, it should certainly protect him. "The L. A. W. must keep the dirty professionals off the track. During the National Circuit Races here it was commented that in every professional race that Major Taylor entered he had more than his share of trouble. There appeared to be a deliberate effort by certain riders to throw him. He was tossed once successfully, and the man who did the job was loudly hissed, and Major Taylor was roundly cheered in front of the grand stand. He was very badly scraped and bruised. The same dirty tactics have followed the plucky little colored rider all around the circuit, and it is to the everlasting discredit of the men who are in on the schemes.

"It does not appear to be the big riders so much as the cheap riders who are out for a fraction of the purses that they can steal from the big riders who may have an off day now and then. If a referee now and then saw these offenses and ruled off a rider it would add much to the interest of the sport. Major Taylor's last episode at Newark, when he had won the one-mile open in a great finish was openly threatened. He asked to be excused in the next race, but the referee compelled him to get up and take the chances. He did, but kept out of the bunch and did not try for a place.

"Attention was recently called in the New York *Sun* to the fact that Major Taylor in all his big races is in deadly fear of his racing companions. He was recently thrown at Worcester and badly injured, and it was charged that the accident was the result of a conspiracy.

"At the Circuit meet at Waverly, N. J., on September 20, Taylor captured the one-mile open event handily, and qualified for his heat in the mile handicap, but when the final race of the latter event was called, Taylor did not show up, and investigation by the referee disclosed that Taylor had been threatened and was afraid to start. The referee refused to excuse Taylor and the colored boy started reluctantly but made no effort to win.

"The situation calls for prompt action on the part of the Racing Board. Major Taylor now ranks with the fastest men in this country, but the racing men are envious of the success, and prejudiced against his color, and aim to injure him whenever he competes. This conduct robs Major Taylor of many chances to secure many large purses and endangers his life besides."

About this same time the New York *Journal* carried this article: "Fears of Major Taylor. Much talk is going the rounds about the unfairness on the part of the other riders toward Major Taylor, the colored boy, and he is said to be in fear of bodily danger if he continues to keep in the front. Possibly there may be little ground for complaint by Taylor, but in the Metropolitan district in which he has competed he had not been sinned against. The colored rider has a very dangerous habit of crowding in on the pole, no matter how narrow the opening is in the finish down the home stretch, and on a couple of occasions the holder of the third desirable position has upheld his rights with a bit of elbow work that was provoked by the offender.

"In the record race at Springfield there was a stiff fight between Tom Butler and Taylor, but Tommy was not in any combine to do up the other, but was simply having it out with him on a personal score. They both come from Boston. The success of the colored boy (and he has done some excellent riding) was sure to arouse bitter opposition and feeling among the other riders, but officials of the meets have been particularly vigilant in seeing to it that Taylor got all that was coming to him. In baseball and fistic circles the color line has caused any amount of trouble, and the same difficulty is now being experienced in bicycle racing.

"One prominent rider declined a match race with Taylor for a substantial share of the gate receipts, and it was not because he was afraid, but simply through his unwillingness to be singled out in a match race with one he considered his social inferior. But for Major Taylor it must be said, however, that he is the most modest and retiring youngster with which his race was ever favored."

My First National Championship
(1898)

Aside from the unpleasant experiences which I encountered from time to time because of color prejudice, my success of my first year's work as a professional was very satisfactory indeed, not only from a point of speed but financially as well. I won several thousand dollars and gained valuable experiences, besides making many new friends, by riding all my races entirely unassisted, and doing my utmost to win every time I got up. I was especially determined to go after the Championship of America in the season of 1898.

There was a plan on foot to bar me, as a colored racing cyclist, from future racing on all tracks under the jurisdiction of the L. A. W. It was grounded on the fact that the League had refused to admit professional membership, but placed a tax of $2 on them and compelled them to register, also it did not admit Negroes to membership.

Naturally I was somewhat disturbed by these conditions until I signed up with the American Cycle Racing Association which was headed by Wm. A. Brady, James Kennedy and Patrick Powers, to ride as a member of a racing team with Fred Titus, "French" Edward Taylore, and under this management I was sent South to engage in about two months of training, but owing to the racial prejudice my stay in Savannah was somewhat brief, as this New York newspaper will show.

"The Cyclists of Savannah, Ga., are congratulating themselves on the fact that Major Taylor, Champion Cyclist was driven out through a White-cap letter sent him during his recent brief stay there, but such is not the case. Taylor left Savannah by order of the American Cyclist Racing Association with whom he is under contract as told in the *Evening Journal* last week.

"Major Taylor did receive a letter supposed to be written or rather printed, as an effort was made to conceal the identity of the writer, by the city's crack triplet team with whom he had some words while training on the road. The letter which bears the postmark of Savannah under date of March 2nd, is now made public for the first time. It is as follows: 'Mister Taylor, If you do not leave here before forty-eight hours you will be sorry. We mean business. Clear out if you value your life. Signed, White Riders.'

"This letter concludes with a very poor attempt on the part of the writers to portray a skull and cross bones."

In 1897 the L. A. W. decided to permit me to register for races under their sanction. But this by no means ended my racial difficulties for I was barred from several tracks in the North on account of my color. I quote the following from a newspaper.

"The announcement made by Tom Eck to the effect that all colored riders including Major Taylor, The Dusky Champion, would not be allowed to race on the Woodside track, Philadelphia, has stirred up a big row, in which the National Racing Board may play a prominent part. While Eck says he has no personal objection to the colored champion's arrangements the owners of the track give him the right to say who or who shall not race on their tracks, and they are against permitting colored men to compete, and so entry blanks will be marked 'For White Riders Only.'

"The peculiar racing rules this year may be the means of causing considerable trouble for the gray haired manager for he cannot very well bar Major Taylor from racing without the risk of being heavily fined by the racing board and also having his track blacklisted. The question is fully covered in Sec. 13, Clause C of the racing rules which are as follows: 'A legal entry is one which cannot be rejected by the promoter, one which complies with the racing rules, and is accompanied by the required fee for all entries of the meet.'

"Major Taylor is in good standing with the L. A. W. and has a perfect right to enter races as the League, while it does not admit Negroes to membership, does permit them to enter races to be held under their jurisdiction. Billy Brady who looks after Major Taylor's interest, has expressed himself in no measured terms as to what he calls unjust discrimination and he has issued a sweeping defy on behalf of the colored lad for any style of racing in sight, and with Eck's best foreign stars preferred. Eck's partner, Senator Morgan, stated yesterday that he had no desire whatever to bar Major Taylor from any of his tracks and he will see if matters cannot be adjusted to the satisfaction of all parties concerned.

"He accepted Brady's challenge on behalf of Jaap Eden, Sissàc or Boulay. The fight for public favor between the Morgan-Eck combination and Brady, Kennedy and Powers interest, promises to develop plenty of enthusiasm before the season is over."

I somehow used to imagine that if I won my first race of the season I was due for a big year. So in the spring of 1898, the year in which I won the Championship of America for the first time, I bent all my energy to win my initial start in the Asbury Park, N. J., one-mile open event. I won that race and continued on my winning way right through the season winning the Championship that I had longed for since my boyhood days. This Asbury Park event was the opening of the Grand Circuit races, it being stipulated that the rider scoring the highest average throughout the season would be declared the Champion of America. During the year, however, much jealousy and dissension cropped up in the racing of the professionals and some of the leading riders in the Grand Circuit seceded from the L. A. W. under whose control all riders and tracks had come for years. This step caused a bitter fight for the Championship honors, five of the leading riders including myself claiming the title, Eddie Bald, Arthur Gardiner, Tom Butler and Owen Kimble.

When I began racing in the 1898 season, my one great ambition was to win the National Championship of America on my merits. After making a hard fight for it against great odds, I was within 14 points of Eddie Bald, who was leading, and had a splendid chance of defeating him in St. Louis when my entry was rejected, thus giving him a decided advantage, but I still had hopes of evening up the score at Baltimore. However, the promoters there also refused my entry which practically shut me out of all possibility of winning the title, which I believe was the object of their conspiracy.

If the L. A. W. accepted my entry for the Championship races I could not understand how it could be lawfully rejected.

I then offered to make a match with Eddie Bald, the possible National Champion, for a purse and a side bet of $500, winner to take all. However, Bald refused to compete against me. He also declined to participate in a race with Jimmie Michaels, the famous diminutive Welshman and myself on the Manhattan Beach track.

Commenting on my being barred from the Baltimore races, John Barnett, the Baltimore representative of the L. A. W. racing board, had this to say. "No race promoter holding a National Circuit sanction from the L. A. W. has the right to bar out any competitor who is in good standing and a regular competitor on the National Circuit, unless for some flagrant breach of the rules. When promoters accept L. A. W. sanction they accept L. A. W. rules and as the L. A. W. draws no color line in racing circles they cannot refuse the entry of a colored rider who has qualified to compete, even though they may have ground rules to the contrary. Major Taylor is a regular follower of the Circuit and is a recognized competitor for the Championship, and he has as much right to compete in the Championship races at St. Louis and Baltimore as Bald, Cooper, and Gardiner, or any of the rest of them."

The Philadelphia Press in speaking of conspiracy aimed at me said that the fact that my rivals on the National Circuit had entered into a conspiracy to prevent me from winning the National Championship was not without foundation.

"Of course," read the Press, "it will be a hard matter to prove but, nevertheless, Chairman Mott would be doing something for the benefit of a great sport if he begins an investigation at once. Major Taylor is the greatest sprint rider in America and his white rivals all know it. Personally they all speak well of the little colored boy,

but there is not one of them who has not at one time or another
expressed the hope that Major Taylor will be kept from winning the
Championship honors.   They have pocketed him at every opportunity
and ran him wide on the turns, and used other foul tactics in order
to defeat him, but as yet not one of them has been punished.   The
L. A. W. recognized Taylor when Chairman Mott accepted his
registration fee and the League should give him all the protection
necessary.

MAJOR TAYLOR—Champion of America, 1898

"St. Louis cannot have the Circuit sanction until it promises to
accept the entry of Major Taylor, and the National Circuit date of
October 9th, originally granted to Berkeley Oval, N. Y. C., has been
transferred to this city.   The sanction covers the National Five-Mile
Championship and 60-point score. Bearing in mind the fact that the
race-meet promoters have refused Major Taylor's entry for the last
Circuit meeting, Chairman Mott granted the sanction on the condition that Major Taylor's entry should be accepted."

With the closing days of the cycle racing season of 1898 rapidly
drawing near the newspapers of the East gave a lot of space to the
discussion as to who should be declared the National Champion. Some
of them frankly declared it was a case of black or white.   It was
pointed out that two men stood out head and shoulders above the field
for the honors—Eddie Bald, the three times winner of the title, and
myself.

I quote from a Metropolitan newspaper: "There is a grave question as to who is champion cyclist of America for the season of 1898. Is it Eddie Bald, who from the League tables was leading when the professionals seceded from the League practically as a walk-over, or Arthur Gardiner who won more firsts at National Circuit Meets than any other rider, or Owen Kimble, whose points under the L. A. W. and other outlaw organizations makes the largest total, or is it Major Taylor who in all classes or races throughout the season scored the greatest number of victories?

"A table has been compiled by Charles M. Mears, the Ohio State Handicap official, showing the net results of the efforts of all the riders, and according to it Major Taylor is the most logical one to have the honor of being called the Champion of America for the year of 1898. This table shows the number of times that each rider has won first, second and third place in any race either on the National Circuit or under the outlaw jurisdiction. This table simply counts firsts, seconds and thirds, figuring four points, two points, and one point respectively for the place, which is the system which is mathematically just.

"According to this calculation Major Taylor heads the list, and thereby wins the title of Champion of America after the table:

	1sts	2nds	3rds	Points
Taylor, Major	21	13	11	121
Gardiner, Arthur	21	12	5	113
MacFarland, Floyd	16	15	13	107
Bald, Eddie	19	17	8	98
Fisher, Johnnie	18	11	0	94
Simms, Fred	16	10	5	89
Eaton, Jay	16	9	4	86
Walthour, Bobbie	12	11	7	87
Stevens, Orlando	14	5	10	76
Titus, Fred	13	11	1	75
Freeman, Howard	8	17	6	72
Cooper, Tom	10	11	7	69
Lawson, Iver	9	12	4	64
Johnson, Johnnie	14	3	1	63
McDuffee, Eddie	15	0	0	60
Bowler, Jimmie	10	4	6	54
Butler, Tom	10	2	5	49
Kimble, Owen	7	7	7	49
Martin, Bill	8	5	7	49
Elks, Harry	11	2	0	49
Butler, Nat	7	8	3	47"

Rivals Try to Keep Me Off Tracks
(1898)

In the spring of 1898 war was formerly declared against the League of American Wheelmen by the cycling champions who followed the National Circuit. Fifty or more famous racing men formed an association to further and protect their interest at the same time. This meeting was held at Trenton, N. J., and was one of the most interesting events in the history of cycle racing in America.

Eddie Bald, the great Buffalo (N. Y.) rider who won three American championships in as many seasons, was among those present. Another at the meeting was Tom Cooper, also champion of America, Floyd MacFarland, Orlando Stevens, Arthur Gardiner and every other bicycle racer of note in this country.

Champion Bald was named chairman, F. Ed. Spooner, circuit correspondent, was chosen secretary. The executive committee comprised A. G. Batchelder, former New York state handicapper, F. Ed. Spooner, E. C. Bald and Arthur Gardiner. This group was appointed to meet track promoters and track owners of the country. At their sessions it was voted to organize an American Racing Cyclists Union.

While this meeting was in progress the L. A. W. officials kept the wires hot as they posted each other on the developments at Trenton. While the new organization was deliberating a telegram was received from the L. A. W. officials imposing a ten-dollar fine on Bald, MacFarland, Stevens and all the riders who had been suspended for training on a blacklisted track in New York. The officials were instructed to permit the riders to race after the fines were paid, thus raising the suspension which had been placed upon them. The riders considered this action a backdown on the part of L. A. W. and a clean-cut victory for them. However, Bald and the other riders refused to pay their fines, but Secretary Muirhead of the L. A. W. did so for them. Next day all of the riders competed in a big bicycle meet in Trenton.

Although practically all of the star riders of the country were in favor of a change of government for the sport not all were ready to jump from the L. A. W. Fred Titus, Fred Simms, "Doc" Brown, Nat Butler, Owen Kimble, Howard Freeman, Tom Butler and several others, including myself, wished to continue to ride under the auspices of the L. A. W. until we were sure that the control of bicycle racing was to be turned over to competent men.

Due to the revolt against the L. A. W. and the formation of the

American Racing Cyclists Union came the organization of the
N. C. A.—National Cycling Association—which body is still in control of bicycle racing in this country. With the N. C. A. in control
of the bicycle racing events in the country that year, 1898, the
L. A. W. practically passed out of the picture. However, there was
a fly in my championship ointment through no fault of my own.
While I was winning the N. C. A. title the L. A. W. circuit continued its championship races and Tom Butler was declared champion of that season under the auspices of that organization.

Prior to my signing up to race under the N. C. A. auspices I entered into a gentleman's agreement with all of the riders in that
group, whereby we promised to do no racing on Sunday. However,
I was doomed to keen disappointment when I was informed that that
agreement was to be considered a scrap of paper and the very first race
that I was to ride in under the N. C. A. colors was scheduled for
Sunday in St. Louis. At the time, Eddie (Cannon) Bald was leading
me by a very narrow margin for the championship honors; therefore,
the race at St. Louis was all important to me. Had I won in the
Mound City, Bald and I would have an equal rating in the standing.
It was my intention to then bend every effort to beat Bald in the
final championship race of the year (1898) at Cape Girardeau, Mo.,
but a rainstorm in St. Louis on the Saturday on which the race was
to have been held, caused a postponement. I insisted that the race be
held any day but Sunday but my fellow riders, forgetting our agreement, favored its being held on the Sabbath, as did the promoters and
it was held on Sunday. I had won my heat on Saturday, thereby
assuring myself of a place in the starting line when the final event
was called, but I steadfastly refused to ride on Sunday as it was
against my religious scruples.

Within a few days all of the riders moved along to Cape
Girardeau which was to stage the final championship races of the year.
Naturally, they were all bent on doing their very best on this occasion,
as between Bald and I lay the distinction of being the champion of
the country for the season under the N. C. A. auspices. However, I
was doomed to another keen disappointment.

While we were still in St. Louis one of the promoters of the Cape
Girardeau race meet came to me to secure my entry for that event.
He knew that the color line had been drawn on me so tightly in St.
Louis that I was unable to get hotel accommodations, which placed
me at a great disadvantage, as any athlete in strict training may well
appreciate. It forced me to secure lodgings with a colored family and
even though I was on a very strict diet I did not feel free to ask my
hostess to rearrange menus in my favor. Instead I made a long trip
three times a day for my meals which I secured for several days in a

restaurant at Union Station. After several meals at this location the restaurant manager very rudely informed me that I would not be welcome henceforth and so instructed the head waiter who was one of my own color. This, however, the waiter refused to do and was promptly discharged for that reason.

Smarting under this shameful treatment I had about made up my mind to pack my racing bicycle and make tracks for my home in Worcester, Mass. It was while I was pondering the question that Mr. Dunlop, the bicycle race promoter from Cape Girardeau, appeared on the scene. He stated he sympathized with me in the rough treatment that I had received in St. Louis at the hands of the hotel and restaurant men. He told me he was proprietor of a hotel in Cape Girardeau and he promised me faithfully that I would receive the same treatment and attentions in his hotel as the rest of my fellow racers. Spurred on by that offer and still bent upon winning the championship, which I felt was at stake in the Cape Girardeau meet, I reluctantly signed an entry blank for that fixture, but upon arriving in Cape Girardeau, I found Mr. Dunlop had made a complete turnabout toward me. All of the racers went to his hotel, signed the register and were alloted rooms. When it came my turn to affix mv signature Mr. Dunlop stated he was sorry, but had to inform me that he had made arrangements for me to stay elsewhere. He had arranged that I would stay with a colored family in the neighborhood during my stay at Cape Girardeau. When I informed him that this was not in accordance wth our gentleman's agreement he again stated he was sorry but the new arrangement would have to stand. With recollections of the inconveniences that I suffered at St. Louis a few days prior still fresh in my mind I did not welcome a second encounter with the color line. In order to avoid any argument at the hotel I made my way to the house designated by Mr. Dunlop and was most royally entertained by my colored host and hostess. However, I felt that since Mr. Dunlop had broken faith with me first that I was under no further obligation to participate in his championship races the next day. Early that morning I made my way to Union Station and purchased a ticket for Worcester, Mass. As I waited on the platform for the train to start, Mr. Dunlop, several of the racers and one of the N. C. A. officials approached me. They told me that if I failed to ride in the races that afternoon they would see to it that I was barred forever from the racing tracks of the country. I replied I was not interested in the future but was deeply concerned with the present, and since Mr. Dunlop had not lived up to his agreement with me I felt free to absent myself from the championship meet that afternoon and was going to do so regardless of consequences.

As time went on I became convinced that the color line was drawn against me in St. Louis and Cape Girardeau by hotel proprietors when in reality the strings were pulled by my co-racers. They evidently felt that I was a good enough rider to land the championship out on the track and that the best way to insure one of their number corralling the honors was to have me kept off the race course through some ruse. I was suspicious that this plan was afoot following my experience in St. Louis. When the brazen Cape Girardeau trick was pulled on me I became convinced of their diabolical plan and had made up my mind that I would never ride in another race.

True to their word the group of officials and bicycle racers who saw me off at the Cape Girardeau Union Station did their utmost to have me barred for life from the tracks of the country. They put every pressure they could muster into service at the N. C. A. meeting that winter with but one thought in mind—to bar Major Taylor for life from all the tracks. I had been automatically suspended for my failure to ride in the Cape Girardeau championship meet, and this well-developed plan to have the sentence carry life suspension against me followed my application for reinstatement.

Meantime the facts of the case had been thoroughly presented to the public through the press. I had always received the fairest treatment at the hands of the newspapers of the country, regardless of the unfair tactics that I was almost continuously facing at the hands of most of the racers on the track. Now the press again came to my rescue and when I sorely needed assistance. News items and editorials in most of the leading papers in the country, from both above and below the Mason-Dixon line, crystallized public sentiment in my favor.

The fact that I refused to desert the L. A. W. arrayed a large number of riders against me. The case was stated thus by the Philadelphia Press: "Major Taylor was the last professional to desert the L. A. W. and join the outlaw movement. It required a considerable amount of argument to move him, and he was never satisfied with himself after he flopped. He rode the outlaw races in the fall of 1898, and his failure to win a clear title doubtless added to his discomfiture, and when the riders reached Cape Girardeau, Mo., he was thoroughly disheartened. His failure to secure desirable accommodations was the straw that broke the camel's back, and he packed his grip and returned east. Therefore the riders' independent movement knew him no more.

"He went back to the L. A. W. and remained there until the League abandoned cycle racing and left him without a guardian. Now he wishes to ride under the N. C. A., but before the N. C. A. will register him he must make his peace with the riders, or fail in this appeal to the N. C. A. Board of Appeals, and abide by its decision. Treason is the charge against him, and life suspension is the threatened verdict.

"The riders have drawn the color line, which is unconstitutional, un-American and unsportsmanlike. It is wrong in the abstract, unrighteous in the concrete, and undefensible, particularly at a time when dealing with something other than a theory, and all the more so since the color line will not be accepted by the American public as a valid cause for the ruling off of a champion.

"Major Taylor is a stern reality. He is here in flesh and blood, and must be dealt with as a human being, and he is entitled to every human right. His case cannot be settled on the color question, but on its actual merits, and this we believe the riders so agree. That being the case, the question arises, what punishment does he deserve? In answering this query, the judges must be unprejudiced, to gain for themselves the hearty esteem of the public. It is required that they make due allowances for the unique and trying position Major Taylor has always held, and take into consideration the admitted shortcomings of his race. If they (the judges) would win golden praise, they should temper justice with mercy, and then turn in and prove, if they can, his inferiority as a racing man, by defeating him fairly and squarely in the championship competition.

"Major Taylor is no angel, his faults are no fewer than those of any racing man, but he has always been the subject of a natural prejudice, and at all times due perhaps to his good work. He has always thought himself an unwelcome competitor. Had he felt at home among the Governors themselves, the professionals, he never would have deserted them, a fact not to be overlooked.

"Then also when Taylor displayed weakness in deserting the riders because of malice on his part, had it been proven? This, too, must be considered, furthermore he should have been dealt with in a spirit of consideration for his inborn shortcomings. We might go on still deeper into this matter, but feel there is little necessity for it. The racing men have triumphed and as victors they can afford to be merciful. Not one of them wants it said next fall that he won the championship because Major Taylor was barred or prohibitally fined. Nor will the riders' committee give anyone the opportunity to cause aspersion of the champion of 1900.

"The committee will, we believe, even be more lenient to Major Taylor than its members would, were he a white man, if for no other reason than to disprove the public suspicions of unfair play, and to prove their manhood and their confidence in their ability as racing men, and their right to govern themselves to the degree vouchsafed them."

More to the same effect was echoed by many other fair-minded newspapers, for the case excited widespread comment. The Syracuse *Journal* goes after them in an editorial. It says, "If a colored man can ride a bicycle as well as a white man he should not be denied the privilege of displaying his ability." The Syracuse *Journal* further goes after the outlaws with a big editorial stick, under the caption: "The Negro should be made to know that He is a Man." The *Journal* prints the following strong editorial, founded in the decision of the American Racing Cyclists' Union, not to allow colored men in its competitive events:

"Ordinarily little interest is taken in the action of bicycle racing associations. They are usually formed and controlled by those who have not yet reached a period in life to treat things seriously. The young and frivolous are the moving spirits and the indulgent parents pay for the moving, but when a cycle association makes a rule denying a colored man the right to ride on the track it behooves the indulgent parents to be less indulgent.

"Such an act as performed by the American Racing Cyclists' Union is a dangerous thing. It would be, of course, better if the colored man spent his time on the school primer instead of on a bicycle track, but that is not the intent of the act. It is an evidence of antipathy, and the condition of the colored man in America is one of the greatest questions for us to handle. All intelligent people know that we do not benefit the condition of the colored man by denying him the privileges that we enjoy, he has been treated like a beast too long, and we must make him know that he is a man before we educate him.

"The colored man has always been denied the rights to share the fruit of civilization with the white man. The school doors have been closed against him for generations, and he has been allowed to propagate in ignorance. He has been forced to toil, and not to study, and that is the reason why the ordinary Negro lacks the mental power of a white man.

"Education is the remedy that the Negro needs, and the remedy cannot be obtained by him if he is deprived of the opportunities of receiving it that his white brothers enjoy. The practice has been pursued for years with the result that makes us wince so often at the shocking news from the South.

"Uncle Sam allows the Negroes to serve him, and if he can pass the civil service examinations he can handle our mails, and if he is qualified he should have the same position a white man can have, and if he can fulfill all the requirements, his color should have no weight against him. If he can ride a bicycle or a horse or play baseball as well as a white man, why should he be denied the privilege of demonstrating his ability?

"The public sentiment is with Taylor, but its sympathy is not pronounced enough to have much weight with a body of riders who are jealous of Major Taylor's successes, and are determined to keep him out at all costs. Track owners would unquestionably like to see Major Taylor riding again, and in every cycle racing center of the country there are many who go to the races simply to see Major."

The *Cycling Gazette* had this to say:

"Boycotting against Major Taylor too long delayed. The white bicycle racers have drawn the color line. They assert they will no longer compete against Major Taylor, the black whirlwind of the cycle tracks. It is all very well for these speedy white gentlemen to insist upon the proper respect for their color, and the *Morning Telegraph* is pleased to see this much delayed but emphatic assertion of the superiority of the Caucasian over the Ethiopian. Still, in the interests of the L. A. W. and to the end that there might be no invidious criticism on the action of the white riders, we could have wished that they had boycotted Major Taylor before he had defeated them all. It looks now as if the ease with which this ebony wonder cut down records and carried away first money in all the big contests in which he entered had as much to do with the action of the white flyers as their active self-love.

"It is, of course, a degradation for a white man to contest any point with a Negro. It is even worse than that, and becomes an absolute grief and social disaster when the Negro persistently wins out in the competitions."

I cannot begin to quote the newspaper opinions on both sides, but at last the matter came to an issue, when the Executive Committee of the American Racing Cyclists' Union met, the organization being affiliated with the N. C. A., at Newark, New Jersey. These officials took notice of this sweep of sentiment in my favor and instead of life sentence, which was sought by several of my fellow riders and a number of officials of the parent organization, I was ordered to pay a fine of $500. Since I felt this was a very unjust verdict, I made up my mind that rather than pay the fine I would hang up my racing togs forever. It was the principle of the thing that I was fighting, and it would have made no difference to me whether the fine was $5 or $5,000, I would refuse to pay it. To me the payment of any fine under the circumstances would be an admission of guilt on my part for doing something which I felt in my heart I had never done.

About this time Mr. Fred Johnson of Fitchburg, Massachusetts, President of the Iver Johnson Arms & Cycle Company, made me an offer to ride his company's bicycle in the coming season. When I agreed he promptly sent a check to the N. C. A. to wipe out the unjust fine which had been imposed upon me.

It gave me no little pleasure, however, to note that the members of the executive committee of the A. R. C. U., Earl Kiser, Tom Cooper, Orlando Stevens, Howard Freeman, Johnnie Fisher, and Jay Eaton, voted unanimously in favor of my reinstatement. I felt that was a complete vindication for me.

A newspaper of the day printed this paragraph which I believe is pertinent to the case in hand: "All the racing men agree that Major Taylor should be barred out, but the Eastern riders have come to believe it is in the best interest of the racing game that he should be reinstated. Track associations, clubs and promoters everywhere feel that Major Taylor is a big attraction, and really demanded his reinstatement."

Fulfilling a Prophecy
(1898-99)

While the moguls of bicycle racing in this country were determining my fate in the winter of 1898–1899, I kept in the pink of physical condition. Naturally, I was somewhat worried as they maneuvered back and forth in an effort to stall my case, but I felt that the scales of justice would eventually swing my way so I kept hard at work at the gymnasium preparing for a busy season in 1899.

No sooner had I been fined $500 for my failure to participate in the Cape Girardeau, Mo., race meet, which wound up the 1898 championship season, than I started to work in earnest for the ensuing campaign. I made up my mind that 1899 would be my banner year, and that I would extend myself more than usual, if that were possible, to pick up any extra prize money, and the excessive amount that I still claim was unjustly levied against me in the guise of a fine.

I also determined to vindicate myself in the estimation of those good friends who had stood by me, and who had done everything possible to assist me in regaining my standing once more, and also to justify the good opinion of the press that had come to my rescue, and forced my opponents to let down the bars and reinstate me, as well as that of the public, whose sentiment was with me from the start.

Down in my heart I felt disappointed at the way the championship season terminated in 1898. Although I was declared the champion there were claims advanced for the honors by Eddie (Cannon) Bald, Tom Cooper, Arthur Gardiner and Tom Butler.

So as the 1899 championship season dawned I redoubled my efforts to establish myself as champion of America, and to make the margin wide enough between myself and my competitors to leave no room for doubt. Since such sterling riders as Bald, Cooper, Kiser and Gardiner, who were considered the four fastest riders in the country, and such other good men as Kramer, Eaton, Freeman, Kimble, Stevens, the Butler brothers, MacFarland, Bowler, Fisher, Simms, Terrill, Newhouse, Cutler, Wilson, Taylore, Jaap Eden, Mertins, Weinig, Collette, and Bobby Walthour were all competing for the championship title that season, I felt I had in that field foemen worthy of my steel. Incidentally the fact that I was competing against such a galaxy of racing stars as these, spurred me on to my greatest efforts, and 1899 will always live in my memory as one of my greatest seasons because I won the championship that season beyond a shadow of a doubt—my keenest competitors conceding me the laurels.

Before I won the American championship I competed in the world's championship meet at Montreal, and there won the world's one-mile sprint championship title. In Chicago I established a world's record for one mile.

My first race that season for the championship honors came at the King's County Wheelmen's Meet at Manhattan Beach (L. I.), June 23. The quarter-mile national championship event was the feature of the program. It attracted more star riders than had ever competed before in a race at this distance. Among them were Bald, Cooper, Gardiner, Taylore, Kiser and Tom Butler, the "big-six" of the racing world, together with Jaap Eden, Mertins, MacFarland, Stevens, Newhouse, Eaton, Weinig, Terill, and Kiser.

The final heat found Jaap Eden, champion of Holland, Fred, Howard Freeman, Arthur Gardiner, and myself lined up at the starting line. I have never seen a group of crack riders that seemed more fit than the five of us, and each was keenly anxious for the pistol to send us away. After I had gotten away with a very bad start, things seemed to be breaking exceedingly bad for me, each of my opponents having a whack at me as they passed, and I found myself in a bad rut and was the last man to enter the home stretch, Eden leading at a furious clip.

After being bumped, jostled, and elbowed until I was sorely tried, I felt sure that as we entered the last straightaway, I must have looked like a 1,000 to 1 shot. However, I quickly found myself and went after the bunch with every bit of vitality that was in me. I pedalled down the home stretch at two kicks to every one, slipped in between Eaton and Simms, despite their efforts to close in on me and won by a scant foot with Eaton second, Simms third, Freeman fourth and Gardiner fifth. The entire field with the exception of Gardiner went over the tape within a half wheel's length of each other.

This was one of the most sensational sprints I had ever made and the crowd was not slow to appreciate it. My trip about the track immediately upon the close of the race became a triumphal march as the enthusiasts in the grandstand gave me one of the greatest ovations that had ever fallen my lot.

Shortly after this event I participated in a one-mile championship race at the Quill Club meet at the Manhattan Beach track.

Tom Cooper, Gardiner, Butler and myself won our trial heats and faced the starter's gun in the final. Butler led me over the line while Cooper trailed me, and Gardiner finished fourth. In this race I was again on the receiving end of some of the foulest tactics that I ever encountered in my more than sixteen years of racing. While I was able to offset them in the one-quarter mile championship event, which I won, I found the odds were all strong against me in this second race at the Manhattan Beach track, and considered myself very fortunate to finish in second place.

A week later I went to Philadelphia to take part in the Castle Wheelmen's event on the Tioga four-lap cinder track which was remarkably fast. Following the rough treatment I received in my race a few weeks previous at the Manhattan Beach track, in my race against Eden, Simms, Freeman and Gardiner, and later on the same track against Tom Butler, Cooper and Gardiner, I decided on a plan of action to offset any rough tactics that my opponents might attempt to pull on me in future races. My trainer bitterly opposed my putting the plan into practice, but I insisted and it so happened that they were to be tried out in this Philadelphia meet. In the first race referred to above I was the object of some clever pocketing. My strategy now was to avoid both in my future starts by beginning my sprint from the front of the field. Hitherto I had always started my sprint from the rear of the field, and naturally in doing so had to sprint past all my rivals giving them an opportunity to elbow me or force me into a pocket, or otherwise make me the victim of rough riding tactics.

"In this Philadelphia meet," said the Philadelphia Press, "besides Eddie Bald, three times winner of the cycling championship of America, there were 25 of the fastest racing men in the world, including the pick of America's best sprinters and the recognized champions of Europe." I won the third of a mile championship event from that field and was mighty proud of my conquest, but I believe I was more pleased at the way my new tactics worked out for me in this hectic dash.

Now to explain my new tactics. In the finish of the quarter-mile championship race at Manhattan Beach, a short time before, the riders, including myself, covered the last 200 yards in faster time than we covered the same distance in this Philadelphia event. The Manhattan Beach race was a much more difficult one to win than that in Philadelphia. The reason was that up to and including the one-quarter-mile championship event, all of my races had been ridden and won in the most difficult manner possible—namely by trailing along in the rear of the field in order to avoid pockets or a fall until the last lap, by which time the riders would be sprinting for all they were worth for the tape. Then I would undertake to ride outside the field in my dash to the finish line. Even if I was successful my victory would be only by a very narrow margin, and in many close finishes I saw a well-earned victory wrest from me by the officials. It is a fact that the verdict rendered against me in one of these so-called blanket finishes, caused me to adopt my new riding tactics.

My plan of action henceforth was to start my sprint from the front of the field rather than from its rear.   In a word I was to maneuver into the front of the field (in second or third position) as we came into the home stretch on the last lap.   I reasoned that in my hard sprint, which won me the one-quarter-mile event at the Manhattan Beach track a few weeks previous, had I started my dash for the tape from the front of the field, instead of the rear, I would have won by between eight and ten wheel lengths instead of the ten-inch margin that separated me from Eaton who was in second position.

As I made my way to the starting line for the big race I heard my trainer urge me not to try out my new tactics that afternoon.   I rode in my customary style until the bell rang announcing the start of the final lap, and then I forgot the good advice of my trainer and started riding on my own initiative.   At the sound of the bell all of the racers started to maneuver for what are generally considered the choice positions, known to riders as the winning positions.   As we entered the back stretch I slipped into second position being on Arthur Gardiner's rear wheel.

Let me quote from the Philadelphia Press:—"As the bunch took the turn into the home stretch at terrific speed, Bald jumped from the middle of the bunch and plowed into the lead like a shot, for he was coming like a champion never came before, and the spectators were yelling like mad for the boy from Buffalo, but in the midst of the excitement in the grand rush for the big purse which was to be the winner's end, the little black form of the colored boy was seen to forge rapidly to the front.   He overtook Champion Bald halfway down the home stretch, passing Eaton like a flash, beating him out by 10 lengths.   In an instant the crowd was on its feet and the cheering for Bald was quickly changed to wild cries for 'Taylor, Taylor,' and Taylor it was for sure.

"The colored boy just flew past the champion while the band played, and the crowd cheered and cheered.   Long after the race was over the applause kept up, and Major Taylor was obliged to ride around the track several times bowing his acknowledgment of the cheers of the spectators."

Naturally I was elated at having won such a great race, but I was even more proud because of the fact that my strategy had worked out so well.

While I was heartily congratulated by many of the riders and officials, not one of the racers that I had defeated, however, saw their way clear to shake my hand.   That some of them at least were peeved because of my victory became apparent while they were racing for the honors in the one-mile handicap event which was held shortly after the championship number.

Again I quote from the Philadelphia Press—"Hon. Albert Mott, Chairman of the L. A. W. racing board and generally considered the outstanding figure among the bicycle racing officials of the country, who refereed the races, saw something in this one-mile handicap event which was not just right, but was not in a position to see who should be punished for it. Major Taylor, the colored boy whose wonderful riding made him the idol of the meet, and who caused the crowd for once to forsake Champion Bald, and applaud the efforts of a hated rival, was crowded from his position in the center of the track until he was nearly run into the press box occupied by the reporters.

"Mr. Mott demanded to know who was responsible for it, but was unable to learn, although the judges admitted that Taylor was crowded out of his course. This was one of the unfortunate events of the day, but one for which the Castle Wheelmen were in no way to blame, as the officials of the meet were carefully selected from the best known wheelmen in the country through whose mistakes Major Taylor must suffer."

As a matter of fact, my position on the track as a result of this foul was so precarious that I had to back pedal for all I was worth over the tape, whereas, were it not for the rough tactics employed against me, my pathway would have been cleared to the tape, and I would have pedalled to a well-earned victory, as is indicated by the fact that I finished in second place, despite my back pedalling.

Incidentally, the Philadelphia Press conceded that I was in the best position of the field to win up to the moment that the foul occurred.

My Greatest Race
(1898)

I have been asked thousands of questions relative to my career on the bicycle track that range from how I happened to start riding a bicycle to what I considered my hardest race. What was my fastest time for a mile, and how I got the name Major, how I managed to get out of pockets. Since every heat leading up to every final that I figured in during my almost 17 years of racing was desperately fought every inch of the way, because of that color business, it is no easy matter for me to answer that last question. However, my special match race against Jimmie Michaels at the Manhattan Beach track in the summer of 1898 was perhaps my greatest achievement. Incidentally, I believe it was also my most spectacular victory.

As I delved into my records and scrap-books to get data on which to base my answer to that greatest question, I came across a number of entries including the following:—"Major Taylor easily won the championship" and "Major Taylor easily breaks world's records." I might say at this time that the impression that I won my races easily was perhaps due in a great measure to my own peculiar position on my wheel. It was distinct from that of any other rider on the track—in fact, it was my own invention which was made necessary when I adopted extension handle bars for my sprint races. I was a pioneer among the sprint riders to adopt the extension handle bars. Today the extension handle bars and the position I perfected for myself on my racing wheel, are accepted as the standard by bicycle sprinters the world over.

My racing position was made conspicuous because of the absence of any unnecessary motion of the head or body, awkward or otherwise, which was so noticeable in some riders. I reasoned that any unnecessary motions only tended to impede the rider's efforts, whereas, if the same amount of exertion were employed in the only motion necessary, from the hips down, with a light, quick motion of the ankle, it would not only produce a maximum of efficiency, but by constant practice it would produce an easy, graceful celerity of motion that is pleasing to the eye. It would also conserve the rider's energy for the final lap where it is most needed. So carefully had I worked out my racing style that newspaper men in general always conceded that I was the most graceful rider on the track.

But to get back to what I consider was undoubtedly my hardest race. Jimmie Michaels, the famous little Welshman, and myself were in excellent physical trim for this race of races on the historic

Manhattan Beach track on a mid-summer afternoon 28 years ago.

We found the three-lap cement track at Manhattan Beach light-ning fast on that torrid afternoon, because of the absence of the usual gale which swept the track. In the grandstand and strewn out along the rail that bordered the track was one of the greatest throngs that ever witnessed a sporting event in this country. Newspapers had

JIMMY MICHAELS—Champion Middle-distance
Rider of the World, 1901, and
Floyd MacFarland

devoted considerable space to the event because of the spectacular way in which this special match race was brought about. Mr. William A. Brady, of New York, who was manager of James J. Corbett when he was the heavyweight champion boxer of the world, was looking after my interest at the time. His challenges on my behalf fell on deaf ears as regarded the other crack sprinters of the day. The great Eddie (Cannon) Bald refusing to be matched against me on grounds that it would affect him socially. In desperation he assembled the sporting editors of the New York daily papers and requested them to broadcast his willingness to wager $1,000 on a winner-take-all basis, and that I could defeat any one of them in a one-mile paced sprint race. Jimmie Michaels was the only one of the bunch that accepted the defy. It was agreed between Michaels and myself that the prize would go to the rider winning two out of three races from a standing start with pace.

I daresay no bicycle race that was ever conducted in this country received the amount of space in the daily sporting pages that this one did. The outstanding reason for this keen interest was the fact that Michaels was at the moment the King of the paced riders of the world while the experts generally conceded that I held the same position among the sprinters. As a matter of prestige, however, the victory meant far more to me than to my worthy opponent, as the event in which we were to participate was classed as a sprint race even though it was to be paced. Michaels stepped out of his class when he consented to ride a short distance while I did likewise by undertaking to ride behind pace. Michaels through his long experience riding behind pace entered this match race with a decided advantage over me, inasmuch as following pace was an innovation for me at that time.

The inside story of Mr. Brady's anxiety to arrange a match race between myself and the cream of the sprinters of the country, including Eddie Bald, Tom Cooper, Earl Kiser and Arthur Gardiner, widely known as the "big-four," centered about the rough treatment accorded me on the Brooklyn track one week before my race with Jimmie Michaels. I quote the following paragraph from one of the New York papers to explain Mr. Brady's attitude on the race referred to and his determination to match me against those who would have prevented my winning any of the prize money at the Brooklyn event:

"On Saturday last the bicycle racers seemed determined to prevent Major Taylor, the colored youth, from winning any prize money in the Brooklyn track meet. However, Major Taylor was equal to the occasion, wiggled in and out of pockets set for him and won the one-mile handicap event in addition to finishing second in the one-mile national championship event.

"Mr. Brady was indignant at the show of race prejudice against the colored cyclist in the Brooklyn events. He claims that under his handling Major Taylor will develop into a world-beater. He has been riding very fast this season and is now up in fourth place in the percentage table, and only a few points behind the leader. Brady claims that if the rest of the racers give Taylor a fair shake he will win every sprint race in which he starts. 'Unhampered, Major Taylor is the fastest man on the track today. Just think of the great odds he has to ride under and then give a thought to the great number of races he wins year in and year out against the cream of the world. Of course it is humiliating to have a colored boy win over them, but Taylor turns the trick honestly and carefully and in racing parlance there is not a whiter man on the track, he is game to the core, and you never hear him complain or protest about his ill treatment,' said Mr. Brady."

It was due to the observations Mr. Brady made at those races in Brooklyn that he challenged the sprinters to meet me in a match race for $1,000. He told the newspaper men that he had implicit confidence in my ability and that if he had not he would never put up $1,000 on me.

Now to get back to this all important race between Jimmie Michaels and myself on the Manhattan Beach track. The press conceded that the rider who got away in front in our race would have a slight edge on his opponent in the dash for the tape. Again I quote further from the same clipping referred to above:—"But this does not mean to say that he will necessarily win the race which will be the best second and third heat struggle with quintet pacing. It will be a wild rush on the part of the two contestants to locate themselves behind their big pacing machines at the getaway and the same sort of a wild scramble will ensue in the concluding few yards when they leave the protection of their multicycles to sprint for the tape."

"The colored rider gets away very fast and the Welsh boy is not negligent in this respect. The battle between the two will be the first of its kind ever staged in this country, and should prove to be a heartbreaker."

The following article appeared in the New York *Journal* the morning after our race:—Major Taylor a winner. Phenomenal performances in Special Match Race. Major Taylor runs away from Jimmie Michaels and establishes a new World's Record of 1:41 which will, no doubt, stand for years."

"The Welsh Rider was hissed while the Colored Rider was cheered."

"Major Taylor, the colored cyclist, met and defeated Jimmie Michaels in the special match race yesterday afternoon at Manhattan Beach. Michaels winning the first heat easily. Major Taylor's pacing quintet going wrong in the final lap. Major Taylor's riding was wonderful both from a racing and a time standpoint, having established a new world's record, which was absolutely phenomenal. For the first time in his racing career Michaels was hissed by the spectators as he passed in front of the grandstand deserted and dejected by Major Taylor's overwhelming victory.

"Immediately after the third heat was finished, and before the time was announced, William A. Brady, who championed the colored boy during the entire season, quickly issued a sweeping challenge to match Taylor against Michaels for any distance up to 100 miles, for from $5,000.00 to $10,000.00 a side. The challenge was received with tumultuous shouts, yelling and continued applause from the large assembly, and the colored rider was lionized when his time was announced.

"Edward Taylore, the French rider, had held the world's competition record of 1.45 for that distance in a contest paced from a standing start. The world's record against time was made by Platt Betts, of England, which was 1.43-3. Michaels broke Edward Taylore's record by four-fifths of a second. Major Taylor wiped out this new mark and tied Betts' record against time. In the second heat Taylor rode on the outside for nearly two and one half laps, it can be easily seen that he rode more than a mile in the time, and shrewd judges who watched the race said that Major Taylor would do even better in his third attempt.

"That he justified this belief goes without saying. After taking up his position on the pole, Taylor jumped away at a hair-raising clip and opened up a gap of 10 lengths. In the first lap of the last heat Michaels never had a 'look-in' after his adversary entered the second lap, as Taylor skimmed along as swiftly as the flight of a swallow, and on the back stretch of the last lap Michaels sat upright and pedalled leisurely to the tape, for he saw it was useless to attempt to catch his speedy rival. The Welsh rider was as pale as a corpse as he jumped from his wheel, he had no excuse to offer for his defeat, for at no time could he keep up with the terrible pace set by Taylor.

"Major Taylor's wonderful performance undoubtedly stamped him as the premier sprinter of the world and judging from the staying qualities that he exhibited in the six-day race, the middle distance championship may yet be his also before the season is over."

After having lost the first heat because of a mishap to my pacing machine, I went to the tape for the second heat fairly bubbling over with confidence that I could take my opponent's measure this time, providing my pacing machine gave me no further trouble. I felt this way even after Michaels had again won the toss for the pole position which gave him the advantage.

After two or three false attempts to get away, due to the snapping of chains on our pacing machines, which was caused by over anxiety on the part of our pacemakers, we finally got off to a perfect start.

I will now relate the most amazing part of this widely advertised match race which the press did not get, and which is told here for the first time.

I was always credited with being the fastest man in the world, off the mark, among the sprinters, while my opponent enjoyed the same distinction among the paced riders. Michaels, having won the favored position on the pole in this heat, the second, experienced little difficulty in getting away first, well in the lead, but my pacers dashed after

them with a vengeance. As we turned into the back stretch they were
confident that I could hang on to them regardless of their speed and
with this thought in their minds they tore down the back stretch and
around the turn at a rate of speed that must have given the crowd a
rare thrill.

After the most furious efforts ever seen in pace-racing, we succeeded in closing the big gap gained by Michaels at the getaway. We
were on even terms crossing the tape at the end of the first torrid lap,
when fresh teams picked us up with desperate though marvelous ac-
curacy, because in changing pace from one machine to another the
slightest possible miscue means certain defeat. Michaels and I were
both struggling for dear life to hold on to our big machines as the
pace was waxing hotter and hotter with every turn of the pedals.
Being obliged to fight around on the outside of the track for the
entire distance, the heart-breaking speed was now beginning to have
its affect on me.

Immediately after I had changed over to my fastest pacing team
steered by Austin Crooks with Allie Newhouse coaching on the rear
seat, this team having been held in reserve to cover that last feverish
lap, I felt my strength ebbing very fast. It was just as I was turning
into the last lap and despite my utmost effort the rear wheel of my
big quintet was getting away from me, inch by inch. My pacemakers were straining every muscle and fiber in their well-trained
legs and were pedalling with perfect rhythm, apparently satisfied that
I could take all the speed that they could give me. At this tense
moment when we were in the back stretch of the last lap, Michaels
was slightly ahead, although our elbows were almost touching, and
we were racing neck and neck.

Our coachers on the rear seats of the big pacing machines were
shrieking frantically, "C'mon, C'mon." It now seemed only a
question of which of us would be shaken off first, and it really
seemed that it would be me, for at this point in the race I was more
than a yard off the rear wheel of my quintet after having failed in
my last super-effort to regain it. In another fraction of a second I
would have been defeated and badly crushed, but at this point the
unexpected happened.

Michaels, who was now leading by more than two yards, could
withstand the great strain no longer. He yelled frantically to his
coach, "Steady, Steady" which was synonymous for "Slow, Slow."
When I heard Michaels' cry "Steady, Steady" to his pacemakers I
could scarcely believe my ears. That proved to be the psychological
turning point of that race, the one I now consider my greatest
achievement.

Michaels' urgent plea of "Steady, Steady" sounded his death knell and simultaneously inspired me to my supreme efforts which were shortly culminated by a remarkable victory. Up to the moment that I heard Michaels direct his pacemakers to slacken their speed I felt certain he would defeat me. I was absolutely burned out.

Just how I ever managed to kick up to the rear wheel of my pacing machine will always remain a mystery to me, but in a flash I got it and was yelling like mad, "Go, Go," and go they did, with every ounce of energy they had left in them. They were delighted to hear me call for a faster pace and on they dashed as we rounded into the home stretch. It was a glorious sensation to see victory now within my grasp, when only a few seconds before inevitable defeat stared me in the face. As we made for the finishing line I was even bold enough to jump from the rear of my pacing machine and beat it across the tape, breaking the record established by Michaels in the preceding heat, and leading him over the line by 200 feet.

Both my pacing-team and that of Michaels were pedalling desperately in that heat for supremacy of speed and low score. For that reason Michaels' pacers disregarded his distressful cry of "Steady, Steady"—their one thought being to lead my boys over the finishing line. This they did but only because my pacers had to fight hard all the way around on the outside of the track. However, it gave my pacing quintet no little satisfaction to know that they had finished the race with me hanging onto them while the rival quintet had left their star away back on the track.

I never heard such applause as that which greeted me when I dismounted and started for my dressing room. I was pretty well "baked," and nearly dropped twice, but the cheers of the crowd did much to revive and stimulate me and by the time I reached my cot I was in pretty good condition. At this point I resorted to some strategy which I always regarded as one of my best cards. It was in effect to have the third and final heat of the race run off as quickly as possible. I always felt that since I was in such perfect physical condition throughout the racing year that I could recuperate more quickly after a gruelling race than any of my competitors. Therefore, my anxiety was to get Michaels out for the final heat at the earliest possible moment. Mr. Brady, my manager, saw to it that we were called out again in short order. Excitement was at a high pitch as Michaels and I took up our positions to start the final heat. Interest in this final sprint for the $1,000 prize, was at fever heat since each of us had won a heat with a record attached to each whirl around the track. I have seen enthusiastic gatherings at bicycle race tracks all over the country but I never saw one more on edge than the assembly that witnessed the final heat in this great race with

Michaels. Incidentally thousands of dollars were waged on the outcome with the odds being two to one on me.

I noticed that as Michaels came to the tape for the final test his face was colorless. His countenance plainly showed that he had been through a trying ordeal in the last heat. When I won the toss for the pole position Michaels seemed to grow even paler. That position gave me a slight advantage such as he had over me in the other two heats. As he stood over on the track it was apparent that Michaels realized that all the breaks were in my favor, and he seemed especially conscious of the bad defeat he had received in the last heat. The mental suffering and physical strain under which Michaels was laboring at the moment seemed to bewilder him. I felt I had him beaten even before the race started.

I jumped to the front at the crack of the gun, taking the lead by 10 or 12 wheel lengths, which I steadily increased as the race continued. The pace in this heat was terrific and I could tell from the outset that we were travelling in record time. Still it did not seem to have the same strenuous effect on me that I had experienced in the second heat and several times I called for more pace.

After the start I did not see my opponent again until the race was concluded. Michaels quit somewhere on the last lap, and for the first time in his life he was roundly hissed as he rode past the grand stand. I felt sorry for him, because Michaels was the best man in the world at middle-distance racing. But he had made the mistake of his life by going out of his class just as I did sometime later when he defeated me in the 20-mile paced race which was his favorite distance. As I made my way to the dressing room it dawned upon me, as never before, that the public is always with the winner, regardless of color.

It was a well-known fact among trainers, managers, riders and newspaper men that Jimmie Michaels was practically unbeatable as long as he could maintain the lead. However, it was agreed among them that if for any reason he lost the front position he was at that moment a beaten man. In a word he could not fight an up-hill battle to win a race. I knew this before we started that epoch-making race referred to above.

As a result of this extraordinary match race with Jimmie Michaels I gained a distinction that never befell the lot of any other racing cyclist in the world, and created a precedent in bicycle racing that has never been equalled, let alone excelled in the history of any athletic sport as far as I have been able to learn.

In all three heats the world's record for the one-mile competition, standing start, 1.45, which was established by Edward Taylore, the famous French rider, was broken. In the first heat Michaels turned the trick in 1:44-1; in the second heat I set the new mark at 1:43-3, and in the final heat I lowered that mark to 1:41-2, a world's record which has not been bettered in the 29 intervening years. Incidentally in the second heat I set up a mark of 1:43-3 equalling the world's record established by Platt Betts in a mile race with a flying start behind human pace several years before. In the final heat I not only lowered the world's record for the standing start competition to its present figure, 1:41-2, but I also shaved 2:1-5 from Betts' world's record. Therefore, I had the honor of having tied the world's record and beating it in successive heats.

So highly elated was Mr. Brady, my manager, that he made me a present of $1,000 for defeating Michaels. Of course, I was delighted with such a material token of his appreciation for my efforts, or as he so generously put it, "Just a little present from one good sport to another."

Deeply mindful of the important part played by my pacemakers leading up to my victory over Michaels, I decided to split Mr. Brady's thousand dollars with them. At first they were reluctant to do this claiming that they were amply repaid for their efforts by the sincere thanks that I had bestowed upon them as soon as we had entered our dressing room. They also took no little pride in the fact that in that furious second heat they were able to furnish me speed and more speed when I really needed it in my mad dash for the tape and victory. Nevertheless, I insisted and Mr. Brady's generous gift was split among them.

Incidentally, no man was ever more grateful to a group of co-workers than I was to those pacemakers who served me so loyally and well in my defeat of the great Jimmie Michaels. Had any one of them so desired he could have brought about my defeat absolutely without one of his team mates even suspecting a plot. I will always be grateful to my pacemakers on that occasion as they played no small part in what is considered the greatest paced race in the history of the sport in this country.

All of my pacemakers in my race against Michaels were white while I was black, but color evidently was neither a burden, handicap or drawback in this instance. Those fine sportsmen, who paced me in that epoch-making race against Michaels, admired me as an athlete, respected me as a man, and gave their utmost in as trying a race as has ever been ridden, that I might achieve victory over the remarkable Jimmie Michaels.

The following paragraph is quoted from a New York newspaper:

"Major Taylor's victory over Jimmie Michaels, coming as it did just after the unsuccessful efforts of certain race meet managers to debar him from their tracks on account of his color, and for no other reason, has established fortune for him. Now the colored boy's services will have to be sought after by the race track promoters as he is among the very best, if not the very best drawing card among the racing men of the country.

"In view of his newly acquired standing, Major Taylor will doubtless know how to deal with those who have sought to retard his progress and injure his prospects as a National Circuit rider. As for those circuit riders who have heretofore given Taylor the cold shoulder, and sought by unfair and unsportsmanlike methods to compass his defeat in past races, they will now do well if they entertain the slightest hope of defeating or making a creditable showing against this new star, to get a match with him without delay. Their mere suggestions in arranging a match with the colored boy will bring most of them greater prestige than they have ever enjoyed in their careers, while to defeat Major Taylor would make them famous."

Winning Tip from an Ex-Champ
(1898)

One of my first tests on the Grand Circuit in 1898 came at the Asbury Park (N. J.) track. The final heat found the five following riders who were the leaders in the battle for the championship crown:—Tom Cooper, Eddie Bald, Orlando Stevens, Arthur Gardiner and myself, opposing each other in this championship event. I won the final heat but great as that victory was in itself, it remains in my memory merely as an accident to one of my greatest achievements on the track.

As I stepped from the train at Asbury Park the afternoon preceding this race I was met by appointment by Arthur A. Zimmerman, the ex-champion of the bicycling world, the hero of all boyhood, as well as my own ever since I was able to read the newspaper. Five years had elapsed since I saw the great Zimmerman. In my capacity of errand boy for "Birdie" Munger in his Indianapolis home in 1893, I was privileged with a personal introduction to Zimmerman who at the moment was riding on the top wave of his wonderful career. He praised me for my having won a road race in Indianapolis as a boy of 13, tidings of which I later learned were furnished him by my good friend, Mr. Munger, who in after years became my manager.

At dinner that night my joy knew no bounds when Mr. Zimmerman requested that I share the guest's place at the dinner table with him. I wore the gold medal which I had won in the above mentioned road race of my boyhood days and it frequently evoked compliments from Mr. Zimmerman. In the course of the dinner Mr. Zimmerman questioned Mr. Munger closely on my bicycling achievements. Mr. Munger said, "I have told Major Taylor that if he refrained from using liquor and cigarettes, and continued to live a clean life I would make him the fastest bicycle rider in the world." Mr. Zimmerman replied that I had a long way to go before I could hope to acquire those laurels, but he added, "Mr. Munger is an excellent advisor and if he tells me you have the makings of a champion in you, I feel sure you will scale the heights some day."

Through the intervening years Mr. Zimmerman's path and mine had never crossed. However, he kept close tabs on my race track activities and invited me to be his house guest as soon as he learned of my entry in the Asbury Park mile championship race. Incidentally, Mr. Zimmerman was to be starter of the title race.

While the riders were limbering up on the track on the forenoon of the race day, Mr. Zimmerman approached me. He told me again and again how pleased he was at my success on the race tracks. Several times he mentioned what an excellent prophet Mr. Munger proved to be when he forecasted my becoming a champion. "I am very anxious to see you win the championship event this afternoon, Major," said Mr. Zimmerman, "and I feel sure you will, even without a suggestion from me, however, I have one to offer, which aided me greatly in my heyday, and I trust you will give it consideration." Mr. Zimmerman then pointed out the spot on the track at which he advised me to make my "jump," and it was on the back stretch halfway to the last turn. "If you can lead the field into this turn, nobody can pass you before you cross the tape. I made all of my successful sprints from this identical spot." This suggestion on the part of Mr. Zimmerman was to govern my racing tactics in the final heat, the arrangement being that I was to use my own judgment in the qualifying heats.

I thanked Mr. Zimmerman for his kindness in offering this suggestion and assured him I would employ his strategy at all costs in the final heat. I kept my word and won the race which stands out even today as one of my greatest. Hardly had the cheering of the immense throng died away before Mr. Zimmerman and myself repaired to a telegraph office and wired the particulars of the race to our mutual friend and admirer, Mr. Munger.

No group of racing horses ever faced the barrier in a more nervous state than the five riders who were on edge for this championship mile event. Cooper, Bald, Stevens, Gardiner and myself were straining every muscle in an effort to win this classic and thereby get an early edge on the rest of the field for the season's honors. As an indication of how fast the qualifying heats were for our race I might mention that such sterling sprinters as Howard Freeman, "Doc" Brown and Bob Terrill were eliminated, and the speedy Gardiner only won his place in the final heat by winning the extra heat for second man.

The first three laps of that mile race were as hotly contested as any I ever rode in. The pace was terrific. As the bell rang announcing the start of the last lap, and the pacemaker slid out of the picture, there was a mad scramble for final positions. Halfway down the back stretch I made my jump and was leading the field when the turn was made into the home stretch. Bald nearly closed up the gap in a wild sprint but he was not quite equal to the task, falling short by less than a length. Cooper finished at Bald's wheel while Gardner finished fourth, Stevens bringing up the rear. I had kept faith with Mr. Zimmerman and started my sprint at the exact spot he had pointed out to me as he gave me some wonderful advice that forenoon.

Of all the ovations that I ever received the one that crowned my efforts at the Asbury Park track on this memorable occasion will re-

main fresh in my memory forever. I can hear it now. I honestly
believe that Mr. Zimmerman got as much pleasure out of the ovation
as I did myself. I have never seen a more happy man in my life than
Arthur A. Zimmerman as he shook my hand warmly at the conclusion
of the race. Our friend "Birdie" Munger was right, he kept saying.

The Bicycle Fan

An Unequaled Feat
(1898)

I had always considered my physical condition my greatest asset and simultaneously my one and only real weapon of defense. Throughout my racing career I was so fine that a matter of ounces over or under my normal weight would have put me out of the running for the honors.

So when I arrived at the Tioga track in Philadelphia on that summer's afternoon in 1898 I was as near physically perfect as an athlete could be. On top of my excellent physical trim I was bubbling over with confidence with the memory of my victory of the previous week over Bald, Cooper, Gardiner and Stevens.

However, I had no idea that before the sun would set that afternoon I was to make race track history by winning two national championship events on the same program.

When I won those two championship events that afternoon I established a record that has never been equalled on any bicycle race track in this country. During my long period of racing I frequently won two first places on the same program and on numerous occasions I won three firsts in a single day's racing which was the equivalent of winning nine races when one considers the qualifying heats which in many cases were even harder and faster than the finals. Of course, such strenuous racing meant that a man had to be in excellent physical condition at all times and nobody knew this better than myself. I was known as one of the most consistent performers on the track and this was due in a large measure to the excellent care I took of myself.

But to get to my record-breaking performance of winning two championship races in the same program. Let me quote the following paragraphs from the Philadelphia Press:

"Two Victories. Major Taylor rode in front in Circuit Meet. Worcester Boy beat Bald in clever style. Major Taylor, the unbeatable colored boy, took both National Championship events, the one-third mile and the two-mile, at Tioga track today. He won out over the best fields of the season, not excepting the National Meet at Indianapolis, and his excellent work placed him 10 points nearer in the race for the championship fight.

"Major Taylor won his heats and finals under the greatest difficulties, he was third and fourth place in the bunch as they rounded the last turn into the home stretch, and again and again managed to win out in spite of the fact that the very best men in the country were ahead of him on entering the stretch.

"Major Taylor was superior to his fields today, as was Zimmerman superior in the days of long ago on the same track.

"For the one-third mile championship battle, Eddie Bald, Major Taylor, Tom Cooper, Arthur Gardiner and Howard Freeman were the most excellent line-up. Gardiner rushed off in the lead with Taylor and Bald just back of him, side by side, Taylor on the pole and Freeman and Cooper following, with Freeman on the pole directly behind Taylor. It was the Detroit man, Cooper, however, who made the jump for the tape and shot to the front, gaining two clear lengths. Taylor jumped from the side of Bald, then Freeman came up from the rear, Taylor quickly catching Cooper and gaining his side. At this point Freeman came to the front making the battle a three-cornered one to the tape, with Taylor winning out by inches over Freeman while Cooper was third. The three finished within half a length, Gardiner was fourth and Champion Bald last."

I was given such a splendid ovation at the conclusion of that race that I determined to enter the two-mile championship event. However, some of my opponents were not anxious to have me start in that event and as I made my way to the dressing rooms one of them openly threatened me with bodily harm if I dared to start in that event. His objection was not based on anything that I had done to him because he did not even ride in the final of the one-third mile championship. Had there been any question in my mind about riding in that two-mile championship it would have been cast aside when I heard that threat. I decided on the spot that I would participate in that race, come what may, and it gave me no little pleasure to lead the field across the finish line for my second championship win of the afternoon, the time owing to excitement was not taken.

Again I quote from the Press account of the meet:

"For the two-mile championship Eddie Bald, Orlando Stevens, Major Taylor, Arthur Gardiner, and 'Plugger' Bill Martin formed the second block of five and a most excellent field. Bald jumped the gun but Taylor beat him in a good race for the pacemaker. Taylor was followed by Bald, Stevens, Gardiner and Martin.

"The pace was so fast that there was no change in positions until the bell lap, when Gardiner came from the rear with Martin on his rear wheel. The pair rounded Taylor and took the lead. Then Bald gained the side of Taylor, placing him in a bad pocket. Stevens made a hot sprint from the rear but was stalled off by Martin, who broke for the tape, which gave Taylor his liberty, the latter being in fourth place on entering the home stretch.

"With a clear field, Taylor jumped with a most wonderful burst of speed, but it was not before the tape was reached that he snatched the lead and won by two feet with Gardiner, Martin, Stevens and Bald close up in that order."

Just before this two-mile race was started a spectator came to me and asked if he could say a few words in private. He was highly excited but I granted his request and we moved off a few feet. He told me he had overheard the other riders planning to throw me. He

Eddie "Cannon" Bald—Champion of America,
1895–1896–1897

implored me not to ride in this race, but I thanked him and told him I was determined to participate regardless of what might happen. However, the information together with the threat one of the riders had made to me personally, had its affect on me and I became nervous. I went to the officials and asked if they would put in double pacemakers for this final and place a very low time limit on the race that we might attempt to establish a world's record for the distance. "I am feeling tip-top today," I told the officials, "and if you will grant this request I assure you that you will see the greatest race you have ever witnessed on this track, or ever will witness on it, and this, regardless of who wins."

Reluctantly they agreed to my plan. However, I had to explain to them my reason for making these unusual requests. I explained to them that the other riders were out to injure me and the only chance

I had to prevent their doing so was to set such a hot pace from the crack of the pistol that they would have their hands full trying to hang on, let alone endeavor to throw me down.

After hearing my extraordinary plea the officials were intensely interested to see how my plan would work out and picked the best and strongest riders for pacing that were at the track. They were instructed to set as fast a pace as possible—and they certainly did. One of the requests that I had made was to have the first pacemaker placed out on the 50-yard mark. When my opponents saw him at that mark they complained that he was out too far but the referee waved aside their protests. They knew all too well that this was a point in my favor because I could jump away from the mark faster than they.

Since there was considerable more than usual at stake in this race I beat the gun a little. So did Eddie Bald, the champion, but in the scramble between us for the pacemaker I gained the advantage and we were off at a terrific rate of speed. Bald was out to redeem himself for having suffered defeat at my hands in the preceding race and he was putting forth his greatest efforts in an endeavor to square himself.

The pace was a scorcher but the race was going exactly the way I had figured it would. The positions were unchanged right up to the bell lap. With the sounding of the bell the monster crowd was in an uproar. There was a mad scramble for the tape but in it the riders had to be very careful in their tactics as the slightest miscue meant certain defeat for them.

As we tore into the back stretch, each rider straining every nerve and muscle in an effort to get the advantage, I was in fourth position and I held that place as we fairly flew into the last turn and rounded into the home stretch. With the most frantic effort I had ever made I fought my way through that bunch of madly sprinting riders and took the front position just as we burst across the tape. My margin of victory was narrow but there was no question about my having won and I received the most thundering ovation that has ever been my lot as I rode an extra lap around the track. The band played "Dixie" and there was a shower of straw hats, fans and programs on the track before I could dismount and make my way to the dressing room.

Every one of the officials of the meet congratulated me warmly on the great race I had just turned in. They all reminded me that I had kept my promise to show them the best race they had ever witnessed. However, down in my heart my greatest thrill centered not so much in having won the race, and I prized the victory highly, but in the fact that I had thwarted the "frame-up" planned by my fellow riders.

Shortly after I had reached my dressing room and was being rubbed down by my trainer, all of the riders who participated in the program that afternoon came rushing into my quarters. Naturally I was frightened, having in mind the threat I overheard, and the warning given me by one of the spectators just before the two-mile race started. However, I was due for a very pleasant surprise when every one of the riders shook my hand in turn, and congratulated me on my two championship victories during the afternoon.

It was the first time in my career that any of my so-called "big" competitors had ever congratulated me for any of my achievements on the track. I was elated, naturally, at this turn of affairs and the satisfaction that I had in having my rivals congratulate me for my successes that day was worth considerably more to me than the prize money I took home. It was the first manifestation of good sportsmanship on the part of my opponents. I felt that their action was a demonstration of their admiration and respect for me as a man and that meant far more to me than even the special purse which was offered the winner of this two-mile race. Incidentally, their action proved my contention that the spirit of true sportsmanship will bring out, or at least should bring out the highest qualities and very best motives that a man can possibly possess. I also beat the field out at a night meet on the Woodside track, Philadelphia, in a hard run mile open event, making a total of three first places in the same day.

A Tribute from an Opponent
(1898)

Disgusted by the foul tactics that some of my rivals had used to prevent me from winning the one-third-mile and two-mile championship races in Philadelphia, Howard Freeman, one of my fairest and fastest opponents, wrote a tribute to me in a local newspaper, including:

Major Taylor has a wonderfully quick jump and when he finds an opening, he manages to jump through it so quickly that it is impossible to close in on him. He has won a number of races this season in this manner but the majority of his races have been won in the cleanest possible manner, apparently without effort and by a pure burst of speed.

The fact that most of the racing men hate him is anything but encouraging. Eddie Bald threatened to thrash him several times this season, but owing to interference he did not get a chance to disfigure the Major's Black countenance.

On August 16, at Green Bay, Wis, Taylor won all the professional races on the entire program and in a most decisive manner. During the entire season he was shown that he is blessed with an almost superhuman burst of speed. The Major cannot stand a race paced fast and jerky as well as Eddie Bald, who excels in this kind of race, and the majority of defeats that Bald has administered to the Major has been in races of this class.

Major Taylor, however, deserves a great amount of credit for the splendid manner in which he has ridden this season, as it has been done under the most discouraging circumstances. All the boys willingly acknowledge him to be the fastest rider on the track and also as a splendid fellow personally, but on account of his color they cannot stand to see him win over them. If it were possible to make him white, all of the boys would gladly assist him in the job, but try as they may, I think it will be almost impossible to keep this little Negro boy, who came into the cycling world entirely unheralded, from winning the cycle championship of America for the season of 1898.

How My Strategy Foiled "Pockets"
(1898)

A few weeks after I had won the one-third and two-mile championship races in the same afternoon at Philadelphia, I practically repeated those performances at the Green Bay, Wis., track. On this occasion I won the one-third mile event and the one-mile national championship race. Prize money amounting to $2,500 was offered for this meet and it attracted the crack riders of the country.

A short time before the final heat of the one-mile championship race the trainer for another rider informed me that there was a plot afoot among my opponents to pocket me. I made my way to the officials and told them of this plan. They asked for a suggestion as to how they could overcome that conspiracy and I replied by ordering double pacemaking for the event. They readily agreed.

The following clipping from a Green Bay newspaper will show how my strategy allowed me to again lead the field across the tape in two finals:

"Major Taylor, the colored boy from Worcester, Mass., easily proved himself to be the king of the pedal-pushers at the local track today. By his magnificent riding he gained second place in the championship struggle for points and finished his day's work only 14 points behind Bald, who failed to qualify, as did MacFarland and Kimble, who failed to gain recognition in their respective heats.

"In the final of the one-mile professional championship race a field of seven as good men as could be found in America today qualified, and double pacemaking was employed. The contestants caught on behind them in this order: Eddie Bald, Orlando Stevens, Major Taylor, Arthur Gardiner, Johnnie Fisher, Howard Freeman and Owen Kimble.

"There was no change of positions until the pacemakers dropped out, at the last quarter, when Taylor made a jump for the front. Fisher then made a dash past him for the lead which he immediately lost again to Taylor. Freeman watched for the rear wheel of Taylor, who finally made his jump for home winning again by two open lengths, with Freeman second, Gardiner third, Kimble fourth and Bald last.

"In the final of the one-third mile race Freeman, Gardiner, Cooper, Fisher and Taylor lined up in that order from the pole. Taylor with Fisher at his side, jumped to the lead right from the start. Cooper tried to come around them, but failed. Then Gardiner also tried but with no better success.

"At the quarter, Taylor made his famous jump but Fisher went after him hot-foot while Gardiner dropped back in single line and shot down the home stretch. It was too late, however, as Taylor finished, an open winner, by two lengths with Fisher second, and Gardiner and Cooper at his rear wheel, only inches apart with Freeman last. The time was 42 seconds which was close to the record despite the poor condition of the track."

Realizing that the entire field was out to pocket me in the one-mile championship race, which was the feature of the program, I decided to employ my so-called Philadelphia strategy to nip their plot in the bud. My tactics centered about having the officials put in double pacemakers.

They had little chance to deal with me in the one-third mile race because the distance was so short. A race of this distance calls for a mad scramble from the crack of the pistol to the tape with no opportunity in between to jockey for positions.

Although I told the officials of the race track that I desired the double pacemakers in an effort to forestall pocketing and other rough tactics on the part of my competitors in the one-mile championship race I really had something else in mind. My thought was to have the pacemakers set such a terrific pace from the outset that the scheming riders would be so busy holding the pace that they would not have time to carry through their foul plans. As the officials seemed a bit skeptical about my reason for making this unique request, I played my trump card. It was, in effect, that I was feeling in exceptionally fine form that afternoon and felt that with the proper pace a world's record might be established. They swallowed my line of reasoning, hook, line and sinker. That's just what the crowd wanted—and the officials also. I received a wonderful ovation.

Despite the fact that I had number "13" wished on me by the racing officials in that season of 1898, and notwithstanding the foul tactics of my opponents, the press of the country was almost unanimous in declaring me the sprint champion of the country. My record for the season, covering 49 starts, included 29 first places, nine second places, and 11 third places.

The official standing of the leading sprinters of the country that year credited me with 121 points to 113 for Arthur Gardiner, 107 for Floyd MacFarland, and 98 for Eddie Bald, who was Champion in 1895-6-7.

Breaking a World's Record
(1898)

After having participated in about 50 regularly scheduled bicycle racing events in 1898, there was an insistent demand that I try to reduce the one-mile record behind human pace. It had been established a short time previously by Edward Taylore, the famous French flier, at 1:32-3 as against the 1:35 mark created by J. Platt Betts in England some time previous. It is a coincidence that three Taylors figure prominently in the assaults on Betts' record as the following newspaper story will indicate:

"Three Taylors have figured in reduction of the One-mile World's Record. It is an interesting fact that since the days of Willie Windle, when that wonderful record breaker from Millbury, Mass., brought the world's bicycle (ordinary) record for one-mile across the Atlantic wresting it from Fred J. Osmond, the English Champion in 1892, whose best time was 2:15, the one-mile has been held by no less than three Taylors. Windle's record was 2:25 3/5.

"The first of these Taylors was George F. Taylor of Ipswich, Mass., a Harvard University graduate. He made two trials; and when he finished the record was 2:14, behind human pace. Later he went out to lower this 2:14 mark and succeeded in 1894, setting up as his final record 2:11. He was satisfied with having lowered the mile mark and after devoting some time to competitive racing he retired to private life in 1894 and is now a prosperous dentist.

One of the first things of vital importance that I learned after joining the big pros, which gave me a world of confidence was that no rider on the track could handle his machine with greater dexterity than I, which was due to the fact that I had formally been an expert trick and fancy rider. Another thing equally important to me was that all of the top-notchers were extremely afraid of a fall, and if forced into a pocket, or suddenly bumped or elbowed, many of them would actually sit up, or quit cold rather than risk bumping the track.

I was not so much in fear of a toss from the big riders as by the second and third class men, who were in the pay of the big riders for a cut of the purse, and they would stop at nothing. Knowing these vulnerable spots in the big sprinters was a great advantage to me, and now that I had mastered the scientific and technic of bicycle racing, "pockets" and "elbows" no longer had any terrors for me. I have been asked numerous times how I got out of a pocket.

In order to be able to get out of a pocket successfully, is to do it without interfering with or bringing any one down. To pull this stunt a rider must have a lightning like "jump," and he should also develop a wonderful bunch of nerve to put it over. I actually had the trick down so fine at certain times that I have often really invited a pocket as a matter of tactics, when I had a dangerous man on my rear wheel I would slip right into a pocket, making no effort to get out until just nearing the tape then timing my jump perfectly I would suddenly hop through leaving my rival in the lurch. The chances were a thousand to one that he would make no attempt to follow me through, and in case he did get through successfully it would be too late, as I would invariably be over the tape yards ahead.

In the middle of a turn I always found the most favorable spot on the track to get out of a "pocket" because it is almost impossible for a rider to tear off a dead sprint at top speed without swerving, or wobbling more or less, and therefore even more difficult and dangerous for three or more riders to engage in a furious sprint on the steep banking and ride steady, and at the same time carry out their part of the plot, then crouching very low, I have often started through with scarcely space enough for my front wheel to pass, and having been so well protected from wind resistance, since the pocket formed a sort of a vacuum I was able to kick through like a cork out of a champagne bottle as I have often heard remarked. As a matter of fact I consider this the most skillful bit of tactics in bicycle racing.

As a rule it requires at least three good men to form an effective pocket, for example, one man leading on the pole, with the pocketed rider on his rear wheel, when the second man comes with a rush and suddenly eases up when slightly in advance of the pocketed rider, the third man quickly comes around from the rear of the pocketed man and dashes for the tape, defeating all the others, the two men forming the pocket sacrificing their chances by holding their victim in the pocket. The winner would of course be expected to split the spoils with the riders who formed the pocket.

What I considered the most vicious practice in the way of foul riding on a bicycle track was often staged by two riders, while we were entering home stretch, or on the back stretch at a break-neck speed, with one leading on the pole, the other close on his right, at this point the man on the right would swerve out just enough to tempt the rider following to pass between them, they would suddenly then close in on him, causing him to bump the track with a terrible crash. If he came through the experience alive it's a safe bet he would never try it again.

These treacherous tactics were nothing less than an attempt to kill, and riders guilty of such fiendish practices should be dealt with severely, or at least permanently eliminated from the sport. I have often been criticised for going through a pocket on the pole, and it was a strict violation of the racing rules, but my answer was this: I was always on the defensive, they were the first to violate the rules by forcing me into a pocket, in the next place it was also an infraction of the rules for a rider, or a number of riders to interfere with another rider. Without such unfair tactics it would not be necessary for me to undertake such dangerous risks, I only took such daring chances as a last resort; they were teaming, which was strictly against the rules, while I was playing the game single-handed in the big majority of my races, so under the circumstances the odds were so overwhelming that I always felt perfectly justified in getting out of a pocket in any manner possible, so long of course as I could do so without bringing anyone down; besides, my own neck was in jeopardy.

In extricating myself from these perilous positions I did not rely entirely on my quick jump but it was also a matter of perfect judgment, skill and daring required in timing a jump, and be able to flash through at the critical moment. At times it might be necessary to force matters by giving the riders' rear wheel directly ahead of me, a side slap with my front wheel by a quick jerk of my handle bar, this would frighten him and invariably cause him to swerve out a trifle, instantaniously I would kick through, and win the race. Incidentally I never once brought any rider down, which was remarkable, considering the hundreds of times I worked it. And I openly challenge and defy any track official to say that I ever willfully, accidentally, or otherwise threw another rider, or in any way did commit a dishonorable act in bicycle racing as long as I was connected with the game. I admit I was no angel, I had my faults, but in my honest opinion a real honest to goodness champion can always win on his merits.

On more than one occasion during my career it was my good fortune to enjoy many rare thrills, such as I imagine comparatively few people have ever been privileged to enjoy. It was the climax that followed a bitterly fought out victory over a vast field of competitors, who with their managers and trainers had concentrated both their mental and physical forces in figuring out and practicing certain tricks, and schemes for weeks, in order to trim the "nigger."

On the day set for the big race every rider trained to the minute and chock full of confidence, and keyed up to the highest pitch of nervous energy, and rareing to go. The stage all set, the final words of instructions whispered by their anxious trainers, the crack of the pistol sounded, and we were off with a wild dash tearing off speed they had never shown before.

I could only figure out the frame up as the race progressed, but instantly I detected their schemes, by a clever bit of jockeying or maneuvering I could invarably upset their crooked plans, and once their moral was destroyed they were thrown in a state of confusion, the rest was easy, I had only to rely on a well-timed jump in the home stretch to complete the job, and sail across the tape a winner amid the roaring cheers of the spectators.

With this victory, came the sublime thrill that was beyond the power of words to express, and the fact of having defeated single-handed the whole crooked outfit, the riders, their trainers and managers, as well, made it a victory fit for the kings. Having won over them in a clean-cut decisive manner I considered it ample compensation for

Quintet Pacing Teams. Before the Days of Motor Pacing

all their unfair and cunning schemes. It was as sweet a revenge as one could wish for.

"The next Taylor to set the one-mile human-paced record was Edward Taylore, the French rider. He spells his name with a final "e," simply to distinguish himself from Major Taylor. Edward Taylore won the honors at Philadelphia in 1898 when he lowered J. Platt Betts' record of 1:35 and set a new mark of 1:32-3. It was thought that these figures would stand for a long time but within a few months Major Taylor had whittled the record down to 1:31-4 and insisted he could lower it to better than 1:30. With that end in view the maker of the bicycle Taylor was riding at the time offered his pacemakers a bonus of $10,000 if they succeeded in aiding Taylor to turn the mile inside of 1:30.

"In the past 20 years the world's record for one mile has been reduced nearly one half. In all, it has witnessed 48 reductions in which no less than 25 riders have taken part. America and England are the only two countries represented in the table and of course this country takes the lead."

Anxious as I was to establish the one-mile human-paced record, I had something else in mind as I turned my sails to lower Taylore's phenomenal mark. I felt that if I could establish a new world's record for the mile that such a performance would go far to dispel any doubts about my right to the American sprint championship honors.

So intent was I upon establishing a new world record for the one-mile that in preparation for my race against time, I hung up new marks for the quarter, one-third, half and three-quarter mile distances. I made these four records on the Woodside Park track in Philadelphia which was also scheduled to stage my race against time in the one-mile event.

I quote from an article printed at the time in the New York *Sun* as follows:

"It is a serious fact that last week, when the horse was monarch in New York, its silent steel-framed contemporary, the wheel, was monarch in Philadelphia, and succeeded in establishing some records for time that throw all past performances of trotters and runners into total eclipse. Indeed, the surprising exhibitions of Major Taylor, the crack colored cyclist, at Philadelphia, have opened the eyes of all wheelmen and horsemen as well. During the week, Major Taylor lowered the paced records for the quarter-mile and one-mile and some of his feats were accomplished under circumstances which would probably have discouraged almost all other riders with reputations for high speed.

"But none of Taylor's remarkable performances equalled the efforts of Wednesday when compelled to exert himself to the utmost because of faulty pacing, he smashed his own record of 1:32, shortening the time for the distance by one-fifth of a second and thus establishing his new one-mile mark of 1:31 4/5. Soon after this achievement Major Taylor sought to lower the figures for the three-quarters of a mile and succeeded in clipping one-fifth of a second from his own record, making the new one read 1:08 2/5. In the same trial he covered the half-mile in :45 1/5 which was one-fifth of a second under the best previous time and :02 2/5 under the record held by Windle. It is worthy of note that Major Taylor's achievements were made in almost continuous riding, very little time being devoted to rest.

"In that respect, as in regard to the number of excellent records established, his performances will doubtless arouse the admiration of all racing men the world over, but it will doubtless startle the cycling fraternity. However, more than anything else, is the fact that four-fifths of a second has been slashed from the old record of the one-mile mark, and further evidence has been given that ere long the 1:30 mark will be easily within the possibilities of the wheel.

"It can scarcely be expected that the one-mile figures will show some drop correspondingly in the next 14 months, as has been shown since September, 1897. In that month J. S. Stocks rode a mile at Crystal Palace, London, in 1:35 2/5. It was that performance which exhibited the bicycle as speedier by one-tenth of a second than the horse. When two or three years previous, W. W. Hamilton of Denver, rode a mile at Coranado, California, in 1:39, it was thought that the bicycle had attained an astonishing speed, but a little over a year after Hamilton's record was lowered almost a second by Eddie Mc-Duffee of Boston, and in about a week after the latter's record ride, J. Platt Betts, the English champion, rode the mile in 1:37 2/5.

"It was thought by many when Stocks knocked two seconds from the previous record that it might remain for some time on the other side of the water, but now our English fliers will have to bestir themselves if they hope to regain past honors."

Another New York newspaper carried the following story on the same day:

"Major Taylor a Cycling Wonder. His Riding at Philadelphia stamps him as the Fastest Bicycle Rider in the World. Colored Marvel will make an Effort to cover the Mile in less than 1:30. No man knows what speed possibilities are concealed in those lithe limbs of the colored boy, Major Taylor, who today is being deluged with telegrams from all parts of the country congratulating him on the annexation of the world's one-mile and half-mile bicycle records, but Taylor smiles and is not satisfied. He is certain of 1:30 for the mile or better, and 44 seconds or better for the half mile is possible.

"Taylor has shown himself a wonder. Other record breakers have again and again tried for the coveted record. Hamilton tried 16 times before he turned the trick in 1:39 1/5 which stood as a record for 17 months. Earl Kiser followed Hamilton in 16 trials, in a great majority of which he lost his pace, and made it in 1:40, and could not come lower. Johnnie Johnson went 12 times for the record of Hamilton, but came no nearer than 1:40.

"While it is true that attempts since that time have been more uniformly successful, as in the case of Eddie McDuffee and Edward Taylore, these have been made at the very height of the racing season when pacemaking teams were at their very best, and after months and months of training and not during the early winter when the cold winds made the teeth chatter, and when officials and spectators would rather have been at the side of a warm stove than at the track side.

"Major Taylor went up against great odds and succeeded. He made his attempts when others would not have done so, and succeeded. He failed but once, and that was the mile which he did in 1:33 3/5,

very near the record.   He twice cut the two miles and finally lopped
13 seconds off the mark, and that within a few minutes after establishing the mile record.   He did quarters, and thirds in these rides
that were records again and again, and he is confident that no record
so far made, will stand if he goes again.   His pacemakers have been
unable to shake him and they, too, are confident."

In that campaign of 1899, covering six weeks of very strenuous
work I established seven world's records, viz.:—the quarter, third, half,

Establishing World's One-mile Record behind Multicycles

two-thirds, three-quarters, one mile and two miles.   However, I got
the most satisfaction out of my one-mile accomplishment as it is
generally regarded as the standard distance for all kinds of speed tests.

While I was delighted with these records I felt in my heart that I
could have broken 1:20 for the mile if my pacemakers could hit up
that clip.   My reason for being so confident was that in all my racing
career I never was in better fettle than when I was making those
successful onslaughts against the long standing records for almost all
distances up to two miles, in the teeth of those November gales.
However, I kept my belief to myself as I knew full well that were I
to mention covering the mile in 1:20 I would have been made the
laughing stock of the racing-track world.

One day just before making my successful try for the new one-
mile record I became convinced that I could never do a faster mile
behind human pace.   The reason for this was that I knew my pacemakers, who were among the very best in the world, gave me every-

thing they had in that race against time, and the best they were able to do was :01 4/5 over the goal I aimed at—1:30. I am confident that they could have ridden several seconds faster on a hot day, but on that cold bleak November day when I lowered the mile record, my pacemakers were absolutely going at their utmost speed when I established the record of 1:31 4/5.

I might mention an incident that occurred shortly before I made my record-breaking ride to establish the mile record to show just how fast I was riding. In my record trials every day I was continuously calling to my pacemakers for more speed. My requests in themselves annoying my pacemakers somewhat and doubly so as some newspaper men overheard me as I called for more speed. The pacemakers unknown to me, got together and decided to shake me off at the next day's trial against time. They purposely held the fastest pacing quintet on the track, all picked men, to take me on the last lap, one-third of a mile, in my record-breaking one-mile race. I had a fresh quintet for each lap in that record-breaking attempt. As a matter of fact, I had another spare quintet take me around the track for the bell lap just prior to the start of the race. This combination giving me a much desired warming up sprint before picking up the team that would take me around the initial lap to my record-making mile.

However, on the last lap I called again and again for more speed from my pacemaking quintet and failing to get the desired results I set out on my own hook, and actually passed that crack combination on the home stretch, leading them over the tape. It was long after that that I was told about the "frame-up" arranged by my pacemakers in their efforts to shake me off in this record-breaking mile sprint. The laugh was certainly on the pacemakers and the newspaper men took good care that it was widely heralded.

A Banner Season
(1899)

Throughout the winter of 1898 I kept in fine physical trim at the Y. M. C. A. gymnasium in my home town, Worcester, Mass. My trainer outlined a course of light exercises for me which I followed to the letter and when the spring rolled around I was in excellent condition for what was destined to be my greatest season on the American tracks. To make sure that I did not get down too fine I carried about six pounds extra weight the same being my reserve in case my opponents started crowding me.

All through that winter season I had four objectives before me. One was the championship of the world, the second was to again win the American championship, the third was to reduce the one-mile world's record to 1:20 or lower, and the fourth was to secure a match race with Tom Cooper or Eddie Bald, leading claimants for the championship of America at the moment and formerly undisputed champions of America. I knew that it was an heroic-sized order and never for the moment did I let up in my training stunts.

I started the ball rolling that season by winning my very first race at Philadelphia. One of my most spectacular victories of the year was winning the big $500 two-mile handicap sweepstake on the Charles River track in Boston on Memorial Day.

I started from scratch with Nat Butler, that great old war-horse who was widely known as the "Handicap King." A last-minute accident deprived me of my sprint bicycle and I was forced to ride a wheel that I only used behind pace. It was geared to 114 inchees which was a tremendous jump from the 92-inch sprinting gear which I had planned to use in this event. Any bicycle racer will appreciate the handicap that that difference of 22 inches means to a rider in a sprint competition race. It is considered an insurmountable handicap. However, I had become so used to doing what seemed to be impossible stunts on a bicycle that I decided to take another chance in this race with my big gear. Again I was relying mainly in this emergency upon my fine physical condition to carry me through.

I left the mark with a jump with Nat Butler on my wheel and we were soon in hot pursuit of his brother, Tom Butler, who had been given a handicap of 50 yards on us. Another brother, Frank Butler, and Watson Coleman started from the 80-yard mark but by alternating pace at half-lap intervals Nat Butler and I managed to overtake the leaders just as the bell clanged for the beginning of the final lap.

Frank Butler was leading at that moment. Then Nat Butler shot to the front of the bunch with brother Tom on his wheel. I made a quick play and nailed Tom's rear wheel as I could see they were relying upon him to defeat me for the big stakes. It was known far and wide that the three Butler Brothers were just about the cleverest combination in regards to team work in the racing world. Thanks to my track generalship I was able to hold my position with that fast field right into the home stretch, and then I cut loose with a great burst of speed that let me break the tape first with several lengths to spare.

There was a tremendous crowd on hand for this special event, the three Butler Brothers being especially popular with the racing fans of their native Boston. Residents of the Hub were well posted in the finer points of the racing game and appreciated full well just how tricky the Butler Brothers were. They were noted throughout the country for their speed and cleverness. With those facts in mind one may well appreciate the ovation that was accorded me for outgeneralling and outsprinting the great trio and the rest of the field in that hectic two-mile race which I won in 4:34.

After a short rest I returned to the track and won the final of the one-mile open race thereby repeating my former successes at Philadelphia and Green Bay when I made bicycle race track history by winning two events on each of those programs, one championship race in each of those meets and the other victories being in open events. Incidentally, I took home $875 as my day's winnings on the Charles River track on May 30, 1899.

The following is an excerpt from the Boston *Post*, printed the day after the Charles River meet.

"Major Taylor Triumphs. Proved a Star. Colored Rider Wins Twice in dashing sprints. Wins Two-mile Sweepstake and One-mile Open. Tom Butler easily beaten. Major Taylor proved to be the star of the A. C. C. meet at Charles River Park yesterday afternoon and succeeded in winning every race in which he competed, his winnings amounting to $875. The Butler Brothers, Nat, Tom and Frank took about everything the Major left on the list. A large crowd witnessed the races which were good and lively with exceptionally fine finishes in the two professional events. The weather was perfect and conditions were never better for fast racing except for a heavy wind on the back stretch.

"In both the one-mile open professional and the two-mile A. C. C. sweepstake Major Taylor was on scratch with Nat Butler and won both his heats and finals leaving the other scratch men behind. James J. Casey of Worcester was out on the 120-yard mark in the sweepstakes and ran fourth in the final. The Major raced under difficulties by being compelled to ride a machine geared up to 114 inches.

This is the first time a sprinter ever used such a high geared wheel in a sprint race, and manage to win out in a sprint with it.

"Tom Butler, who is to ride Taylor a match race at Westboro on June 10, ran second in the sweepstakes, he having 50 yards on the man whom he is to ride from scratch with. Butler rode well, however. Major rode a splendid race in the two-mile sweepstake. He started from scratch with Nat Butler and the pair caught the bunch on the sixth lap and the Major set the crowd wild by a magnificent sprint down the home stretch which carried him in first. The time was 4:34. Tom Butler on the 50-yard line was second, Frank Butler on the 80-yard line was third, and James J. Casey, 120 yards, fourth. Watson Coleman and Eddie McDuffee also ran."

On June 10 I lost the match race to my great rival Tom Butler at Westboro, Mass. Naturally, Butler was elated at this victory over me and especially since it was by a very wide margin, thereby removing considerable of the sting attached to my victory over him at the Charles River Park meet 10 days previous. I always considered my loss of that race due to the fact that I was obliged to ride my wheel with the big gear, which I had used in the sweepstakes race in Boston, only a short time before and partly to the fact that the Westboro race was run on a four-lap dirt track making it impossible for me to jump as fast as Butler. He was at his best in that race and as a result he led me over the line for the first time in his life.

In addition to the purse offered for the race at Westboro, which was divided 75 percent to the winner and 25 percent to the loser, the winner also was to get 25 percent of the gate receipts. On top of that Butler and I placed a side bet of $200 all of which was to go to the victor.

Three weeks later, July 2, I more than atoned for this defeat at the hands of Tom Butler. This match race was held on the Charles River Park track, Boston, and in it I had the use of my sprint wheel which was geared to 92 inches.

My Triumph Over Tom Butler
(1899)

On July 2, 1899, I participated in one of the greatest match races of my career when I defeated my old rival Tom Butler in straight heats on the Charles River Park track, Boston, for a purse of $1,000. Coming three weeks after his defeat of me on the Westboro, Massachusetts track for a purse that aggregated $500, this victory was especially pleasing to me. I felt that the fact that I was obliged to ride a wheel with a big gear brought about my downfall at Westboro,

Tom Butler—One of the Famous Butler Brothers

as it was impossible for me to jump as fast as Butler on the four-lap dirt track there. An accident to my 92-inch sprint wheel caused me to shift to the big gear at the last moment.

My match race with Tom Butler at the Boston track was the feature of the L. A. W. meet on that occasion. It was arranged that we would ride one-mile heats, the winner of two of them to have the purse of $1,000. I won the first two heats but had to ride the second one over again as the spectators were not educated to the French method of riding the unpaced mile heat, and insisted that the second heat be re-run. I readily consented to do this and the newspaper men present agreed that I showed Tom Butler as fast a sprint, in that re-run heat, as he had ever seen.

In the first heat Frank Gately furnished the pace and when he dropped out at the last quarter Butler and I sprinted for ourselves. We flew into the home stretch about even but I quickly jumped, and shot across the tape, winning by a half wheel length. No pace-makers were used in the second heat, as is the custom in France, the riders loafing along until within 200 yards of the tape. At this point the pair of us made a gallant effort for first place. I won by a wheel's length. I received a wonderful ovation.

My next race, which marked the opening of the Grand Circuit, was held in St. Louis, in July 1899. No rider ever received a greater ovation than I when I won that championship.

I quote this account of it from a St. Louis newspaper:

"Major Taylor a Champion. Beats Them All In One-Mile Championship. Major Taylor won the one-mile national champion-ship this afternoon. A large crowd was present to witness the post-poned races.

"Tom Butler was a favorite with many of the spectators, who looked to him to win, but he disappointed their expectations by fin-ishing fourth in what was a comparatively slow race. But the real race of the day was between Jerry Woodard, Major Taylor and Charles McCarthy. All three stayed together all through the race until the colored rider by a plucky jump managed to leave them at the finish line by a wheel's length. The crowd cheered the Major heartily and he evidently has many friends in this city.

"The final of the one-mile national championship was won by Major Taylor first, Woodard second, and McCarthy third. St. Louis has for years been a great cycling town, and has turned out many famous riders, such as, Charles McCarthy, Jerry Woodard, Dute Cabanne, the famous Coburn brothers, and many other fast riders." I received a most flattering ovation from the spectators, and officials.

Next I went to Chicago for the L. A. W. meet. In those days Chicago was a hotbed of racing. The city had turned out such famous sprinters as, Bliss, Githens, Diernberger, Lumsden, Was Sicklin, Spooner, Munger, Barrett, Tuttle, Rhodes, Gardiner, Bowler, Leander, Peabody, the wonderful amateur champion, and a host of other star riders. It was my first appearance in Chicago since I won the 10-mile road race against Henry Stewart, "the St. Louis Flyer," back in 1894. I was anxious to show the bicycle fans of that city how much I had improved in the meantime.

The one-mile professional championship event was the feature of the card and it was one of the greatest bicycle races that Chicago had ever seen. The starters included Tom Butler, Nat Butler, Jimmie Bowler, Charlie McCarthy, and myself, all having qualified in the four preliminary heats. In the final Bowler and myself were so close together at the finish line that the judges declared it a dead heat although a number of the newspaper men declared positively that I had won.

It took two starts to get us away for the final heat and it was nip and tuck all the way. Bowler had the lead on the last lap and kept it into the stretch. "Fifty yards from the tape," read a Chicago newspaper account of the race, "Major Taylor began a magnificent spurt. It looked as if Bowler was a sure winner, but the colored rider came with a great rush and passed him at the tape. The crowd yelled for both Bowler and Taylor, and some for a dead heat, according as the finish impressed them, but a dead heat was declared although it looked to many as if Major Taylor had fairly won the decision. The riders divided the purse, and tossed up for first place, which was won by Major Taylor, Nat Butler was third."

I believe I won that race, but Chicago was Bowler's home town. On top of that I had never received the benefit of a close decision. I offered to ride the race over again right on the spot, the winner to take both first and second money, and also the championship points, but Bowler refused. Much to the disappointment of the public.

Janesville, Wisconsin, was the scene of the next National Circuit Championship event in which I figured. Tom Butler defeated me in the one-mile title event, that being the first time I trailed anybody in a national championship race that year. Nat Butler was third in this championship, while Bowler, the Chicago man, who rode a dead heat with me the preceding week in Chicago, finished fourth, with Eddie Llewellyn fifth. However, I made up for that loss by winning the one-mile open and the five-mile handicap events, Tom Butler being second to me in the five-mile race, in which he startd from the 25-yard mark, with Barney Oldfield, who later won undying fame as an automobile racer, third, and Dunbar fourth.

That made still another occasion in which I won two races on the same program, tossing in a second place for full measure.

An Unexpected Win at Ottumwa

(1899)

I decided to give up riding on the National Circuit for a week or two, following the Janesville program, so that I might go to Chicago to make an attempt to once more lower the one-mile world's record. That meant I would skip the Circuit races which were scheduled to be held at Ottumwa, Iowa, July 26 and 27.

Arriving in Chicago, I met "Birdie" Munger who was to take charge of my record trials. My objective was the world record for the mile, which was held by Eddie McDuffee, who was the first bicycle rider to ride the distance under 1:30. As I trained for this trial against the world record something went wrong with my big steam pacing tandem which had been specially built for me for this occasion.

Since it would take several days to make repairs to my pacing machine I decided to jump to Ottumwa and participate in the Circuit races there. I had been working out on the Chicago track for two weeks with a big gear, it measured 114 inches. Shifting from that 114-inch gear back to my usual sprint gear, 92 inches, would, I felt certain, prove too much of a handicap for me against the fast field that were entered in the Ottumwa Races. Followers of bicycle racing will readily appreciate what it means to have a rider drop from a 114-inch gear to one of 92 inches, after having practiced for a fortnight exclusively on the higher gear.

Nevertheless, I won two first places and one second place in the Ottumwa two-day program, using the 114-inch gear. One of the events that I won was the one-mile national championship. I also won the one-mile open and finished second to Nat Butler in the two-mile championship race.

I quote from an Ottumwa newspaper as follows:

"Major Taylor Wins National Championship of the Iowa State Meet on the Ottumwa Track. Major Taylor, the far-famed Negro, was a great surprise to the crowd that attended the National Championship races of the Iowa state meet on the new Ottumwa track yesterday. He is a perfect wonder on the wheel, which he rides much easier than any other rider on the track, and yet he always seems to have a reserve force that would land him a winner. Although the people could not help but admire his riding he was given a marble heart at the start. The crowd did not like him and did not want to see him win, but in spite of this he carried off his share of the honors.

"When that doughty old warrior, Nat Butler, undoubtedly one of the finest men on the circuit, won the prettiest race of the entire program putting Major Taylor down to second place, winning the two-mile professional championship, the crowd demonstrated its approval by a roar of enthusiasm. The two Butlers, McCarthy and Gibson all qualified for this event and from the very outset the race

NAT BUTLER—The "Handicap King." One of the Famous Butler Brothers

was hotly contested. The final heat was paced by Davidson and Lavin, alternating two laps each. Tom Butler took the lead in the second lap. His brother, Nat, caught his rear wheel immediately with Taylor following, McCarthy and Gibson hanging on in that order. Gibson looked like a possible winner until Taylor arrogantly swung ahead and took the lead, even trying to lead the pacemaker. This caused his defeat as the two Butlers crowded him so closely he was exhausted.

"On his last lap-and-a-half Nat Butler suddenly jumped ahead of his brother Tom with Taylor closely following. Tom Butler held the lead for the first half of the final lap but dropped out and finished fifth. The cleverness of the sacrifice was apparent at a glance. Taylor exhausted by his long lead, could not catch Nat Butler while that clever rider sprinted over the tape as fresh as a daisy with a full wheel to spare with McCarthy third."

In the one-mile open race, Tom Butler won the first heat and Llewellyn was second with Phillips third, the time being 2:40 4/5. I won the second heat in 2:41 3/5 with Dunbar second, Harley Davison third. Nat Butler won the third heat with McLeod second the time being 2:08 2/5. The fourth heat was won by McCarthy in 2:08 2/5 with Gibson second. I won the final heat in 2:06 3/5 with Tom Butler second and Charlie McCarthy third. This was an especially closely contested race, as the fast time will indicate. There were no pacemakers used but there was plenty of team work. I believe that my good judgment rather than my speed, enabled me to win this race. From the outset I was determined that the other riders would slip nothing over on me as I had a very vivid recollection of the pocket they had driven me into in the two-mile championship race just finished.

Close as were the two-mile championship and one-mile open events, the national one-mile championship race excelled them. It was arranged in advance that only the winners of each heat would ride in the final. I was fortunate enough to land my heat and then in that hair-raising final I led the field across the tape winning by a wheel's length from Nat Butler with Harry Gibson third. The time was 2:00 2/5, the last quarter being clocked in 26 2/5 seconds which was the fastest quarter ever ridden on the Ottumwa track.

Tom Butler won the first heat, George Llewellyn second with Dunbar third, the time being 2:43 2/5. The second heat was won by Nat Butler with Wood second, time being 2:26 4/5. I won the third heat with McLeod second, and Phillips third, time being 2:26 4/5. Gibson won the fourth heat with McLeod second and Shook third, time 2:29. Harley Davison led the field home in the fifth heat with Lavin second and the time was 2:57.

"Dunbar paced the final heat," reads a clipping from an Ottumwa daily. "Tom Butler jumped away at a hair-raising clip. He held the pace, which was hot from the start for eight laps, after which the race was between Major Taylor and Nat Butler, the Major making a great jump at the last lap."

In commenting on my showing at this meet the same Ottumwa paper printed the following:

"Major Taylor demonstrated that he is a wonderful rider in this event. He has tremendous power and his ebony legs seem to fairly fly around the short circuit made by the pedals. He rides with apparent ease, and a lack of exertion that brands him as a true athlete. He seems to have a reserve force behind him at all times and can put forth an effort at the very last moment when it seems as though he must be completely exhausted.

"Major Taylor is a queer specimen. He is supremely arrogant and egotistical and does not readily make friends. He imagines that he is the whole performance. The sympathies of the crowd were naturally with the white riders, yet they could not help admiring Taylor's wonderful speed, his marvelous endurance and his doggedness, which makes him cling on in a race as long as there is any hope to win."

In passing I might say that the above attack was the only one ever launched against me in my career. I feel that in justice to myself I should explain the motive behind that charge of egotism and arrogance. The writer was connected with the Ottumwa track and in common with the other officials thereof, he was peeved somewhat because I had not sent my entry for the meet several days in advance. This I was unable to do as I had tried to make my attack on the world's record for the paced mile at Chicago on the very day that the Ottumwa meet opened. This writer-official was keenly perturbed because, had he known of my plan to participate in the Ottumwa program, an advertising campaign would have been launched to center about my participation therein. Therefore, my eleventh hour entry did not give the track officials an opportunity to advertise my entry as they would have had I arrived with the rest of the riders. The inference was that my failure to reach Ottumwa with the other riders caused the track hundreds of dollars loss as it was felt that many more would have attended the program had I been advertised as a starter.

The riders were also surprised by my sudden appearance and greeted me very coolly. Something on the order of that lawn-party and the skunk business. Thinking I would not be on hand they imagined that they were going to have everything their own way, but much to their chagrin I spoiled their little party, and just about cleaned up the program.

This same writer declared that the sympathies of the crowd were with the white riders. Still I recall receiving one of my greatest ovations the moment I set foot on the track to take a warming up spin about its surface. This was the first time that I had ever been in

Ottumwa. The reception accorded me as I won the one-mile open event fairly swept me off my feet.

This victory in the one-mile open event came after Nat Butler had defeated me in the two-mile championship race. It was so apparent to the spectators that I was beaten because of a pocket the riders forced me into that they fairly howled with glee as I led the galaxy of stars home in the mile event, so far in front of my competitors that they were unable to attempt to box me or otherwise bring about my defeat by unfair tactics of any kind. I was delighted with the treatment accorded me by the public of Ottumwa despite the belief expressed by the writer quoted above.

Setting a World's Record
(1899)

I went direct from Ottumwa back to Chicago to resume my attempts to lower the world's motor-paced record for the one-mile. This mark, 1:28, was made by Eddie McDuffee on the New Bedford, Mass., three-lap board track one week before I established the new record.

In my first two attempts to lower McDuffee's record I was balked by the failure of my pacing machine to function properly. But let the following clipping tell the story of my efforts to establish new figures for the mile. I quote from one of the Chicago newspapers as follows:

"Major Taylor Fails in Record Attempt but Wins One-mile National Championship Race. Major Taylor in his trial against the world's record for one-mile proved to be a disappointment at the Ravenwood Park track, Illinois, last night. Three attempts were made but the machine broke down each time. However, the other events on the program were run off in fine style.

"Major Taylor, was, of course, the center of attraction, although Jimmie Bowler came in for a good share of applause. Aside from the attempts at the record the race that aroused the greatest enthusiasm was the one-mile national championship which went to Major Taylor with Tom Butler second and Nat Butler, third, the time being 2:02. A great race was looked for between Bowler and Taylor. The Chicago boy won his heat but was not fast enough in taking up the sprint and did not get a place in the final."

Undaunted by the failure of my first attempt to establish a new world record for the mile, I was more determined than ever to lower McDuffee's mark. In the preceding November I broke the old record, human pace, for the mile, establishing the figures of 1:31. A few weeks before my unusual attempt to still further lower the record for the mile, machine pace, Eddie McDuffee shaved three seconds off my 1:31 mark which I established at Philadelphia.

In my 1899 attempts for a new record I was much better equipped than I was at Philadelphia. I had a specially constructed steam motor tandem, whereas in my Philadelphia race against time I had to depend upon 30 men to furnish the pace for me. I felt that with my pacing machine operating properly I could put the record below the 1:20 mark. In addition to my confidence I knew I was in the very best physical condition, so much so that I was very anxious for this all-important record-seeking test.

No sooner had repairs been made to my pacing machine than I went after the one-mile record again. A Chicago newspaper gave the following account of my second attack on McDuffee's record:

"Major Taylor fails again. Pacing Machine gives out before Half the Distance is Covered. Plucky Colored Boy will go out after Mark once more. After six unsuccessful attempts to lower the one-mile world's record at the Ravenwood Park (Ill.) track yesterday, Major Taylor shifted his affections to the Garfield Park track (Ill.) which is a half-mile cement surface. His manager, "Birdie" Munger, thought that the fewer turns on the half-mile track might possibly benefit the pacing machine. However, this made no difference and Taylor failed again. Everybody who has seen Major Taylor in action declares that the colored rider is capable of sticking to almost any kind of pace, for even when the machine is going at its very best he keeps up to it with the greatest ease. Both Munger and Taylor are anxious to get the job off their hands, so the machine may be sent east where some alterations are to be made in its construction. Major Taylor will join the circuit chasers as soon as possible and try to get in shape for the Montreal World's Championship Meet."

A few days later, August 3, 1899, to be exact, I made my third and successful attempt to establish a new world's record for the one-mile motor-paced event. Again I quote from the above mentioned Chicago newspaper:

"Major Taylor's Fast Ride breaks One-mile World's Record. Made Mile in extraordinary Time of 1:22 2/5. Major Taylor today at Garfield Park clipped 5 3/5 seconds from the record made by Eddie McDuffee last Saturday at New Bedford, Mass. The steam pacing machine was taken to the track early this afternoon and in a couple of trials it worked admirably. Then it went wrong again and the crowd prepared to leave, but at six-thirty the officials announced the machine was repaired and that Major Taylor would make another attempt at once.

"Taylor was sent around the track for a preliminary warming up behind a triplet team steered by Jimmie Bowler. Major rode a fast mile behind the triplet, then the motor picked up the colored rider with him sticking to the rear wheel.

"The speed was gradually increased until the three-quarter mark was reached when Munger who was operating the steam pacer, turned her wide open. The jump was made so quickly that for a moment Taylor dropped back and when the machine and rider crossed the starting line he was a yard behind it. With a final great effort he shoved his front wheel up close to the rear wheel of the big motor a few seconds after the officials' watches had been snapped. The eye of every timer rested on the quarter mark and as the machine flew by it, one of them shouted, 'Twenty and one-fifth.'

This was at the rate of 1:20 4/5. The second quarter was 19 1/5 seconds. This was a 1:16 4/5 clip, or just 2/5 of a second slower than the time made by Joe Downey on the straightaway course. The third quarter was made in the same time as the first. The tripler was in readiness to pick up the Major in the last quarter, but as it turned towards the pole, the pacing machine with Taylor swerved aside and shot by the triplet as if it had been standing still.

" 'Now jump!' Munger yelled to Taylor, who immediately made a greater effort and his wheel crept up beside the pacing machine and they crossed the line almost together, this breaking the record in the remarkable time of 1:22 2/5 much to the pleasure and shouting of the hundreds of enthusiastic spectators who had remained to see this successful trial."

Naturally I was pleased at my performance and was delighted that this series of nerve-racking time trials was over with. However, I had no time to celebrate the establishment of the new record as I was scheduled to participate in the world's championship races at Montreal within only nine days after I broke the world's record for the mile. I was anxious to get to Montreal so that I might engage in practice on the track on which the world meet was to be held August 12, most of my competitors having been there already for several weeks. Entries were received from practically every country in Europe, the United States, Canada and Australia.

I Win a World's Championship
(1899)

Upon my arrival in Montreal for this international meet I read in one of the local papers that I was looked upon as the most likely winner from this country in the short distance events, while McLeod, McDuffee, and McCarthy were named as the likely winners in the long distance events. When I made my first trip to the Queen's Park track I found more than 100 professionals and amateurs from all parts of the world training on it.

As I was now in my very best physical condition it required the best judgment of my trainer and myself to keep me in trim for the big championship race. I knew that if I overtrained or undertrained the least bit it might cause a reversal of form at the last moment and, of course, that would undoubtedly throw me off my championship form. By dint of hard work we happily struck the right combination and I finished up by light sprint practice for several days before the championships on my 88-inch sprinting gear which I changed to my regular 92-inch gear on the day of the big championship event.

I won the world's one-mile championship at this meet shortly after I had been "jockeyed" out of a well earned victory in the half-mile open event for professionals the day before. All through my racing career my one outstanding motive was to win the world's championship—and the same desire inspires every rider to his greatest efforts at all times.

This country furnished about 60 percent of the contestants at this international meet. England, France and Australia sent the cream of their cyclists to participate in this, the greatest bicycle program of the year. So keen was the interest of the public in the meet that thousands of enthusiasts gathered at the track daily to watch their favorites going through their training preparations. In the breast of every one of that contingent of riders, amateurs and professionals, burned the desire to win the world's championship title in his chosen distance, and take the crown back to the country under whose colors he rode.

The first race in which I participated was the half-mile open for professionals. The starters were Nat, Tom and Frank Butler, Charlie McCarthy, of this country, Angus McLeod, D'Outreion, Harley Davison, Blaney, Clarence Carman, Tom McCarthy the Canadian, Harry Gibson, Calgar, Watson Coleman, Jimmie Bowler, James J. Casey and Church.

Through a weird ruling of the judges I was forced to take second money despite the fact that the rank and file in the crowded grand stand insisted that I had won. But let the following clipping from a Montreal daily tell the story as a disinterested reporter saw it.

"The World A'Wheel. Greatest Gathering in the Records of Bicycling. The world's record in a racing way, and the world's attendance in an attendance way—that tells the story in a small kind of way. There were more than 5,000 people who could not get in at the Queen's Park track yesterday for the International Races. Inside were gathered 18,000 bicycle race enthusiasts.

"There was only one mistake and it is extremely difficult to account for. That was, why Major Taylor was deprived of a race that he had won. Just what the judges could have been thinking about no one seems to know. That Major Taylor won his race seemed clear to all the spectators who arose in a mass and cheered the colored rider every time he appeared on the track. This was the only difficulty of the first day's meeting. It was unfortunate, however, for the man who won the race was not credited with his winning. It was 'Taylorian Day.' Color cut no ice at any stage in the game.

"The largest crowd ever seen in Montreal was gathered inside Queen's Park track for the races and the program was worthy of the gathering. Chief interest centered in the half-mile open race for professionals in which the most prominent speed merchants were entered. The leaders were Major Taylor, Nat Butler, Frank Butler, Charlie McCarthy, Angus McLeod, D'Outreion, Harley Davison, as well as a host of other fast riders who gave promise of being heard of in cycle circles in the future.

"The final of this race had a most unsatisfactory termination in that the majority of spectators were of the opinion that the Worcester, Mass., boy had won the race in which he made such a spectacular finish by crossing the tape not less than a foot ahead of McCarthy and Nat Butler.

"The first heat was won by Nat Butler with McCarthy second and Blaney of Toronto, third. The second heat went to Carman, T. B. McCarthy second, and Gibson third in a terrific finish.

"There was a broad smile on Major Taylor's face when he lined up for the third heat. Frank Butler cut out the pace; behind him riding leisurely came Major Taylor who was greeted with cheers at every turn. Woodward and McLean trailed Taylor. There was little interest from a strictly racing standpoint until the last quarter of the lap when the black wonder straightened out his limbs and fairly lifted himself into the lead. He ran away from the Cambridge rider in the sprint and finished easy. The Detroiter, Woodward was second while Butler had to be content with third place. The trailers were Murray and McLean.

"Angus McLeod won the fourth heat, D'Outreion was second, Watson Coleman third with Bowler, Casey, and Church bringing up the rear.

"McCarthy set the pace in the final with Taylor in second place and Nat Butler bringing up the rear. The race was a pretty one until entering the home stretch when Taylor was caught in a bad pocket formed by the other riders.

"Major Taylor saw the trick about as quickly as it was sprung and held himself in reserve, but when he saw an opening he fairly lifted his machine through. McCarthy was leading until within a few feet of the tape when the Major shot in ahead and it was the opinion of 18,000 people in the grandstand that Taylor was the winner by at least a foot. The judges, however, ruled otherwise and awarded the race to McCarthy, giving Taylor second place and Nat Butler third. The time was 1:00 2/5.

"When the foregoing announcement was made on the bulletin board the people in the grandstand set up a vigorous protest, calling upon the Board to reconsider its decision and award the race where it rightfully belonged. Major Taylor also thought that he was the victor and expressed some surprise when he walked up to the Board. He asked one of the judges if that was their honest decision that McCarthy had won. When informed that such was the result of their deliberation, the Major said, 'Well, all right, if that is your verdict, gentlemen, I shall have to abide by it, but I know I won.'"

Still another newspaper clipping reads as follows:

"No More Pockets. Major Taylor runs right away from the Field. Wins World's One mile Championship Title. The Two-mile Open was easy. The last day of the World's Championship Meet was attended by fair weather. Major Taylor of the United States had little difficulty in adding the one-mile world's professional championship title to his laurels. All of the preliminary heats were marked by good finishes save the one won by Major Taylor who easily rode down his field.

"In the final of the one-mile world's professional championship race Nat Butler took the lead at the start, Major Taylor dropping into last position. The pace was slow. On the back stretch of the second lap there was some pretty maneuvering for positions and when it was all over Taylor had gotten the position he was jockeying for —second place on the pole with Nat Butler leading. The others were well bunched behind them. McLeod went to the front with a great rush and attempted to make a runaway of it but the others were not to be denied. They rounded the turn into the home stretch, McLeod still leading; but half way down the home stretch Taylor had the race well in hand and there was a great fight on between Nat Butler, Taylor, D'Outreion and McLeod. They finished in that order.

"Major Taylor was too much for his associates and landed the world's championship by a wheel's length. He was cheered and cheered by an enthusiastic crowd of 18,000 people who loyally greeted the new world's champion, Major Taylor, U. S. A."

Still another Montreal newspaper printed this account of the the world's championship meet: "The most really exciting incident of the world meeting was the final of the half-mile open professional. Major Taylor, the colored rider, for some reason or other, took the fancy of the spectators right from the beginning. He did some marvelous riding in the trial heats and the applause that greeted him was insistent and continuous. He is a very pleasing looking boy when he smiles and his skin, though dark, looks soft and smooth as velvet. Though rather small he is finely proportioned and taken all around, is probably the best developed man on the track.

"In the final referred to McCarthy and Taylor crossed the tape so nearly in a dead heat that it was very difficult to decide who should be awarded the decision. Referee Ingles announced McCarthy the winner and when this finally dawned upon the spectators in the grand stand they went frantic at what they believed was an injustice done to their protege. Some people began to shout for Taylor and it was taken up everywhere. They kept at this for nearly half an hour varying the monotony with some name and yelling scathing remarks to the judges and doing other things to create diversion but always with the idea in view of expressing their disapproval of the decision.

"Finally someone suggested that all those who were against the decision should stand up and in a flash every man, woman and child had arisen. The entire stand was on its feet and Mayor Prefountain, Aldermen Stevenson and Larry Wilson, who occupied a box just opposite the tape, vigorously joined in the protest.

"The referee, however, stuck to his decision and met the remarks of the angry crowd with a look of perfect indifference. It might be well to understand that in the case of so close a finish only the very few that can be actually on the starting line and on the track are in a fit position to judge who wins. In this case there was considerable difference in opinion among the officials, but as the referee decided against Taylor, and the judges, who represented Canada, United States and France, backed up the decision it can hardly be seriously questioned."

While waiting to start in the final of the greatest race that I had ever been called upon to contest, the one-mile world's championship at Montreal in 1899, I was a trifle nervous, perhaps, because I knew full well that I was going to be up against the most formidable racing combination known in the cycle racing world, the famous Butler brothers whose superlative tactics and skill in team work really were perfect.   They were noted for their ability to outgeneral and out-sprint any combination of riders or tandem team in the racing game.

They worked with clock-like precision, and understood each other so perfectly that no signals or secret codes were necessary.   If they had pre-arranged to pull off a certain tactic and their plans mis-carried they were each fast enough sprinters to overcome the miscue, and invariably win out down the home stretch.   I am frank to admit they were the fairest on the track where I was concerned.

I was confident that the other contestants, big Angus McLeod and D'Outreion, would be riding on their "own."   In other words I figured that they would not be in any combination with the Butlers. I was in wonderfully fine form, however, and was never in doubt as to the outcome, my only bogey was being caught in a pocket.

A most dramatic solemnity seemed to settle over that vast audience as we took up our positions at the starting line.   The officials and trainers went about their respective duties in a reserved silence.   The pistol was the first to speak out loud, however, which signified that within only a few moments more that terrible nervous suspense would surely be over.   Then all would know who was really the fastest bicycle rider in the world.

In winning this long-sought title, the highest honor to be obtained in the cycling world, I had at last accomplished my life's greatest ambition. I felt amply repaid for my strenuous efforts in that great race when I was awarded the gold medal which was symbolic of the world's one-mile championship, to say nothing of prestige.

My success in this memorable event was won in precisely the same manner in which I figured it would be.   It proved to be more a matter of tactics and track generalship than speed.   I had my first test in competing under the French style of competition in which victory and victory only counted.   The time occupied in the race being no factor, except that the timers always clocked the last 200 meters.

This type of race puts a premium on the rider's strategy, skill and power.

In the half-mile open race on the preceding day I was caught in a very bad pocket as we entered the last turn into the home stretch, causing me to finish second to Charlie McCarthy according to the de-cision of the officials.   Despite the fact that a reporter at the finish line, who was quoted above, wrote that the grand stand rose en masse and yelled its disapproval of the unfair decision.   They believed I won and so do I, even to this day.   However, I learned my lesson in that race and I decided henceforth never to be caught in a pocket again, especially in the one-mile championship race which came the next day.

Now for the inside story of how I won the world's one-mile championship at the same meet, and it is being told here for the first time.

I was positive that I could win the race as far as speed alone was concerned. But in spite of my very best judgment and after using every precaution I avoided being caught in a pocket only by the narrowest margin. Just coming into the back stretch on the second lap there was considerable finessing and jockeying for positions.

Dashing into the home stretch on the last lap, Nat Butler was leading at a very fast clip. I was following him with Tom Butler on my rear wheel, D'Outreion next, with McLeod bringing up the rear. We crossed the tape in that order as the crowd cheered wildly and were going great guns as we swept around the turn into the back stretch. Everything was going along nicely up to this point when suddenly the positions changed, as we swept into the back stretch.

I quickly saw a pocket opening up for me, but thanks to the big Canadian Champion, Angus McLeod, who at the same instant made a mighty dash for the finish line at about 250 yards from home, I avoided the pocket.

I had an abundance of reserve power, in fact, I did not dare risk putting my full force into my jump for fear of damaging my trusty machine. According to the track rules, if an accident happened on the last lap the race could not be re-run unless the winner agreed to such a procedure as a matter of sportsmanship in case an opponent was put out of the race through a mishap. So I simply unwound a lively sprint and quickly brought the canny Scot, McLeod, back. I instantly realized that the only obstacles in my way at this critical point to the world's championship were the two Butler brothers, Nat and Tom, and I also realized that they were two tough hurdles to take.

I adopted new tactics the moment I overtook McLeod. I knew that McLeod was no longer a factor so I but kept a very close watch on the Butlers from under my arm until they started their last desperate struggle as we flew into the last turn. It was now a thrilling fight with victory almost within my grasp. As we swung into the home stretch our three front wheels were almost abreast. At a glance I realized that for the first time in my life I was going to be able to make that last supreme effort to break the tape first without interference of any kind. In a word, the four of us came down that home stretch much the same as sprinters are confined to their lanes in a 100-yard dash. It was a fair field—there was no crowding or elbowing, it was a case of winning or losing the world's championship on merit alone.

That style of racing suited me to perfection, so with a great burst of speed I bolted for the tape, and flashed across it more than a full length ahead of Tom Butler. In the meantime there was a great fight on between Nat Butler and McLeod and the French rider, D'Outrion, who by a mighty effort in the home stretch nosed out Nat Butler and Angus McLeod for third position. But I had actually won. How the great throng did roar. I was elated with my victory and especially because it was a clean cut and decisive triumph with a margin wide enough to forestall any cause for complaint on the part of my opponents whom I had turned back. They were the cream of the cycling world. It was indeed a glorious thrill.

I shall never forget the thunderous applause that greeted me as I rode my victorious lap of honor around the track with a huge bouquet of roses. It was the first time that I had triumphed on foreign soil, and I thrilled as I heard the band strike up the "Star Spangled Banner." My national anthem took on a new meaning for me from that moment. I never felt so proud to be an American before, and indeed, I felt even more American at that moment than I had ever felt in America. This was the most impressive moment of my young life, and I was a mighty happy boy when I saw my trainer crate my bicycles that evening for I was still three months under twenty-one years of age when I won that world's championship and gold medal.

During that joyous demonstration there was but one regret in my mind—that my manager, Mr. Munger, could not be present to actually witness his remarkable prophecy, "the fastest bicycle rider in the world," become a wonderful reality in such a spectacular manner. I considered my great championship success a big victory for him as well, not only for his confidence in me as a rider, but also on account of his high ideals and true sportsmanship for which he stood.

In my successes at the International Meet in Montreal I once more performed what among bicycle riders is considered a remarkable feat— winning two firsts on the same day, after having been "gypped" out of a first place in a race on the preceding day at the same track. That made two first places and one second place for me in the same program, an unusual feat particularly in view of the fact that one of my victories was a world's one-mile professional championship. The second victory was in the two-mile open event while the much discussed first place I lost at Montreal was in the half-mile open event in which the judges ruled I finished second, whereas the crowd of 18,000 figured I had won first place in this race also.

Foul Tactics, Fair Wins
(1899)

After I had won the world's one-mile professional championship title I centered my thoughts on the next race, the two-mile open event. I had in mind winning this race in order to give me two first places for the day, which would have been the 10th time in my career, up to that moment, that I had won two first places on the same program. Incidentally, on four occasions I turned in three victories in as many meets, a feat seldom accomplished.

I was pressured to race the world's amateur champion at that event, so I declined, partly because of the lack of prize money but primarily to save my strength for the two-mile professional race later that afternoon.

While some reporters noted me a coward and a poor sport, that afternoon I won the two-mile contest and received a flattering ovation at the closing of the race. The 18,000 people present apparently appreciated my work.

However, I soon found that my fame made me a prime target for disgruntled rivals. At Boston's Charles River Park track, on August 16, 1899, I tried in vain to qualify for the final, but the entire field violated every rule of the track at my expense as the fans howled their disapproval of the underhanded methods adopted by my rivals. The officials did not so much as reprimand those who had fouled me in such a daring manner.

Later in the day I tried to qualify for the final of the one-mile handicap event but I was so badly roughed by the field that I failed to win a place. I was a pretty sorely mussed up World's Champion when my rivals had finished with me at the end of the first day's racing.

On the second day, however, I showed my rear wheel to the Butler boys and won the half-mile L.A.W. championship.

But at Brockton, Mass, shortly afterward, I found myself once more in peril from unscrupulous competitors. The result was my hardest race of the 1899 season and a breathtakingly close decision.

In this race, the riders succeeded in getting me into a tight pocket that I could not very well get out of without bringing someone down with a crash, and possibly two or three of them, because every man in the race had a hand in the job. I was obliged to use every trick I knew in extricating myself from my dangerous position. With but 250 yards to go, and the field sprinting like mad, I managed to wiggle my way out of my bad position without interfering with any other rider. It was the tightest box I was ever in.

In the end I was forced to pick up and come around on the outside of the entire field. Once clear, I made a last desperate plunge for the tape and got across the line a few inches ahead of Bowler with Coleman in third place.

As the three of us bolted across the line, a crowd of riders sitting near the tape immediately started shouting for Coleman. It was an old trick, the object of it being to influence the officials and the spectators to favor Coleman. This was one of the most sensational races I had ever figured in and it was extremely difficult to judge. Realizing the shabby deals that had been given me under similar circumstances in other races, I fully expected to be awarded second or even third place. But I was pleasantly surprised when the judges rendered the verdict in my favor—the first close decision that had ever been given to me.

Before the 1899 racing season was over, I had the supreme satisfaction of returning in triumph to Worcester, winnning races there for the first time as World's Champion.

In October, I went out to Peoria, Illinois, where I won three firsts in the course of a single meet. From there, I adjourned to Chicago, and rounded out this memorable racing year by setting a new world record for a motor-paced mile, pedaling the distance in a flashy 1:19.

Praises and Points
(1899)

"Major Taylor is Champion. Colored Youth won L. A. W. and International Championships and set many new records, capturing 22 firsts in 29 races. Has enviable record. If he never had it before Major Taylor this year has gained the title of Champion Cyclist of the World. It would be presumptuous for anyone to question his standing. This is the story of the colored boy who has astonished the world of cycling by his great feats of speed on the cycle tracks, 'Major Taylor, National Champion of the L. A. W., One-Mile International Champion, and Holder of the Quarter, Three-Quarter

MAJOR TAYLOR—Champion of America,
1899

and One-Mile Paced Record,' is the subject. Major Taylor's record this year is one to be proud of.

"Physically, Major Taylor is admirably put together. He has never been sick a day in his life. He has a well knit form, and is agile and supple in all his movements. He has continued to put on flesh since

1895 at which time he weighed 118 pounds. At present he weighs 160 pounds.

"In racing Taylor rides very low, his back arched over his handle-bars which offers but little chance for the wind to impede his progress. Major Taylor's father, Gilbert Taylor, a veteran of the Civil War, having served with the Union Army, is still living in Indianapolis. Taylor finds the racing and record-breaking business profitable, and has cleared several thousand dollars out of it.

"Despite the pleas of the race track managers and the bicycle riders Major Taylor has refused for years to compete on Sunday, as he has felt that all should rest on the Lord's Day. He has held strictly to that theory and in 1898 his decision to refrain from riding on Sunday almost cost him the American championship title.

"Major Taylor has never ridden on Sunday and says he does not intend to. When the International Cyclists' Association was formed in September 1898, Major Taylor went with the other riders in order to finish out the championship series in which he had been competing with the other fast men. Taylor claimed the N. C. A. promised not to hold any races on Sunday if he went with them, but this agreement was not kept, and later the colored boy sought reinstatement in the League of American Wheelmen. The colored champion does not say in so many words that the N. C. A. took this action in order to force him out of taking a big slice of the honors, but that he believes as much cannot be doubted."

The Official Bicycle Record Book gives the following chronological order of my achievements in the year of 1899:

Date		Race	City	Place
May	27	One-third-mile open	Philadelphia	First
"	30	One-mile open	Boston	First
"	30	Two-mile handicap (scratch)	Boston	First
June	10	One-mile match (vs. Tom Butler)	Boston	Lost
June	16	One-third-mile open	Boston	First
"	16	Twenty-five-mile match (paced vs. Eddie McDuffee)	Boston	Won
July	1	One-mile match (vs. Tom Butler)	Boston	Won
"	8	One-mile Championship	Chicago	First
"	12	One-mile Championship	Janesville	Second
"	12	Two-mile handicap (scratch)	Janesville	First
"	16	One-mile Championship	St. Louis	First
"	26	Two-mile Championship	Ottumwa	Second
"	26	One-mile open	Ottumwa	First

"	26	One-mile Championship	Ottumwa	First
"	29	One-mile Championship	Chicago	First
Aug.	12	Half-mile open	Montreal	Second
"	12	One-mile World's Championship	Montreal	First
"	12	Two-mile open	Montreal	First
"	16	Five-mile Championship	Boston	Lost
"	16	Half-mile Championship	Boston	First
"	23	One-mile Championship	Brockton	First
Sept.	3	Half-mile open	Worcester	First
"	3	Five-mile match (pursuit)	Worcester	First
"	3	(vs. James Casey)		
"	3	Fifty-yard match (foot)	Worcester	First
		(vs. Charles Raymond)		
"	20	One-mile open	Taunton	First
Oct.	12	One-mile invitation	Peoria	First
"	12	Two-mile open	Peoria	First
"	12	Five-mile lap	Peoria	First

A New Season's Honors

(1900)

"Who will be the Cycle Champion of 1900? Racing Season begins Thursday and struggle for Title promises to be unusually keen. Experts pick Frank Kramer. American cycle racing season will open next Thursday in Louisville, where at Mountain Ferry track the stars will meet for the first time. One week later Vailsberg will open and several other New England tracks will open about this time. There will be a vast increase in the number of competitors this season which has been apparent in the request for both amateur and professional registrations at the office of the board of control of the N. C. A.

"Big match races will be the feature of the season, but the sprint race field includes more prominent men than ever before. The professional champions of both the N. C. A. and the L. A. W. of last year, and the amateur champions of both organizations will come together in professional ranks this year. The sprinters who planned European trips have decided with one exception to remain at home, but one prominent rider, and one coming champion, Elks and Ross will be missed from the paced ranks. Just at this time there is a lot of talk regarding the probable champion of the season among the professional and amateur sprint riders.

"The decision of Tom Cooper, the champion of last season, and Earl Kiser, his closest competitor, to remain on this side has added great interest to the problem. The entry of the stars in the amateur ranks, and the probability of Major Taylor's name being added to the list of competitors, and Eddie Bald's decision to go out again for the championship has complicated matters and made the discussion even more interesting. Cooper was the N. C. A. champion last season, and the year Arthur Gardiner was considered one of the champions and for three years previous to that Eddie Bald held the honors. Major Taylor was champion last season under the L. A. W. For the past several seasons Orlando Stevens has been a prominent factor in the championship race. Frank Kramer, amateur champion the past season, and Jimmie Moran, who held the same honors under the L. A. W. have both become professionals with the opening of the season. Floyd MacFarland promises to figure more prominently in the race this year, as does Al Newhouse. In addition to these men Howard Freeman is liberally touted and Hardy Downing, the Californian, may give the best of them a rub. These men are all sprinters of the first rank. Among many who have watched the development with interest, Frank Kramer is expected to clean up the whole bunch. Jay Eaton, the board track king, is a close observer and has ridden with many of these stars for years, and speaks by the book on cycle racing matters, and he gives as his best opinion that Frank Kramer will surely win the sprint championship of America, this year, 1900."

Despite the fact that most of the sports editors of the country picked Frank Kramer to win the American sprint championship in 1900, I made up my mind that he would not. As the season opened I felt physically fit and was confident that I would once more top the field of the sprint stars of the country before the 1900 season closed.

The field was one of the greatest that ever set out to win the championship as the 1900 season dawned. There was Tom Cooper, who won the N. C. A. championship in 1899, myself, who won the L. A. W. title the same year, Earl Kiser, Cooper's closest competitor, Eddie Bald, the former champion for three years, Orlando Stevens, Frank Kramer, former amateur L. A. W. champion, Jimmie Moran, who also held the amateur honors under the L. A. W.; Floyd MacFarland, Al Newhouse, Howard Freeman, Hardy Downing, Tom Butler, Nat Butler and Frank Butler, the famous trio of brothers from Boston, Watson Coleman, Arthur Gardiner and Owen Kimble, and a host of other good men.

No less an authority than Jay Eaton, the board-track king, who was one of the closest observers of bicycle riders, picked Frank Kramer to win the laurels that season. Eaton's opinion in this case was highly regarded especially since he had ridden with many of the stars who were to participate in the mad scramble for the sprinting honors that season.

When I failed to win the first race of the 1900 season some of my closest followers started nodding their heads. They knew the controversy surrounding my being dropped by the L. A. W., and my subsequent reinstatement by the N. C. A. upon my payment of a fine of $500 had not only worried me but also caused me to let up in my off season training. This inactivity caused my weight to increase eight pounds, and that was the reason I was unable to finish better than third in the premier race of that season, June 23, 1900, on the historic Manhattan Beach track. I won my preliminary heat and also placed in the semi-final heat. I led the way in the final heat and was well down the home stretch before I started to fade. Jay Eaton was at my rear wheel and we were pushing like mad for the finish line when Johnnie Fisher of Chicago burst into first place about twenty yards from the tape to win by a length over Eaton who beat me by half a wheel.

That was the first time in my career that I had failed to win the opening race of the season. I knew that my poor showing at the Manhattan Beach track was due to the excess weight I was carrying so I set about taking off the extra poundage that I might be in the best possible condition for the remaining races in that campaign.

Since Frank Kramer had recently defeated Tom Cooper his name was on the tongues of all followers of the bicycle racing game. He was looking for new worlds to conquer and on several occasions suggested that he would like to take me on for a sprint or two. Before long Kramer and I were signed up for a match race for a purse of $500, the winner thereof to take all. This race was held on the Manhattan Beach track on June 30, 1900.

I trained hard and faithfully for this race with Kramer and on the eve of it felt I was riding fast enough to give him my dust. Incidentally, I had an additional motive. I felt that if I defeated Kramer and won the $500 purse it would just offset the fine that bicycle moguls had imposed upon me in what I have always considered an unfair manner in the preceding season. So faithfully had I trained for this race that a few hours before I went to the track I weighed but three pounds above my best sprinting weight, indicating that I had taken off five pounds in one week's training.

I quote from a New York newspaper of July 1, 1900, concerning that race:

"Major Taylor Defeats Frank Kramer. Negro takes two straight Heats in decisive Style. The great special match race between Major Taylor and Frank Kramer at Manhattan Beach track yesterday afternoon, was a treat of the first water. Last Sunday Kramer, who has been riding like the wind, administered a crushing defeat to Tom Cooper, the N. C. A. professional champion at Newark.

"Kramer defeated Cooper in two straight heats, but yesterday Major Taylor served the same medicine to Frank Kramer and he turned the trick so easily that his position in the very foremost ranks of the sprinters must be acknowledged.

"The race was single paced. Bob Miller was put in front and he cut out a good fast clip. In the first heat Taylor lost the toss for position and took the place on the rear wheel of the pacemaker. When the last turn was reached Kramer tried to jump by, but Taylor beat him to it and pulled away from him up to the home stretch until there was only a peek of daylight between them as they flew past the tape.

"In the second heat Kramer was obliged to take the pace, and he was outgeneraled by the colored boy in every way. Even as they reached the last turn Kramer made the least bit of a bluff to jump and then tried to get the Major past him, but no, Taylor just simply rode along in second position until they were nearing the home stretch and well out of gale; suddenly there was a dusky streak and Frank Kramer got second place. Major Taylor won by two lengths and he was moving faster when he crossed the tape than he was down the home stretch. The reason—tremendous applause.

"On the whole Major Taylor is King-Pin among the sprinters. There is only one other man now who appears to have a chance of defeating Taylor, and it will take all of the great Eddie (Cannon) Bald's very best speed and tactics to do it."

Immediately after my match race with Kramer I signed up for another with Jay Eaton, famous champion of another era, who was widely known as "Indoor King." I was fully aware that I had my work cut out for me with the clever and speedy Eaton. I knew that a loss to him would offset even my fine performance against Kramer. However, I had no fear of him so far as speed was concerned and I figured that I was as clever otherwise as he, although he was a very tricky rider. On top of that Eaton had worlds of experience and realizing all these things I admit I was a little anxious on the eve of the race. Nevertheless, I tore after Eaton and felt like a new man when I led him over the tape and satisfied myself that he was more tricky than speedy.

This race was held on the famous Vailsburg (N. J.) track. As was the case in my match race with Frank Kramer the purse in my match with Eaton was $500, winner take all. My race with Eaton followed his sweeping defy to all the professional riders of the country. It was inserted in all of the papers over the signature of Fred W. Voigt, Eaton's manager and read as follows:

"Jay Eaton's Defy to All Professional Riders. I will match Jay Eaton, 'The Indoor King' against any rider in the world with or without single paced, one-mile heats, best two in three heats. The match to take place on the Vailsburg track upon receipt of two weeks' notice from challenger. No one is barred, and the challengers will be taken in order of acceptance of this defy, and the winner of the match to receive $500. The only stipulation I make is that the challengers post $100 in the hands of the official referee which shall serve as a forfeit that the match shall take place and subject to the conditions named above. Signed: Fred W. Voigt, Manager Jay Eaton, 'Indoor King.' "

A New York newspaper carried the following story about my race with Jay Eaton on the day following the event:

"Major Taylor Easily Defeats Jay Eaton 'Indoor King' in Special Match Race. Major Taylor, the champion colored rider, is the fastest bicycle rider in the world, which was again demonstrated yesterday on the Vailsburg Track when he defeated Jay Eaton, the 'Indoor King' in two straight heats in a mile special match race for a purse of $500. The fight between these two great riders had been counted upon as being likely to produce some gilt-edge sport, but the dusky-hued champion defeated the Jersey man in two successive heats, in neither one of which did the finish measure in inches. The 'Indoor King' was simply outclassed both times.

"In the first mile heat Taylor followed Eaton to the last lap, until the turn into the home stretch when he came from behind with a perfect jump and beat his rival to the finishing line, the greater part of a length. In the second heat Eaton sat upright on his wheel about half way down on the home stretch when the dark streak flashed along side of him, the Major again crossing the tape two yards to the good, mid the storm of applause from the big crowd."

After these two victories over Frank Kramer and Jay Eaton, I was now in my very best sprinting form, and, if anything, I was perhaps a shade better than usual because I felt stronger than ever, and therefore, could hold a sprint longer. I next went after a matched race with one of my greatest rivals of the day, Tom Cooper, whom I had long been anxious to meet in a match race. In fact I longed for a match with Cooper ever since I witnessed the great race between he and Eddie Bald two years previous at the League of American Wheelmen's meet in Indianapolis, which Bald won.

Immediately after that Indianapolis match race between Cooper and Bald I challenged either of them in a match or that I would take on both of them in a three-cornered race. However, I was promptly turned down by Bald who still insisted on drawing the color line. He made no bones of stating that if he raced me it would hurt his social standing.

Cooper tried to evade meeting me in a match race using the color line as a dodge. However, the fact that he was champion under the N. C. A. auspices put him in an awkward position as I insisted on his meeting me. On top of that the purse of $1000 which was to go to the winner of our match race, proved to be very tempting to him. No doubt, my defy to Cooper would not have borne fruit were it not for the fact that the newspapers of the country got solidly behind me and demanded that Cooper race me or forfeit his title forthwith. That pressure caused Cooper to lower the bars he had set up against the color line and accept my defy.

When we met to make the final arrangements for the match I offered to put a side bet of $1000 with Cooper that we might make a real race of it but his manager refused to cover my money.

Down in my heart I knew that Cooper had taken a leading part in having me fined $500 for my alleged infraction of the racing code in 1899. Cooper was treasurer of the American Cyclists' Racing Union at that time and he was one of the principal instigators who aimed to debar me for life from bicycle racing tracks of the world.

With these facts in mind one can readily appreciate how I felt as I walked on to the track at Milwaukee on July 13, 1900, to race Cooper for the purse of $1000. I felt that after months of waiting I was about to realize one of my most cherished ambitions—that of getting a chance to show one of the men who would have ruled me off the bicycle tracks of the world in an unfair manner, the way to the tape. If ever I was anxious to win a race I most certainly was on this occasion. I felt it was the most important race that I had prepared for up to this time—that is how much there was at stake in it.

However, the fates had decreed that Cooper and I were not to hold that all important match race on the Milwaukee track that day. After both of us had jogged about the track a few times there was a conference of officials concerning the construction of it. This was brought about in no small degree by a fall sustained by Cooper during his workout. The upshot of the confab was that the track was condemned as being unfit to ride upon. The officials of the track asked me, in view of this fact, if I still desired to ride against Cooper. I replied in the affirmative and said I was ready to start to if Cooper was, but the race was declared off.

Return of a Native

(1900)

Knowing that my next appearance on the track was scheduled for Newby Oval, Indianapolis I trained hard that I might make a good showing before the people in my native city. In that event which was held on July 18, 1900, were entered most of the star riders of the country.

Racing in one's home town is incentive enough for anyone to do his utmost to·win. Imagine then my anxiety to lead the pack home in the two races in which I was entered, the two-mile handicap and the half-mile professional championship, as I realized that my father was to occupy one of the boxes at the track. It marked the first time that he had ever consented to see me race and that made me doubly desirous of giving one of my best performances in the track. My father who was a veteran of the Civil War, had as his guests on the occasion a number of his comrades in the Union Army.

Try as I might, however, I was unable to win my heat in the half-mile professional championship race. Fate was kinder to me in the two-mile handicap event and I picked my way through a big field to win first money in a most spectacular manner.

I quote as follows from an Indianapolis newspaper clipping concerning that race meet:

"Major Taylor and Owen Kimble Capture Professional Races at Newby Oval. Major Taylor is still the best of them all. Once in a while he fails to win, as instanced in the third heat of the half-mile professional championship last night, but all in all the black streak comes through first in a big majority of his races, and it matters but little who is competing against him.

"Major Taylor showed all his old time form in his race last night and made such a wonderful finish in the final of the two-mile handicap that he was cheered time and again by the immense crowd at Newby Oval. This was the greatest race of the evening. Major Taylor, Newhouse, Rutz, Maya, and Jimmie Bowler qualified for the first heat. Owen Kimble, Pease, Stone, Barney Oldfield, Stinemetz in the second heat.

" 'Now watch for the race between Major Taylor and Owen Kimble' was the word that went around, and the crowd did watch for it with great excitement. For seven laps all Taylor did was keep his eyes open watching the other riders like a hawk to see that he was not pocketed. On the bell lap he was well in front of the bunch and riding on the outside. Then, quick as a flash, he shot up the

banking and on the famous northeast turn of the oval he dashed down
on the pole again which gave him the lead and he pedalled like a fiend
for the last two hundred yards.

"Kimble, the speedy Kentuckian, set sail after him, but there were
not revolutions enough in his wheel to bring him anywhere near
Taylor, who had gotten in that famous jump of his and he was never
headed. Major Taylor finished by three open lengths, with Al Newhouse second, and Owen Kimble third. The time was 4:28 3/5.

Owen S. Kimble—"Old Kentucky"

"Major Taylor was scratch man in the first of the two-mile handicap
event, and also first in the final. In the first heat he caught the foremost rider, Lew Gorden, who had a handicap of one hundred yards
before the first lap was completed. Taylor, however, failed to qualify
in the half-mile championship, by Kimble getting the jump on him in
the last eighth of a mile and finishing a length ahead. Kimble made a
runaway of the final of this event winning by a dozen lengths."

My set-back in the half-mile championship race made me more
determined to win the two-mile handicap in which I started from
scratch. I won this race after one of the most sensational rides I
ever made; that was immensely pleasing to the public, and I received
a splendid ovation.

My father who had never seen me race before came into my dressing room after the races were over to congratulate me. He had a rather surprised look on his face when he said, "Well, son, there is one thing I don't understand, that is, if you are the fastest bicycle rider in the world, as the newspapers say you are, why in time don't you beat those white boys out further at the finish line?" "Well," I said, "I won by a couple of lengths, didn't I?" "Yes," he said, "but I expected to see you leave them so far behind that you could get dressed and come out and see the rest of them fight it out for second, and third money." The innocence of old age.

I tried to explain to him that I was perhaps not quite as fast as the papers proclaimed me to be, and he readily agreed. Then he wanted to know as to why it was they made me start way back in the last place in the two-mile handicap race, and place all the white boys away out ahead of me. I again tried to blame it on to the newspapers, but he couldn't see it that way; he insisted that I was being picked on again because of my color.

This was my father's idea how fast his boy could ride a bicycle, and also his idea of what I was up against because of my color.

Piling Up Victories
(1900)

Keenly disappointed because of my defeat in the half-mile professional championship in the Indianapolis meet of July 18, 1900, I determined to show the same riders, if possible, the way home in the next race at that distance. My opportunity came on the famous Buffalo Athletic Field track on August 2, 1900. This meet attracted the cream of the country's bicycle stars, including Owen Kimble, Frank Kramer, Earl Kiser, Johnnie Fisher, Al Newhouse, Otto Maya, and Charles Kunkle.

At Buffalo, I obtained sweet revenge. In the half mile, as a local sports reporter described,

> The riders were divided into two heats, four men in each heat, the winners and second men in the fastest heat to meet in the three-cornered final provided for by the rules of the N.C.A. Board of Control. Major found Kimble, Stone, and Kunkle in his heat, and although at one time it seemed as if the Black Streak was safely pocketed, on the back stretch Stone swung a trifle wide just entering into the last turn and like a flash, Taylor jumped through on the pole and was yards away from danger. Kimble was out after him like mad, but not dangerously close. The heat was a loaf and the time was so slow that the riders in the second heat put up a stiff argument for the two coveted places, which meant that the winners thereof were certain of competing in the final. Kramer outsprinted Kiser, who was too much for Newhouse and May.
>
> The management put in Johnnie Fisher to pace the final. Kiser decided the pacemaker's rear wheel but Taylor accepted it with the two white boys trailing. On the last lap Major Taylor swung wide up the bank carrying the other two with him. Frank Kramer shot out in front with a dash for the tape, but Taylor began a terrible sprint that carried him right past the others and landed him a winner by yards; Earl Kiser finished in second place with Frank Kramer third, the time being 1:04.
>
> The victory was so impressive that spectators were convinced that if America is to have a white champion this year, Major Taylor is the man they will have to defeat for the honor. Major Taylor received a thunderous ovation."

Shortly afterward, at the new Velodrome Track in Hartford, I won the two first places in two starts. I then moved on to New Bedford, Mass, where a week later

I participated in the N.C.A. Grand Circuit Meet, in connection with the L.A.W. midsummer gathering. Once more the star professional riders of the country were competing.

One reporter wrote,

"Among them, was Major Taylor, the great colored rider, who is without question the neatest rider who sits in a saddle today, as well as being the fastest sprinter in the short distances. The meet produced the best spring races that have ever been on the local track.

One very fast mile was ridden and it was thought that the track had another low mark. It was the second heat of the semi-final of the one-mile championship. Major Taylor won the heat in the splendid time of 1:45 2/5, which is the fastest mile that has been ridden in the year's circuit races. The national championship event was a very interesting contest, although in each preliminary heat for three laps the riders loafed at only professionals can. The last lap, however, made up for their laziness.

After the first half dozen sprints, the spectators were wrought up to a high pitch of excitement. They were prepared for the semi-finals and the last heat, which was more exciting than the ones which weeded out the slower ones. Major Taylor won the championship and also the five points that went with it. Frank Kramer was second and Al Newhouse was third. Major Taylor now leads in the 1900 championship races with thirteen points to his credit. Frank Kramer is second with eleven.

After the main events, I tried alone for a record in the motor-paced mile. A local sportswriter declared,

"The crowd has never seen a motorcycle before, and went wild over its speed. Major Taylor came out while the motor was circling the track and began riding. He made a pick-up on the lower turn and did it very cleverly. He followed the machine around for a number of laps, the audience marveling at his ability to stick to it so closely. When he passed the officials the second time, he signaled that he would start the next time around and the word was given.

He rode finely and the half was made in :46 1/5 which was close to a 1:32 clip and the speed did not diminish for the next two laps. On the last lap, the second was increased to trifle but Taylor hung right on to the it, and around the turn through the back stretch they tore into the home stretch across the tape in the remarkable time of 1:37. Taylor was given a great ovation.

My Easiest Championship

(1900)

In the three weeks interval between the race meet on the new Bedford track and the next championship race which was scheduled for the Vailsburg track at Newark, New Jersey, on September 3, I spent my time training on the Colosseum track in my home town, Worcester. This track which was on the site which later housed the Worcester Professional Baseball Club attracted some of the greatest bicycle riders in the world to Worcester some thirty years ago. It has long since passed out of the picture but will ever remain a pleasant memory to hundreds of the country's greatest riders and thousands of loyal bicycle fans.

It was heralded far and wide that the quarter-mile championship event would be the outstanding feature of the Vailsburg meet. Knowing that, I set to work in a determined way in an effort to win this event. I knew the field that would start for the laurels in this race would represent the greatest bicycle racers in the United States. With this fact in mind I trained faithfully on the old Worcester track for hours at a time.

A Worcester newspaper commented as follows after one of its reporters had clocked me in practice sprints at the old Colosseum track:—"Major Taylor is doing his preliminary training at the Worcester Colosseum for his next championship race at Newark on September 3, and if faithful and consistent training will win, Major Taylor has the quarter-mile championship already won. In practice sprints at the local Colosseum yesterday afternoon Major Taylor showed wonderful form, he covered a sixth of a mile (or one lap of the track) unpaced in the remarkable time of :16 flat, or at a 1:36 clip for a mile. From a standing start unpaced he finished a lap in :20 1/5."

On the day following the holding of the meet on the Vailsburg track one of the Newark dailies carried the following article:

"Major Taylor Unbeatable. Wins Quarter-Mile Championship Showing Positive Superiority Over All Competitors. The Vailsburg track furnished an afternoon of rare sport yesterday for 10,000 people. The principal event of the day was a quarter-mile dash for the championship of America. This race was won by Major Taylor, the ebony complexioned record breaker, from a field of clever sprinters including Owen Kimble, Frank Kramer, Tom Butler, George Collette, Howard Freeman, and Al Newhouse, the pick of the fastest sprint riders known in this country with the single exception of Earl Kiser who did not appear. The time was :33.

"Major Taylor as usual in such races had everything his own way and won the final easily. Johnnie Fisher took the lead followed closely by Taylor with Frank Kramer bringing up the rear. Major was offered the pole on the back stretch but refused it, he made no effort to begin his wonderful winning jump until the last turn was

FRANK L. KRAMER

reached. Kramer then cut down to the pole behind Fisher and Taylor and rounding into the home stretch set sail for the tape unhindered. Fisher was beaten at the head of the stretch and Kramer did not have enough left in him to overtake and pass the dusky whirlwind, though he made a strenuous effort. The Major was never headed and won by a clean open length, Frank Kramer was second and Johnnie Fisher was third."

The final of this quarter-mile championship race was one of the most popular victories I ever won. This was due in considerable measure to the fact that I considered the Vailsburg bicycle fans far better educated upon the fine points of bicycle racing than any other similar group in the country, and as far as I can learn the same holds true today. The Vailsburg fans liked my style of riding from the very first time I competed there. They seemed to appreciate my efforts, were always very fair to me and gave me very generously of their applause.

I realized these facts very well as I trained faithfully for this quarter-mile championship race, incidentally, I knew I had a man-sized job on my hands if I were to win this big event and anticipated the

A Smile of "Fair Play"

bitterest battle of my life down that home stretch if I were to lead the pack home. I was trained to the minute for this big classic and was never in better fettle than on the afternoon of the race, the weather being well nigh perfect and the fans giving me a tremendous ovation as I came onto the track.

The manner in which the heats were run placed only the three best men in the final, which in a short race of this kind gave each man a good chance, providing there was no frame-up—that is none of that "two-against-one" business.

I was a little nervous when we were called to the starting line for the deciding heat of this big race. However, when I noticed that I was pitted against Frank Kramer and Johnnie Fisher for the laurels I gave a sigh of relief. This was not due to the fact that I underrated these two stars, not by a long shot, as they were two great riders and very smart in tactics. I had the utmost respect for them as sprinters but I knew that they were not on friendly terms with one another and that convinced me that each of them would be out to win on his "own," and that fact gave me a tremendous psychological advantage at the start of the race.

Before we had covered fifty yards, however, I knew the race was being ridden strictly "according to Hoyle," meaning that each man in the race was riding his own race with but one thought in mind —to win, or every man for himself, and the devil grab the hind-most across the tape. My mind was at ease as I realized that for once in my life I would not have to contend with pockets or combinations against me. With that fact in mind I felt I had a big advantage over my opponents especially in view of my fine physical condition. I actually smiled as I realized that this race was to be won by the best man, on merit alone, with nothing to count but speed and good judgment. It was a "fair field and no favor." Incidentally this was the first and only smile of the kind I ever enjoyed of all my many successes.

So confident of victory was I that I actually allowed my opponents to lead me right into the home stretch at top speed before making my jump, when I came from third position and won out by about three lengths. Had I failed to win this race under such unusually favorable conditions I should have felt that the end of my racing days were in sight.

Incidentally this race was the first one I had ever contested in which I was not hampered by pockets or other foul tactics. In a word it was the first race I had ever ridden that was settled on merit, speed and good judgment.

Robbed by a Prejudiced Judge
(1900)

Immediately after the Vailsburg meet, I returned to my home town, Indianapolis, for a big event on the famous Newby Oval there.

I was in fine physical condition as we stepped on to the track for the final heat of the third-of-a-mile championship race, and well I might be, as there was a galaxy of racing stars entered in the event, the outstanding race of the program.

In the final heat of this event the judges decided that Owen Kimble and I had raced a dead heat although I am convinced to this day that I beat him to the tape by a safe margin.

Others shared my conviction that I had been robbed, for on the following day, an Indianapolis newspaper reported that the judges who had officiated would not be asked to serve when Kimble and Taylor rode the tie off, "for it has been reported that one of the judges who decided the race a dead heat afterward declared he believed Major Taylor had won the race, but because he disliked the colored rider personally, he decided against him."

This cowardly judge boasted among some of his friends after the above-mentioned tie race between Kimble and myself how he had trimmed the "nigger." However, the unsportsmanlike conduct of this judge gained many friends for me and his bitter prejudices only caused me to fight all the harder in my next race on the Indianapolis track. It nettled me, however, to think that this low piece of business robbed me of one of the hardest-earned victories of my life. It was a man-sized task at best to beat Kramer and Kimble to the finish line and to turn the trick with those two riders combined against me was nothing short of a Herculean task. On top of the team work of Kramer and Kimble, who were out to best me at all costs, I had this unscrupulous judge to contend with and although I defeated Kramer and Kimble on the track on that eventful night, I was unable to compete with the underhanded methods adopted by the aforementioned track official. That three-way combination was simply unbeatable.

Two Thrillers at Indianapolis

(1900)

I decided to make the best of matters in the meantime, however, and assured myself that the best way to assuage my feelings would be to defeat Kimble on the same Indianapolis track. By some clever maneuvering my trainer and myself drew my great rival into a championship match to decide the dispute over the dead heat business between us. We agreed to ride for a purse of $300, winner take all, and I tried in vain to persuade Kimble to add a side bet of $100 to make an even $500 purse.

I knew that Owen Kimble being a southerner did not like me because of my color. He was naturally imbued with all of the old traditions relative to that perpetual color prejudice and race hatred that are so typical of that section of the country. Kimble felt that in order to uphold those inherited ideals of his forefathers he was obliged to hate me with a genuine bitterness and to do his utmost to defeat me every time we met. Because of this intensity of color hatred for me, Kimble always seemed to be able to develop an extra degree of speed when battling it out with me that he never displayed against any other rider in the world. In fairness to Kimble, however, I wish to state that he took a decent stand against me in all of our races inasmuch as he had never actually put me down by unfair means.

He made a claim, however, that I elbowed him in the championship event the week before, which was declared a dead heat. His claim was not allowed as he was generally known to be very unsteady in sprinting, and was very wobbly even in practice, but he was a very dangerous rider at any stage of the sprint game and I had the utmost respect for his somewhat awkward though powerful sprinting ability.

No sooner had the agreement for the special match race between Kimble and myself been drawn than I set about training as I never had before. I sought to be in my best sprinting form for this big event which was already creating great interest and promised to draw a tremendous crowd. I was now at a point where too much training might prove disastrous by causing me to go "stale." On the other hand if I were insufficiently trained, of course, I could not expect to be at the height of my form. In a word my chief concern at this time centered about my fear of being a little "off color" so to speak, so I trained very carefully and cautiously.

My rival was equally vigilant in his training and was in wonderful condition also. However, I was confident of being able to bring the big Kentuckian into camp again, single-handed and without the assistance of any of the officials. It was while I was training for this championship match that I was credited with tearing off the fastest mile ever recorded on any track under the same conditions, the mark of 1:45 standing to this day.

I quote as follows from an article printed in an Indianapolis newspaper concerning that record mile:

"Major Taylor's Fast Mile. Colored Champion Paced by Other

MAJOR TAYLOR and Trainer, R. W. "Bob" Ellingham

Cracks Does Stunt in Remarkable Time of 1:45. This is the fastest time ever clocked for the distance on any track. The record-ride was made in a work-out, and does not stand as an official mark. R. W. Ellingham held the watch on Taylor as did Earl Kiser, the great sprinter, and several others. They were dumbfounded as they realized what Taylor had done and so were the other riders who were assembled at the track to watch the work-out. None of them seemed to be able to realize that Taylor was capable of such a marvelous performance. Taylor made this mark on a wheel geared to ninety-two inches and Palmer tires.

"Major Taylor was pulled out by the cracks who are in training at Newby Oval. Lew Gordon paced him to the tape with a flying start, and George Leander took him to the first quarter in :26 flat. Owen Kimble paced him for the second quarter in :26 3/5, the half by Taylor being :52 3/5. Jimmie Bowler pulled Taylor to the third quarter in :26 3/5. Taylor rode the last quarter alone in :26 3/5 completing the mile in 1:45. The best previous time for the distance was 1:51 by Orlando Stevens, at Louisville.

"On Friday afternoon Taylor rode a quarter of a mile in the unheard of time of :22 3/5, which stunt startled the riders training at Newby Oval especially when they learned a close tab was kept on the watch while the colored marvel took his work-out."

On the eve of my special championship match race with Owen Kimble, the strong boy from Louisville, I was at the peak of physical condition ready and anxious for the starters gun to send us on our way.

The following article is quoted from the columns of an Indianapolis newspaper the day after my race with Kimble:

"Major Taylor Champion. Takes Both Big Races From the Aggregation of Eastern Racing Talent. $500 in the coin of the realm, the National Professional Championship of 1900, and a permanent place in the estimation of the bicycle race loving public of Indianapolis is what Major Taylor has gained during his present sojourn in this city. One week ago last night he and Owen Kimble demonstrated that they were in a class by themselves, so far as sprint racing is concerned. Last night Major Taylor proved that he is the best man in this class and had he not been pocketed in the half-mile handicap he undoubtedly would have earned $100 more.

"Major Taylor was the prime favorite of the meet. When starter Allison's pistol announced the start of the first race there were thousands of cycle enthusiasts at the track and before the fight for the third of a mile national championship was started the crowd was even larger.

"The first event of importance was the match race between Major Taylor and 'Old Kentuck' Owen Kimble. Pacemaker Watson was placed ten yards in advance of the two men. Hardly had the report of the revolver died away when Taylor tacked on to Watson's rear wheel. When the gong in the official's box announced the beginning of the final lap, the riders were tearing off speed that would make a locomotive envious.

"Around on the back stretch Watson dropped out so as to give the contestants an opportunity for the final spurt to the tape. Down the back stretch they tore, each man straining for himself. Kimble's wheel seemed to fairly leave the track as he made the effort of his life but it was to no avail. He could not shove his front wheel past the colored boy's handle bars. When they flashed over the tape both men were well nigh exhausted. Major Taylor won by a fraction of a wheel's length in :39 3/5. He was cheered loud and long by the great crowd. It was a beautiful race.

"Then came the two-mile national championship. Frank Kramer was an important factor in this event. He defeated Major Taylor in the preliminary heat but the colored boy got in on the final. The second and third men in the two heats rode another heat to decide who should be entitled to start in the final. The starters in this heat were Taylor, Howard Freeman, and Jimmie Bowler. Both gave Taylor something of an argument but he won out hands down. In the final of this event Taylor led Kramer and Owen Kimble over the tape."

The following item is quoted from an Indianapolis newspaper:

"Major Taylor's Early Sprint. Taylor, Kimble and Kramer lined up for the final of this great two-mile national championship race. In the last lap of this event Taylor gave one of the most remarkable exhibitions of sprinting ever seen in this decade. All three were following single pace furnished by the Stinemetz boys and allowing things to take their own course. As they passed the press box Major Taylor was seen beginning to edge to the outside, as he was the last man in the vanguard.

"With a sudden jump on the first turn Taylor passed the other two men as though they were stationary. Usually the fate of a rider who starts a sprint that early is to finish in about the lowest possible position, but it was not so with Taylor, who gained about two wheel's lengths before the other two men were aware that there was anything doing and he kept right on sprinting. They tore after him like mad, Kramer leaving Kimble in the rear as he pushed after the Negro. It was to no avail, however, and Taylor won by over a wheel's length in 4:43." The applause was again thunderous.

Of all the incentives that spur athletes to their best efforts, I believe the most outstanding is the desire to dethrone a champion in his home town before a host of admiring friends. I realize a handsome purse, a diamond-studded medal, a gold or silver trophy and even a champion's best girl seated in the grandstand are wonderful inspirations for any competitor. However, that almost fiendish desire on the part of a field to humble a champion in his native city outdoes them all by a wide margin. I speak from experience as I'm frank to say that no rider ever exerted himself more than I did to beat the great Eddie "Cannon" Bald on the Buffalo Athletic Field Track. Bald lived in Buffalo. I never defeated Bald in Buffalo.

For this and other reasons Kimble and Kramer, my bitter rivals, combined against me in both the championship races on this occasion particularly in the two-mile event. Their tactics in this race were the more noticeable because, the distance being longer, they had better opportunities to pull something.

After his stinging defeat in the third of a mile championship match only a few moments before, the stalwart Kimble's hot southern blood was at the boiling point. He was furious when called out to start in the two-mile championship race final and was counting upon squaring himself in this event. Kramer was also nursing a grudge because of his defeat in the championship the week before. He was out to retrieve his laurels. Besides the purse, championship points and prestige that were at stake, just enough of that "color business" was injected into it to rouse one's sporting blood, giving the race just the right "pep" and the public an extra run for their money. I figured that Kimble and Kramer were out to get me. The big Kentuckian looked grim as we came out to do our "stuff" in the two-mile race. Kramer looked somewhat worried as if a little uneasy about the part he was to play. I must have looked rather serious myself because I was trying to figure out what new joker they had up their sleeves. As I could not foresee this, my best bet was to ride on the defensive, keeping alert to beat them at whatever they tried.

Before we reached the first half I realized what their plans were. To beat them required a burst of speed that seemed almost suicidal. But I knew my "stuff." I timed them perfectly, and threw every ounce of strength into a jump when about 270 yards remained to go. The confidence I felt because of my never failing physical fitness enabled me to gain a lead of two lengths and I gained a third on the way to the tape. It was a furious sprint with a glorious thrill at the end, which was increased by the excited cheering of that frantic crowd. Had I allowed Kimble and Kramer to pocket me I might have had no chance at all.

Neither Kimble nor Kramer offered to congratulate me as such an act of sportsmanship was not in their code. The wonderful ovation given me by the sports lovers of Indianapolis when I scored my second victory on that program again demonstrated that the public always likes to see the best man win.

Once in their dressing room my rivals immediately became involved in a heated argument that almost ended in fist-a-cuffs over the collapse of their plan. That quarrel resulted in a complete split between them which worked out very much to my advantage as it meant just one less combination to battle against.

It was not always the mere excitement of out-generaling, and outracing my opponents around the track and across the tape first that gave me the greatest thrill, but the real climax was the glory of vindication and the joy of retribution following each success, which was always indeed a personal triumph, because of their prejudice and unsportsmanlike methods.

Winning the Name "Major"
(1900)

Hardly had the cheers of the throng that saw me win the third of a mile championship special match race from Owen Kimble and the two-mile championship race from Kimble and Frank Kramer died away before I recalled an objection raised by a prominent Indianapolis merchant over my riding under the name of Major Taylor.

Shortly after I had won my very first race, that ten-mile event on the Indianapolis highways as a boy of thirteen, I received a letter from this merchant asking me to call around and see him. Strangely enough his name was Major Taylor. I knew Mr. Taylor by sight.

For several minutes after I called at Mr. Taylor's office I was grilled by him. Among forty and one other things, he asked me what my christian name was, but he did not give me an opportunity to answer. This third degree business made me very nervous and I was very anxious to get out in the open air. Mr. Taylor accused me, among other things, of appropriating his name, which he led me to believe was a very serious offense. Likewise he alleged that I was receiving his mail, which charge to me was second only to one of murder. As our talk, if it could be called such, came to an end this merchant said to me: "Now I warn you, young man, never to use my name again. If you do I will send you straight to Plainfield (the location of the boys' reformatory) until you are twenty-one just to start with, and after that I am not sure just what will happen to you."

I began to cry. His reformatory talk struck terror into my heart. I was all fed up on that Plainfield business, for years, before I was old enough to know what it was all about. The mere mention of its name caused me to quiver. After I had promised never to use his old name again he then handed me a letter addressd to "Major Taylor." It was mine but he had opened it. I figured he wanted to frighten me out of doing what he thought I might do about this letter, because it was what he would have done under the same circumstances.

Shortly after that interview in Mr. Taylor's office I received a letter from a big law firm there asking me to drop in to see them at my earliest opportunity. In the meantime I had won a number of bicycle races in and about Indianapolis and my name was appearing more or less frequently in the daily papers. These lawyers accused me of using the name of Major Taylor, their client, the merchant referred to above, illegally. They asked me what my correct first name was and I told them "Marshall." They told me to use my right name henceforth or they would land me in Michigan City (penitentiary). I promised them I would but added, "But I can't stop all the kids in town from calling me 'Major,' but I'll try."

Not long after that I left Indianapolis. The next time I returned to the city I was a big "champ," and no longer a little "chump." The name, Major Taylor, was appearing frequently in big headlines in the newspapers throughout the country and on billboards as well.

The day after my success on the Newby Oval track, when I won the third of a Mile Special Championship match race and the Two-mile Championship race, I received another letter. Imagine my surprise when I learned it was from M.̇. Major Taylor, the local merchant. Again he asked me to call to see him, I figured that I was a big champion now and couldn't be bluffed any more, so down I went to see him with blood in my eye. However, I found that Mr. Taylor had evidently experienced a change of heart. He told me that I had performed on the race tracks of the country in such a sportsmanlike manner that I was now free to adopt the name "Major." He also told me that my work on the track had won the honor for me. "I want to congratulate you as champion and wish you every success," said Mr. Taylor as he shook my hand warmly.

When I recovered from my surprise I thanked Mr. Taylor for the privilege of using his name Major, and assured the venerable gentleman that I would always do my very best to uphold with dignity and pride the proud old family name of "Major Taylor," even though the "Major" part of it had been wished on me.

An Indianapolis paper got wind of this meeting of Major Taylor and Major Taylor and ran the following item concerning it in their next issue:

"Major Taylor and Major Taylor. Major Taylor the business man, and Major Taylor the bicycle racer are both of Indianapolis, yet they are two distinct individuals. This could be easily seen if the two were brought face to face.

"The racing man is young and black, while the business man is past the racing age and white, but unfortunately, so Major Taylor the business man says, thousands of people are not aware of this fact and confuse the two. He also says that the use of his name in connection with bicycle racing is causing him no end of trouble, and that he has been obliged to explain to hundreds of his friends that he has not deserted his business and gone into the bicycle racing game.

"Major the racing man, so he asserts, is masquerading around under an assumed name, and that the racing man's correct name is Marshall Walter Taylor. This the racing man admits but claims the right to answer to the name of Major if he likes, although he does not sign his name Major.

"Major is a name in both cases and not a title. Major Taylor the racing man will be in the city next week and promises not to interfere in any way with the business pursuits of Major Taylor the business man. Major Taylor the racing man has made a great reputation this season. No one knows of Marshall Taylor on the National Circuit, but thousands are watching the clever riding of Major Taylor and the clever little colored rider is determined to stick to the name which he has made famous. Meanwhile Major Taylor the business man will continue to send out notices that he is still doing business at the same old stand."

Numerous titles were hung on me by the sports writers of the country when I was in my heyday. Some of them referred to me as the "Black Zimmerman," "the Black Streak," "the Ebony Streak," and the "Black Cyclone." However, I believe the most popular one was "the Worcester Whirlwind."

Some of the riders also had a few choice "pet" names for me occasionally when I flew over the tape ahead of them. These outbursts, of course, were true indications of poor sportsmanship and also showed what hard losers they were.

I Lose to Owen Kimble
(1900)

The last race of the 1900 championship season was scheduled for the Montreal track on September 24. I was entered in three events on that program, the third-mile, the one-mile and two-mile handicap events. Although I had what was generally conceded to be a safe margin to insure my winning the championship title for the season, there was an outside chance that my closest rival, Frank Kramer, by winning the mile championship race at Montreal and the five-mile championship event on the Hartford, Connecticut, track a week later, could tie me for the laurels.

With those facts in mind I determined to put everything I had into my races at Montreal that I might start in the Hartford events with a margin over Kramer that he would be unable to wipe out as we sprinted like mad for the laurel wreath. This marked my first appearance in Montreal since I won the world's championship title the year previous. When I first came on to the Queen's Park track for my warming up sprints I received a tremendous ovation indicating that the crowd had not forgotten my riding to the International honors on the same boards in 1899.

Despite the fact that I was in excellent condition on this occasion Owen Kimble defeated me in the one-mile championship event, the feature number on the all-star program, this being the only championship event I lost that season. However, I won the third of a mile handicap event from scratch, and was very anxious to test my speed in the two-mile handicap event when some water I had drank made me so ill that I was unable to start in that race.

Among the star riders who participated in the Grand National Circuit Meet in Montreal on this occasion were Owen Kimble of Louisville, Kentucky, Frank L. Kramer of Newark, New Jersey, Floyd Krebs of Newark, New Jersey, Saxon Williams of Buffalo, New York, George Collette of New Haven, Connecticut, and C. T. Boisvert of Montreal.

In the one-mile International professional championship race I won the first heat with Saxon Williams second, the time being 2:30 2/5. In the second heat Frank Kramer was the winner with George Collette second, the time was 3:13. Owen Kimble won the third heat in 2:40. I won the first heat in the semi-final in 2:22 1/5. Kimble was first in the second heat of the semi-final with Collette second, the time being 2:14 4/5. Kimble won the final heat with myself second in 3:48.

I won the third of a mile handicap race for professionals, Boisvert being second and Williams third. The time was :40.

Commenting on the meet one of the Montreal dailies printed the following: "There was a monstrous crowd at the Queen's Park track yesterday to witness the cream of the bicycle riders of this country and the United States as they strove for the laurels in the Grand National Circuit Meet. All of the races were hotly contested, in one or two instances the heats nearly resulted in ties. Included in the field of starters was the old favorite, Major Taylor of Worcester, Massachusetts. The appearance of the 'Major' on the track was a signal for a hearty round of applause, which the crack rider politely acknowledged by doffing his cap.

"Several surprises were sprung on the audience during the afternoon, the most notable one being the winning by Owen Kimble of the one-mile championship event with Major Taylor second. It was generally conceded by the knowing ones that the Major had a 'cinch,' but it seems that on the finish Taylor misjudged his sprint with the result that before he was aware of the fact Kimble darted past taking the lead and flying over the line a safe winner. It was a great spurt and although the true merits of the race were challenged by the many, nevertheless, the winner deserved the victory, not only for his plucky fight throughout the race, but the manner in which he grasped the opportunity to turn a certain defeat into a triumphant win when only a few yards from the finish.

"This seemed to act as a tonic on the 'Major,' for in the one-third of a mile handicap which followed, Taylor, who had practically the same men against him as he had in the former race, set a terrific pace from the crack of the pistol and after one of the most exciting and keenly contested bicycle races ever witnessed at Montreal, and probably not surpassed by any other in America for the same distance, flew over the line a winner by ten yards, making the remarkably fast time of :40. Taylor is remarkably popular with Montreal audiences and it seems they have not forgotten the little incident that happened at the World's Meet last year when he was 'gyped' out of a hard earned victory in the half-mile open event through a ruling of an unscrupulous judge.

"When the two mile handicap professional race was announced it was learned with deep regret that the 'Major' was in no condition to contest it as he had become suddenly indisposed, no doubt as a result of the terrible pace he had set in the third of a mile event. This was very disappointing as it seemed to take the interest out of this particular contest."

Following my victorious riding in Indianapolis, and prior to the Montreal races mentioned above I took part in two other programs.

On September 10 I raced at Terre Haute, Indiana winning the one-mile professional open event in the fastest time ever made in competition on the new track there, 2:04. In my second start on that occasion, the two-mile professional handicap, I was unable to place.

In my preliminary heat in the one-mile professional open event I won over Howard Freeman, the time being 2:29. In the final of that race Jimmie Bowler of Chicago was second and Lew Gordon third. Pease won the two-mile professional handicap with Gordon second and Bowler third. I was slowed up in my heat by Freeman for three laps but sprinted the next two laps and caught the bunch. Stinemetz thwarted my efforts thereafter and I was too exhausted to overtake the bunch again. The time for this two-mile event was 4:38.

On September 17, at Erie, Pennsylvania, I was scheduled to meet the three fastest sprinters in America, Frank Kramer, Owen Kimble, and Otto Maya, in a special four-cornered race. It developed to be a case of three against one in this event, however. I knew in advance that the odds were decidedly against me but decided to do my utmost to win especially as I recalled it was one of the last events of the season and my initial appearance in Erie. Fortune smiled on me that day and I led the field home.

On the day after the race the Erie *Dispatch* printed the following article: "Major Taylor, the colored bike star, who attracted so much attention here at the race meet yesterday, is a rare exception to his class generally. He is fairly modest, rather conservative, and not overly proud nor stuck up. He is very white for a colored man and has other qualities that should recommend him to the public generally. He does not drink or use tobacco in any form, never uses profane language, does not race on Sunday and attends church regularly. He is a married man and has saved $25,000 from his winnings and investments covering the past four years.

"Taylor rode in excellent form in the four-cornered special match race yesterday always holding himself back until just before the tape was reached, just to encourage the boys, then he darted ahead with ease and grace that was alone worth going to the track to witness. Later in the season he will ride a special match race with Willie Fenn, the amateur champion, to decide the National Championship for the year of 1900. Major Taylor won about $300 in the races here.

"Major Taylor is not as light in complexion as George Dixon, but he is a dandy in dress and he has a muscular development that is the envy of every slim-jim that sees him."

American Champion Again
(1900)

Under the old order promulgated by the League of American Wheelmen, the winner of each championship event on the National Circuit Tracks was declared the champion of the season for the distance ridden, but in the season of 1900 it was decided that a series of championship races would be held at the various distances on the several tracks of the country in the National Circuit, the winner of each event being allowed a certain number of points. At the close of the season the rider having the most points for the one mile championship races was declared the one-mile champion and so on through the list of other distances. The rider having won the greatest aggregate number of points was declared unreservedly the National Champion of his class, either amateur or professional.

I quote as follows from the "Cycle Age" of October 4, 1900: "American Championship Decided by Points. Now that the championship races of 1900 are over and Major Taylor has been officially declared National Champion, the thought arises that the method of deciding champions under the new regime is much more satisfactory than under the old.

"When a championship depends upon one race it may be won by a rider who is not in reality the champion by merit. For instance, in the International Championship Race at Paris this summer, the French rider, Jacquelin, gained the title of International Champion. Immediately following this International meet came the Paris Exposition of even greater importance from standpoints of competitors, prizes, crowds, etc., and Jacquelin failed to defend his crown, being beaten by Meyers and Cooper. Jacquelin has also been beaten well in several almost successive races since the International meet.

"When a championship is won, as Major has won the 1900 National Championship, by a series of races, it shows conclusively that the winner is the true champion. The champion point table shows forty points for Taylor as against twenty for Frank Kramer his nearest competitor. He is without doubt the best sprint race rider of the aggregation with which he raced."

A New York daily printed the following article relative to the 1900 bicycle championship:

"Major Taylor Is Champion. Worcester Whirlwind Proves Himself the Fastest Man of the Year. The championship among sprinters for the season has been won by Major Taylor, the colored boy, who also was champion last year under the L. A. W. He has now

achieved his fondest hope after a number of years of steady riding
in championship form. He scored the highest number of points in the
N. C. A. series by an immense lead with Frank Kramer second, and
Owen S. Kimble third.

"Major Taylor scored more points than any of the N. C. A.

MAJOR TAYLOR—American Champion, 1900

sprinters and double his nearest competitor, Frank Kramer. Five increased point championships have been run during the season in which
the winner scored eight points instead of four which is the allowance
for the winner of a circuit championship. Major Taylor won four
firsts which gave him thirty-two points, one second gave him four
points, and he won a circuit championship which gave him four points,
making a total for the season of forty points with Frank Kramer
having but twenty. Major Taylor won every championship but the
mile at Montreal in which he ran second. Taylor won the quarter,

third, half and the two-mile, also the one-mile circuit championship events. The five-mile was not contested.

"Major Taylor's supremacy during the season has been unquestioned. His victories being easily accomplished in most cases. It was Owen Kimble, the Kentuckian, who gave the "Major" the bitterest battles of any of the contestants, and he managed to beat Major out occasionally. Whenever they came together in a final it was always sure to be a battle royal. On Monday at Hartford Major Taylor rode a special match against Willie Fenn, the amateur champion, for the National Championship title and defeated the amateur in straight heats. It was a great race.

"The following is an official record of the professional series for the season of 1900. Rank of the riders, championship contestants were rated as follows for the first ten fastest riders in America:

TEN FASTEST RIDERS, PROFESSIONAL SERIES, SEASON OF 1900

Rider	First	Second	Third	Points
Major Taylor	5	1	0	40
Frank Kramer	1	3	4	20
Owen S. Kimble	2	1	1	18
Howard B. Freeman	2	0	0	8
Earl Kiser	0	3	0	8
Johnnie Fisher	0	0	2	3
Jimmie Bowler	0	1	0	2
George Collette	0	0	1	2
Bobby Walthour	0	1	0	2
Al Newhouse	0	0	0	0

Defeating Tom Cooper at the Garden
(1900)

At last the stage was set for one of my most desired races. I was pitted against the famous Tom Cooper of Detroit in a special championship match race over the mile route, best two in three heats for a purse of $500, winner take all. The event was featured on the opening night of the six-day bicycle race in Madison Square Garden in 1900. So anxious was I to race Cooper that I readily agreed to all of the conditions suggested by him with but one exception—that was that a loser's end of the purse be provided for. I insisted on a winner-take-all basis maintaining that the loser did not deserve a share of the purse, and eventually I carried the point.

Since Cooper had but recently returned from a very successful season throughout Europe I realized he would be in excellent fettle for his match race with me. To make doubly sure that I would be in top form for this classic I discontinued my vaudeville engagements on the "home-trainers" and put in two weeks of special training on the Ambrose Park track in Brooklyn.

If ever there were two riders on earth that I wanted to meet in match races above all others they were Eddie Bald and Tom Cooper. Since a match with the former was out of the question, because he drew the color line, my next best choice was Cooper. Now after three or four years of dickering and yearning my opportunity to meet him was at hand. When I signed the contract to race Cooper I was in perfect physical condition and was confident I could take Cooper into camp.

Earlier in the season Cooper and I had been signed to race a special championship match on the Milwaukee track. However, that event was called off when municipal inspectors declared the track unfit. In all my years of waiting to oppose Cooper in a match race that Milwaukee engagement was the first in which we were actually signed to an agreement. Our Madison Square race was, therefore, the first in which we had ever been pitted against each other in a special match.

I quote the following article from one of the New York papers relative to this special championship match race:

"Major Taylor, the Marvelous Colored Sprinter, Upholds His Supremacy. Defeats his old rival, Tom Cooper, in Straight Heats. Major Taylor by a clever jump on the eighth lap of the first heat gained a lead of ten yards on Tom Cooper, and beat him out badly at the tape in the first heat of their championship match race.

"The first heat was unpaced and both men held back at the pistol, shortly Cooper reluctantly took the lead, Taylor trailing until they entered the back stretch on the eighth lap. Then he suddenly dashed down the banking and took the pole and a lead of ten yards with it. The ex-champion pedalled pluckily and pulled up a few yards, but he could not catch and pass Taylor who won easily, time 3.06. There was tremendous shouting and cheering.

Tom Cooper—and trainer "Mother Webb"

"Taylor also won the second heat of his match with Cooper, but only after a great finish, which brought the large audience to its feet with excitement. By agreement a pacemaker was put in, Louis Grimm. Taylor caught his rear wheel and followed closely until the pacer dropped out at the end of the seventh lap, and then the real fight began. Struggle as he could Cooper was unable to pass Taylor. The white champion made his final effort at the bell. He drew up along side Taylor on the back stretch and they swung on to the stretch and over the tape with Cooper lapping Taylor's back wheel, Taylor having won the heat and the match in the time of 2.08 4-5. The colored champion was cheered wildly.

"Tom Cooper used very poor judgment in both heats. In the first he opened up a gap on the pole allowing Taylor to jump through and take the lead. In the second heat he permitted Taylor to have the lead on the last three laps and all Major Taylor had to do was to hold the position of advantage on the pole to the finish.   But it was a great race and a most popular victory."

As I tore over the finish line in the final heat of my race with Cooper my thoughts flashed to the night a comparatively short time previous when as a New York paper put it, "he electrified the immense throng in the same old garden by outsprinting the great Eddie (Cannon) Bald in a hot finish in his first professional race."

This race stands out in my memory as one of the greatest victories I ever won.   It is as fresh in my memory today as it was on the night of the championship match race with Tom Cooper in the old Madison Square Garden.

I clearly recall an incident that occurred as I was leaving my training quarters for the first heat of that great match race.   It centers about Tom Eck, the white-haired veteran and mentor, who was acknowledged trainer and manager of numerous bicycle champions in that era.   On this occasion he was handling Cooper.   I can see him now carrying Cooper's wheel on his shoulder toward the starting line.

As Eck passed my trainer and myself he called out to the former, Bob Ellingham, "Well, Bawb, Tawm will now proceed to hand your little darkey the most artistic trimming of his young life.   In this first heat Tawm is going to give the Major his first real lesson on the fine points of the French style of match racing.   Tawm has a fine assortment of brand new tactics, fresh from Paris, and if the Major will practice the strategy in this heat until he has it down fine, coupled with what he already knows about the game, he may in time be able to give Tawm a pretty smart race.   However, Bawb, I have cautioned Tawm that in the best interest of the sport and for the good of all concerned, not to beat the little darkey badly."

Of course this comment by Eck was designed solely to get me nerved up.   He felt that it would so upset me that I might possibly lose my head and make a false move or slip-up in the race thereby bringing about my downfall.   Eck's comments served an entirely different purpose, however, as it made me all the more determined and confident.   I smiled as I heard my trainer inform Eck as follows: "It is true, Mr. Eck, that Major Taylor has never raced in Paris and will, therefore, be obliged to ride this race on what he has been able to pick up on this side of the pond.   What he may lack in track strategy he will have to make up in gameness and speed.   However, he is always willing to learn and never lets an opportunity slip by to teach the other fellow a point or two if possible."   Cooper smiled confidently as he overheard the repartee between our two trainers and I reflected Cooper's broad grin.

The six-day riders were called off the track proper but continued riding on the flat surface inside the track. There was an understanding among them that there would be no attempt at lap stealing until the heat of the match race was over when they would be given the pistol signal to renew their six-day argument in earnest.

At the start of the first heat Cooper attempted to force me into the lead. After trying every trick he knew, including an assortment of French numbers, he gave it up for a bad job and took the lead and settled down to business.

I can recall every move he made in this heat as vividly as though it were run only yesterday. I actually measured the revolutions of his pedals in comparison with my own to determine what gear he had up. When I was satisfied that it was an 108-inch gear I could tell from experience just what tactics he would employ. My forecast was strengthened when I discovered he was using a seven-inch crank. I figured he was relying more upon the difference between his 108-inch gear and my 92-inch gear and his seven-inch crank as compared to my six-and-three-quarter-inch crank, to quote a jibe given by Cooper's trainer a few moments before "to teach me the fine points in the art of the French style of racing," rather than through a burst of speed. It was apparent to me that Cooper figured he had an edge on me through the size of gear he was riding as compared with mine together with the advantage he thought his crank held over mine rather than a display of speed and good judgment.

Cooper evidently figured that if he could get the jump on me down the steepest part of the banking, he should get his big gear wound up in fine style and I would never be able to get around him in the last lap and beat him to the tape. I knew that once he got that big gear rolling it would be a very difficult task for me to beat him out at the finish line. Therefore, as we rode I was very busy figuring out his plan of action and planning my campaign to meet it.

Sure enough with three laps to go Cooper gradually edged away from the pole toward the outside of the track. At the same time he began to pick up his sprint as he mounted the banking at a lively clip just after crossing the tape at two laps to go. This strategy Cooper planned would aid him materially in making his great plunge *à la Française* on entering the back stretch. However, I had him timed perfectly and beat him to it by jumping from low right into high speed so that by the time I reached the pole I was going at top speed. I gave him everything I had. The spectators cheering frantically.

I gained about ten or twelve lengths with only one and a half laps to go. When I saw I had Cooper hopelessly beaten and that it was unnecessary to extend myself further I was about to ease up, and then I suddenly recalled Tom Eck's sneering remarks about his warning

Cooper not to beat me too badly for the good of the sport. Riled by that taunt I kept right on tearing to the tape. Meantime Cooper sat up down the back stretch—he had been badly outgeneraled, outsprinted and outdistanced. It was not my usual custom to do business in this way. This was the first time I ever really tried to distance an opponent.

Shrewd old Tom Eck hadn't a word to say as he and Cooper walked to the latter's dressing room, neither did my trainer nor I.

As Cooper and I were called out to resume hostilities in the second heat, he looked nervous and pale. Eck looked worried but this time failed to utter a sound. Louis Grimm was put in as pacemaker and a very fine job he made of it. As the pistol barked I made a bid for his rear wheel and I held it for seven laps after which I went to the front and taking it easy watched Cooper closely from under my arm.

I saw every move he made and when he noted that I was not going to mount the banking he started to do so. As a matter of tactics and in order to keep him on the pole I started to sprint the moment he started up the banking. My move forced him to come along with me on the pole and as soon as he was back there I eased up again. Twice this trick was repeated and as Cooper sensed my strategy he made a desperate effort to jump past me. That was physically impossible as he could not pick up speed as quickly down on the pole with his big gear as I could with my smaller one.

So I kept him fighting furiously around on the outside of the track for a lap and a half. When he began to weaken I jumped for the tape which was then a lap away. My jump gave me about two lengths lead which advantage I maintained to the finishing line. In the excitement incident to that mad dash for the tape, the old Garden fairly ringing with thunderous cheers, I made a very serious error that came very nearly causing me the heat after all.

I made a mistake in the number of laps to go and sat up as I crossed the tape. As the bell clanged to designate the last lap, however, I realized my error and quickly regained my stride. Cooper meantime had not miscalculated on the number of the laps and he tore after me with a terrific burst of speed. We had a desperate neck-and-neck struggle for the honors throughout the entire lap. His big gear was now wound up in fine style but I managed to hold my advantage and led him across the tape by half a wheel's length. That margin settled the race and squared for all time my score against Tom Cooper. My principle grievance against Cooper centered about his strenuous efforts to have me debarred from the race tracks of the country in 1899. The drive being camouflaged cleverly to cover up its real cause, color prejudice, on the part of my rivals who realized I was their peer on a bicycle.

Had the purse been $5,000 instead of $500 it would have been a mere bagatelle compared with the supreme satisfaction that I felt over my defeat of Tom Cooper. If ever a race was run for blood this one was. Incidentally, world-wide prestige went hand in hand with the victory. Neither Cooper nor Eck offered to shake hands with me at the close of the race nor did they utter a word of congratulation. I have never seen a more humiliated pair of "Toms" in my life than were Cooper and Eck as they marched silently to their dressing room.

As a matter of fact, I was equally silent as Ellingham and I repaired to our dressing room. I had never indulged in boasting over my conquests either within the hearing of my opponents or elsewhere. I felt that real sportsmanship demanded that an athlete wear his laurels modestly. I know very well that some of the greatest riders of my day had a different idea about that, and I am also aware, that many of the present-day stars do not share my theory in this respect. It is still my belief, however, that no real champion in any line of sport could or would resort to such ungentlemanly conduct. But many times I have had all I could possibly do to refrain from handing out a bit of the old sarcasm.

Cooper was keenly disappointed at the outcome of our championship match race. Naturally he was anxious to win the $500 purse, but he was far more desirous of defeating me on this occasion as he had planned to retire after the race—provided he had administered a crushing defeat to me to mark the end of his brilliant racing career.

In response to a general demand on the part of the six-day bicycle enthusiasts in New York, the management of the Madison Square Garden signed me to race two exhibitions on the track while the grind was on. Apparently I had got the public fancy in my spectacular victory over the great Tom Cooper. So high was the enthusiasm of the moment that the management of the track practically permitted me to name my terms for the exhibitions. I rode the quarter of a mile in 2/5 of a second under the world's record and later covered the half mile in 4/5 of a second lower than record. One of the New York dailies commented as follows on my victory over Cooper:

"Major Taylor's Great Victory over Tom Cooper makes him Equal to the Great Jacquelin. Major Taylor's victory over Cooper places him on a par with the celebrated French rider, Jacquelin. The merits of the two have been compared as far as could be without an actual race. Jacqueln defeated Tom Cooper in a match race this summer in Europe, and had Cooper been able to defeat Taylor in the Garden the French champion would be considered faster than the 'Worcester Whirlwind.' "

My thrilling victory over Tom Cooper paved the way for my first invasion of Europe in 1901. Tom Cooper had made a very fine impression in Europe through his great riding in 1900. Therefore, the bicycle enthusiasts of the Continent were deeply interested in my welfare and whereabouts following my sensational victory over him in Madison Square Garden that winter. Hardly a day passed thereafter that I did not receive a cablegram asking my terms for a series of championship match races with the stars of Europe in 1901.

European riders who participated in the 1900 six-day race at Madison Square Garden were eagerly sought out by newspaper men upon their arrival home. It was apparent that they were anxious to get first-hand information on my riding ability. Very favorable comment caused track promoters all over Europe to seek my services for match races forthwith.

The following article was printed in a Paris sporting newspaper shortly after the 1900 six-day bicycle race in New York had become a matter of history:

"Jean Gougoltz and Other Foreign Stars Have Arrived in Paris. Contrary to the general rule of returned cyclists they declare that they were treated beyond expectation by the American riders. Robert Coquelle, the French newspaper man, who was with the invaders said upon his return to Paris that America is a great country and the riders are very fast. Major Taylor, he said, is built like a bronze statue. He simply played with Tom Cooper in their match race, and he will defeat every champion in Europe. He has signed a contract and is coming to Paris next spring."

It was arranged that I would race Jacquelin, the sprint champion of Europe, in a series of special matches. The first two to be held in Paris, May 16 and May 27. I was also signed to meet Willie Arend, champion of Germany, Thorwald Elleggarde, champion of Denmark, Momo, the champion of Italy, Grognia, champion of Belgium, Gougoltz, champion of Switzerland, and all of the leading sprinters of Europe. Other American invaders in Europe that season were Billy Stinson, Johnnie Nelson, and Harry Elkes, all of whom were motor pace followers.

Beating a Middle-Distance Star
(1900)

Now that I had defeated all the topnotchers among the sprinters, I drew some attention from the middle-distance riders. Chief among them was Harry Elkes, and a few weeks after defeating Tom Cooper, I signed up to oppose Elkes at Boston in three varied heats for a purse of $500, winner takes all.

"The first will be a one-mile spring, single paced, which ought to be won by Taylor," a Boston daily predicted. "The second will be a five-mile pursuit race in which Elkes should have a little the best of the argument. If each should win a heat, the toss of a coin will decide whether the third will be a one-mile spring or a five-mile pursuit race. If Taylor should win the toss, he will prefer the one-mile sprint; provided Elkes wins the toss, he will choose the five-mile pursuit race. The match will be for blood as neither man can afford to have his reputation suffer by a defeat."

On the night of the match, at Park Square Garden, I won the fateful coin toss. A Boston newspaper summarized the outcome as follows:

Major Taylor won his match against Harry Elkes last night, but had no easy time doing it. In the one-mile heat, paced by Oscar Babcock, Taylor won through a sprint on the last lap and down the home stretch which enabled him to cross the tape a length ahead of Elkes.

The second heat, a five-mile pursuit race, was won by Elkes. Taylor stopped riding in the third lap, his rear tire having been wound too thickly with tape causing it to bounce and skid so badly that the Major was obliged to give up the race.

The last heat was a mile unpaced in which both men started from the tape. In this race Taylor again demonstrated his superiority, but Elkes was at his rear wheel when the tape was cross. Major Taylor was cheered to the echo.

Triumphant Invasion of Europe
(1901)

In the short space of two months I participated in fifty-seven races in various European cities. In view of the fact that I refused to ride on Sunday one will readily see that my schedule called for almost one race a day while I was on the Continent. There wasn't one race in which I participated that could be called easy by the widest stretch of the imagination. It was one of the most strenuous campaigns that I ever took part in and this despite the fact that I had planned to compete in the championship circuit races in this country as soon as I arrived home from Europe.

Among the cities in which I rode against the champions of Europe were: Roubaix, Bordeaux, Nantes, Orléans, Paris, Toulouse, Agen, Lyons, France; Verviers, Antwerp, Belgium; Berlin, Hanover, Leipzig, Germany; Turin, Milan, Italy; Copenhagen, Denmark; and Geneva, Switzerland.

Among the riders whom I opposed in my sweep through Europe, which compares in a measure with the recent trip through this country by Paavo Nurmi, the great Finnish runner, were: Edmond Jacquelin, champion of France; Quivy, one of the best French riders; Dutrieu and Fouaneau also of France; Thorwald Elleggarde, champion of Denmark; Willie Arend, champion of Germany; Louis Grognia, champion of Belgium; Charles Gascoyne, champion of England; Palo Momo, champion of Italy; Muringer, one of the topnotchers of Germany; Ferrari and Bixio two of the greatest sprinters in Italy; Van den Born who was recently defeated by Grognia for the championship of Belgium which Van den Born had formerly held.

Other well-known riders of the day were: Poulain, who became champion of France in 1902; Marteles, former champion of France, Bonnevie, Coutenete, Dangla, Chodeau, LeVeler, Marsollies, all great French riders, and the famous French tandem team, Lambrecht-Legarde; Protin, former champion of Belgium; Huber, former champion of Germany; Crause, a great German sprinter; Sidel, former champion of Germany; Cornelli, former champion of Italy; Anzani, former champion of Italy and now world famous as a builder of airplanes; Dei, former champion of Italy, now a bicycle manufacturer; Tommosillo, former champion of Italy; Gougoltz, champion of Switzerland; Sid Jenkins, the British champion.

I shall never forget my first race in Europe. It took place in Berlin on April 8, 1901, and the distance was one kilometer, and all hands started from scratch. The German champion Arend won this race, Elleggarde champion of Denmark was second and I finished third.

My greatest handicap on this occasion was the cold weather as I was always at my best when it was extremely hot. On top of that drawback I arrived in Berlin the day preceding the race and was unable to take a practice sprint on the track until the day of the race. I also found myself at a disadvantage in not being able to speak the

WILLY AREND, the German Champion

language of the country—this being a novel experience for me since the race was run according to French tactics. This meant loafing until the last two hundred or three hundred yards when a furious sprint for the tape was the order. It allowed considerable loafing until it was time for the jump. This enabled my opponents to confer as they rode the race and make their plans out in the open because they knew I could not understand them.

No sooner had Arend crossed the finish line to win the race than the greatest demonstration I had ever seen on a bicycle track took place. He was presented a monster horseshoe of roses after which the officials, the band, and the public filed out on to the track in perfect order. One section of the crowd carried Arend's wheel while others bore the champion on their shoulders. The band played the "Watch on the Rhine" while the entire gathering sang the words of the German

national anthem as they made a complete circuit of the track. I
added my bit to the festive occasion by shaking hands with Arend as
I congratulated him warmly on his splendid victory. Down in my
heart, however, I felt that it would not be long before the tables
were reversed with Arend seeking me out to shake my hand as he congratulated me over leading him across the finishing line.

My chance to even up the score with Arend came a few days later

Start of the Final of the International Championship Race

on the same track and I trained as I never had trained before for my
come-back stunt. Besides Arend and myself the promoters secured
Sidel another great German rider and Elleggarde, the Danish champion, to ride in this four-cornered International Championship race.
My three opponents on this occasion were all great sprinters and were
in excellent physical condition.

On the day of the race the weather was all that one could wish for
and my form was vastly improved in the intervening week. It was
agreed that the race would be decided on points. I won the first heat
scoring one point on Arend who finished second, one point above
Elleggarde who was third while Sidel was last. Elleggarde, Arend
and myself lined up for the final. In the deciding heat I pulled a neat
little trick on the field that worked out perfectly. I had my trainer
pace off about one hundred yards from the tape down the home
stretch and make a mark in the sand along side the edge of the
track with his foot to mark the spot. True to my calculations my
three opponents started to sprint for the tape with almost two laps to go.

That was just what I wanted them to do. They thought I was going to make my jump from the spot that my trainer had made in the sand and they planned to speed me by it so fast that I would be unable to start my jump therefrom. When I pulled frantically for the last lap they had already sprinted a full lap and as we reached the last turn I made my jump. After a most furious effort I had won by about two lengths.

The applause that greeted me was as great as that accorded Arend a few days previously when he defeated me. The "Star Spangled Banner" never sounded sweeter than it did on this occasion, the band playing it as I rode my lap of honor around the track. Arend, Elleggarde and Sidel congratulated me as did thousands of American admirers who appeared at the track to cheer for me.

One week later I made my début in Verviers, Belgium, the home of Louis Grognia, the champion of that country. It was a championship match race between Grognia and myself. I won the first heat after a desperate fight in the last two hundred fifty yards. Grognia won the second heat and I took the final and the race.

In the second heat an incident occurred that had never before fallen my lot in my racing career. I had forced Grognia into the lead and was watching him closely. I allowed him to mount the banking on leaving the tape in the final lap and even permitted him to start his jump down the banking first, feeling certain that I could beat him to the tape even after giving him those advantages. When we reached the pole he had a length's lead on me which he increased to another before he reached the tape beating me by about two good lengths.

Grognia's defeating me in this heat gave me the surprise of my life and incidentally threw a scare into me that I shall never forget. I was dumbfounded as I realized all too well that Grognia had gained on me in the home stretch, a feat that no opponent of mine in my years of racing had ever been able to do. The thought kept running through my mind that if Grognia defeated me in the third and final heat of this race in the same manner my invasion of Europe might just as well end then and there. My chief objective on my trip to the Continent was a race with the great Edmond Jacquelin, who had acquired his title as champion of Europe by setting back all of the champions I was to do battle against, and should one of them lead me home in the interim, the zest would naturally be out of our big match race. With these facts in mind one may well realize I was completely upset by Grognia's terrific sprint which enabled him to win the second heat.

As we were called out for the final heat I had my mind all made up as to the style of race I was going to ride. In the breathing spell between the second and third heats I delved into my bag of cleverest tricks and tactics and extracted therefrom my outstanding favorites.

I finally decided that I would ride practically the same style of race in the final heat that I followed in the second with one exception— I made up my mind to jump off the banking first. This strategy enabled me to reach the tape first, a little more than a length ahead of Grognia. I breathed a sigh of relief as I rode my lap of honor. It was one of the most trying races that I had ever contested in Europe. However, I felt amply repaid as the Belgians gave me a splendid ovation despite the fact that I had dethroned their idol, Grognia, who was the last stumbling block between Jacquelin and myself.

Louis Grognia—The Belgium Champion

Turning the Tables on a French Idol
(1901)

After having competed in ten races in the various sections of Europe I was called upon for the feature event of the tour—the match race with the French champion Edmond Jacquelin. This race of races was held at the "Parc du Princess" in Paris on May 16, 1901.

At the time of this match I felt I was in excellent physical condition for the big fuss and desired only a warm day for the race. I was doomed for a disappointment, however, because the day was cold and raw and despite the fact that I wore an extra heavy sweater I shivered as I took my warming-up trips over the track. The fates had also decreed that I was to be beaten on this occasion by the great Jacquelin and I took my reverse gracefully. I offered no excuses.

EDMOND JACQUELIN—Champion of France

Although Jacquelin defeated me in our first meeting I learned a very valuable lesson while he was turning the trick. That was that Jacquelin's well-known mental hazard (that deadly jump) through which he gained his margin of victory in most of his races availed him naught when he pulled it on me. From experience I learned that try as he might Jacquelin couldn't jump away from me and in each of our heats I was right at his rear wheel as we crossed the finishing line. Incidently, I realized that Jacquelin was as good a rider as I had heard him proclaimed and that with a warmer sun and balmier air I could have given a far better account of myself.

At the conclusion of the second and deciding heat of our match race Jacquelin astonished me by his childish antics. He was so carried

MAJOR TAYLOR—Champion of America

away with his victory over me that he lost his head completely and thumbed his nose at me immediately after crossing the tape all the way around the track. As I stood bewildered by Jacquelin's actions his thousands of friends and admirers poured out of the grandstands and carried him about the track on their shoulders. In all my experience on the tracks of this country and Europe I had never before suffered such humiliation as Jacquelin's insult caused me.

However, Jacquelin's conduct was to react as a boomerang. I was hurt to the quick by his unsportsmanlike conduct and resolved then and there that I would not return home until I had wiped out his insult. My opportunity to square the balances came in a fortnight and I did little else but plan for that race in the interim. I made up my mind that I would lead Jacquelin home in this championship match race by such a margin that there would be no doubt, even in his mind, as to who was the better rider.

So on May 27 I had planned my campaign in a way that I figured would bring the best results. I was in prime condition for this race and was still further favored with a hot day. So pleased was I at the weather conditions that I felt this was going to be my day.

Upwards of thirty thousand eager, impatient bicycle race enthusiasts

Start of First Heat of Second Grand Challenge Match

greeted Jacquelin and I with a storm of applause as we came out to face the starter. The Frenchman had his same arrogant smile as he mounted his wheel. As we rode slowly from the tape in the first heat there was great cheering. After some maneuvering Jacquelin and I tried to force each other into the lead. In so doing both of us came to a dead stop. We were practically side by side, Jacquelin being slightly ahead. Balancing a few moments, I backed slowly half a revolution of my crank until I brought myself directly behind Jacquelin. That's just where I wanted to be. The grandstands were now in a frenzy. Realizing I had out-maneuvered him on this score Jacquelin laughed out-right and moved off in the lead prepared for business.

I was so satisfied that I could bring him into camp on this occasion that I again allowed him to ride his own race. I played right into his hands and actually permitted him to start his famous jump from his favorite distance, about two hundred fifty yards from the tape. However, I was very careful to jump at the same instant and the sprint down that long straight stretch must have been magnificent. Jacquelin was four lengths behind when I dashed across the tape. The applause was deafening.

Twenty minutes later we were called out for our second heat.   It proved to be the final heat, as per my plans.   I worked in a bit of psychology after both of us had mounted and were strapped in.   I reached over and extended my hand to Jacquelin and he took it with a great show of surprise.   Under the circumstances he could not have refused to shake hands with me.

I knew from the expression on his face that he was well aware

That Bewildering Hand Shake—Start of Second and Last Match

of the fact that my hand-shake was a demonstration of sarcasm pure and simple.   My motive was to impress on Jacquelin that I was so positive that I could defeat him again that this was going to be the last heat.   Followers of boxing will recognize my action as a parallel to what happens at the boxers' meet at the start of the final round.

As the French idol gathered the full significance of my gesture he mumbled something, shrugged his shoulders, and set his jaw.   His sneering smile disappeared and a frown encompassed his face.

No sooner had the starter's gun sent us away than Jacquelin seriously accepted the lead without the usual jockeying.   However, as we came to the last quarter I took the lead and with two hundred fifty yards left to go we tore off the steep banking together, and as we entered the home stretch and dashed for the tape, I kicked away from him—the resentment I bore towards Jacquelin for the insult he offered me

Finish of Revenge Match

serving to pace me as I never had been paced before. When I crossed
the finish line Jacquelin was again four lengths behind.

As I crossed the tape I quickly pulled a small, silk American flag
from my belt and waved it vigorously in front of the vulgar Jacquelin
while we circled the track.   Meantime the people were howling their
approval and tossing their hats into the air as I deftly turned the tables

My "Military" Salute

on the French hero.   It appeared that the vast audience, although stunned for the moment by my victory over their idol, were delighted to have me take some of the conceit out of him.   They were also elated at the method I pursued to even up the insult he had offered me at the close of our first match.   Jacquelin was severely censored by the press and public for his ungentlemanly conduct.   He made a gesture that was merely a military salute, so I thought it only fair and quite proper to return my salute in this manner as ample revenge for his insult.

Meantime the band struck up the "Star Spangled Banner" as I rode my lap of honor with a big bouquet of roses on my shoulder which were symbolic of my victory.   Hundreds of Americans poured onto the track and gave me a splendid ovation as did thousands of natives, men and women.   This was my greatest triumph in Paris.

My Hardest Match Race

(1901)

From Paris I journeyed to Copenhagen where I met Thorwald Elleggarde, the sensational Danish champion, in his home town in a championship match race. He was the peer of the stars of Europe in open competition while Jacquelin was the king of the field in match races. Elleggarde won the world's sprint championship on several successive occasions prior to my match race with him. Arend the German crack was possibly more brilliant than Elleggarde but the latter was the most consistent performer among the European stars. Although I arrived in Copenhagen only a day before my race with the great Dane and so had little time to get accustomed to the track, which was a third of a mile and built of cement, I had no fear of the outcome. Nevertheless, I was in my best form as usual. Elleggarde won the first heat, I took the second while the big Dane captured the third and the match.

There was a tremendous attendance at this race the weather being well-nigh perfect. Notwithstanding the fact that the first heat was called for nine o'clock P. M. the use of artificial lighting about the track was superfluous. I recall that the track, thanks to the midnight sun, was lighted almost as clearly at midnight as it would be at midday.

In the first heat, being unaccustomed to the track, I forced matters with Elleggarde a bit too soon and was beaten by inches to the tape. There was a wild demonstration on the part of the Danes present, so overjoyed were they at his victory over me. However, I reversed the tables by winning the next heat by a length after a terrific sprint right over the tape. The big crowd awaited breathlessly for the final heat anticipating another hectic duel on that last lap.

However, these Danish people got a thrill as Elleggarde and I rode on to the last lap that they had not looked forward to. As we swung onto the back stretch I started my jump and was just kicking past him when my rear tire blew out with a bang and I went down with a crash. Elleggarde hesitated for a moment as though making sure that I was down for the count and then dashed for the tape for all he was worth, evidently fearing that I might remount and tear after him. Since my feet were strapped to the pedals I could not free myself and had to be content with raising myself on one elbow and watching the big Dane sprint like mad for the tape.

The thought went through my mind at the moment that Elleggarde had displayed a very poor brand of sportsmanship under the circumstances.

Right then and there a feeling sprang up between us and it continued to grow more and more bitter as time went on. Our sentiments as a result of this fluke race brought about a revenge match on the famous Agen (France) track in which I was the victor.

It was the consensus of opinion among sports writers of Europe that as a matter of sportsmanship Elleggarde should have volunteered to ride the final heat over in our Copenhagen match race. Their

THORWALD ELLEGGARDE—Danish Champion

criticism of his refusal to do so hurt the big Dane and brought about our being signed up for a return match which would, the newspaper men claimed, determine the real victor of the Copenhagen race and the Agen match at one and the same time.

Just three weeks to a day from the date of the Copenhagen fiasco Elleggarde and I hooked up in our revenge match race at Agen. It proved to be the hardest match race that I ever competed in. Elleggarde was determined to wipe out the stain of his fluke victory over me in Copenhagen, while I was out to prove that I would have led him home in that race only for the accident to my tire, had he been sportsman enough to ride it over again after I had been painfully hurt in the last lap.

The Agen track was a beautiful course, built of concrete and measured three laps to the mile. Ideal racing weather greeted Elleggarde and I as we went to the starting line, while the immense throng gathered about the track gave us a rousing reception. It was apparent that all hands wanted the better man to win this momentous race and I knew that the French bicycle enthusiasts would acclaim the winner regardless of whom he proved to be, provided he won the race on merit alone.

The first heat was paced by single riders—which was just to my liking. However, I was greatly surprised when Elleggarde led me home in this dash by six or eight inches in a manner that left no

Start of the Deciding Heat of the most bitterly fought Match Race I ever contested

doubt in the minds of all who saw the race as to who was who. After a brief rest we came out for the second heat which was unpaced. This time Elleggarde appeared to be more confident and determined than I had ever seen him before. I decided to ride a different style of race this time and we fought it out for a full lap, neck and neck, with a heart-breaking finish down the home stretch and right over the tape. I had just about the same advantage over Elleggarde in this heat that he had on me in our first heat, not more than half a foot. There was great excitement.

Then came the most trying test of all, the one that would tell the story, and settle for all time the question of supremacy between Elleggarde and myself. Incidentally, I felt positive that this heat would decide two matches simultaneously—my race with Elleggarde in Copenhagen as well as the current one and judging from the way he rode this race in Agen he must have felt the same way. It was a grudge fight and there was no friendly hand-shaking either before or after our heats on this track. The enormous throng was cheering frantically as we came out.

In this third heat I allowed Elleggarde to take the lead for the first two laps. Then I suddenly jumped past him just coming up to the bell on the last lap. After taking command of the situation I eased up a trifle until he challenged me, then I made my final jump for the tape. He had me timed just about right. It was anybody's race down the back stretch, around the turn, down the home stretch and right over the finish line. It was a savage fight but I had the advantage again by about six or eight inches. The cheering was deafening. I can never forget it.

We were nearly exhausted at the close of this heat despite the fact that we were both in perfect physical condition. Judging from the physical expression on Elleggarde's face, and from subsequent events this race must have settled for all time any hope he might have had of ever defeating me in a single man-to-man race. As a matter of fact we met a number of times after that gruelling race but I never again experienced a great deal of difficulty in defeating him. It is apparent to me now that my victory over Elleggarde on the Agen track on that eventful day broke his morale as far as I personally was concerned. The outcome of this great match proved that it was the hardest match race that I ever won.

Soon after my races with Elleggarde I jumped to Berlin where I defeated the champions of four countries in a five-cornered international match race at 1000 meters. It was arranged that we would ride three heats, winner to be determined on a point basis.

The field included Momo, the Italian champion, Elleggarde, champion of Denmark, Protin, Champion of Austria, Arend and Huber, the premier sprinters of Germany, and myself.

From Berlin I next went to Leipzig where I won a three-cornered match race over Willie Arend, champion of Germany, and Huber, the former champion of Germany. At Antwerp I defeated Grognia, the champion of Belgium, Momo, the Italian champion and Protin, the champion of Austria, in a four-cornered international match race. At Toulouse I scored another victory over Van den Born, the former champion of Belgium, and Cornelli, the former champion of Italy.

In a match against the tandem team composed of Grognia and Prevost at Bordeaux I was defeated, but won out against Lambrecht and Legarde, another tandem team in Lyons. On this same occasion I won the 1000-meter handicap event from a field of stars which included Lambrecht, Legarde, Grognia, Prevost, Marteles, Van den Born, Cornelli and others. At Geneva I rode my final engagement of that season and defeated Gougoltz and Henneburn another famous tandem team.

My first European tour had proven even more successful than the trip made by Arthur Augustus Zimmerman, my famous predecessor, when he was champion of America.   All told I competed in 16 cities, most of them being the capitals of European countries, and was successful against the champions and leading riders of six countries.   I was defeated in only two single man-to-man match races, Jacquelin and Elleggarde turning the tricks as has been explained.   Incidentally, my first invasion of Europe, in 1901, netted me 42 firsts, 11 seconds, 3 thirds, and 1 fourth prize.

High Tension at Worcester

(1901)

Through the strange turn of affairs the most outstanding incident of my career was staged in my home city, Worcester, Massachusetts, in the summer of 1901. It followed the National Circuit meet races at Springfield, Massachusetts, and brought to Worcester the pick of the bicycle riders of the country, as the program included the one-mile championship event.

This one-mile national championship event with its increased points was the feature event of that program. Great as was this incentive the real motive that sent all of my rivals to participate in this big race at Worcester was their desire to humiliate me before my fellow townsmen. As a matter of fact the winner of a national championship race secured eight points whereas in a circuit championship event he would only gain four. That fact had no little bearing on my desire to win before my thousands of friends in Worcester, and it also served to spur on my rivals.

As usual there was the customary combination trumped up to bring about my defeat regardless of cost in this race. MacFarland, of course, was at the bottom of it and he had such able assistants as Owen Kimble, Frank Kramer and Tom Cooper to aid him in putting across his underhanded tactics. In addition to that MacFarland entered the races himself to make sure that his instructions were carried out to the letter. It would have been a great feather in his cap to have caused me to trail the field in my home town. The feeling had become so strained that the riders in MacFarland's clique felt that to defeat me would bring admiration that would dwarf the prize money and even the victory in the race itself.

Knowing that the final heat of this national one-mile championship classic would virtually result in a match race of the two best men in the country, I had no fear of the outcome provided I got into the final. The immense gathering at the old Colosseum track was right on edge with excitement. Likewise the crowd knew that there would be some excellent racing in the trial heats and semi-finals in which none but the best riders could survive. Since the final was scheduled to be ridden without pace of any kind the throng also knew it would be a test of brains as well as brawn. The people anticipated a scorching race in case Owen Kimble, Frank Kramer, Tom Cooper or even Floyd MacFarland opposed me in the final, and they were not disappointed. They all conceded that I would be in the final but they could not decide whom my opponent would be, so evenly matched were the other riders in the big race. They knew that MacFarland and Kramer bore ill will towards me and that Kimble being a southerner had no use for anybody of color. I was, therefore, on my best behavior. Physically I was well nigh perfect.

In the course of this meet in Worcester one of the most unpleasant incidents of my life took place, but for fear of hurting the sport the fracas did not reach the public print and I am making it known

FLOYD MACFARLAND—Handicap Champion and
"Mentor"

now for the first time. In the heats of the mile championship, Mac-Farland, my most formidable adversary, resorted to every unfair means he had at his command to have me eliminated. He carefully instructed the riders in my heats as to how to trim me, but I managed to win each time despite their scheming and after some very furious riding I got into the final. MacFarland's underhanded strategy came to naught and all bets were off when his *protégé*, Kramer, gummed things up completely by failing to get into the final. He was so anxious to oppose me in the final that he actually fouled Owen Kimble in his semi-final heat and was promptly disqualified. That meant that Kimble and I would battle it out for the laurels.

In the dressing rooms immediately after Kramer had been disqualified a rumpus started. It centered about the efforts of MacFarland and Kramer to attack Kimble. Only the timely arrival of a squad of policemen prevented bloodshed.

As Kimble and I were leaving our dressing rooms going out for the final tussle, MacFarland yelled to Kimble as a parting shot, "The nigger will trim you, the nigger will trim you." Kimble boiled and wheeled about as if to rush at MacFarland but policemen prevented that step.

I felt badly for Kimble despite the fact that I knew he disliked me very much because of my color. In order to relieve the pressure somewhat I made the finish as close as possible and I know that Kimble appreciated the stunt. I knew what Kimble or any of the other riders would have done to me under similar circumstances even in my home town, but I sympathized with Kimble and made it a close finish although in the perfect physical condition I was in that night I could have easily distanced him. I was given a royal ovation.

MacFarland and his crowd gave me a cheer as I made my way to the training quarters at the end of the race. I knew they were only acting and paid little attention to them. But I plainly heard them aim cutting remarks at Kimble to further humiliate him. The worst one of them was voiced by MacFarland himself, it was, "So you'd rather be trimmed by a nigger than to be defeated by a white man, would you? Well, how do you like it, how do you like it, you ————!!!!———— southerner?" Three times MacFarland yelled this at Kimble.

It was a tense moment, the rest of the riders, their trainers and their managers stood breathlessly awaiting developments. They knew such taunts would rouse Kimble, the southerner, to action and they were not disappointed. Kimble suddenly sprung from his cot and pleaded with me to come with him. I refused saying it was not my fight, but he insisted saying that he did not want to fight but only wanted to show "Mac" and his yellow bunch up.

Once in the presence of MacFarland and his gang Kimble placed his hand on my shoulder, and addressing particularly MacFarland and Kramer, said, "Yes, Major Taylor did defeat me and he didn't have to run me off the track or foul me to do it either. He did it like the real champion that he is and although his face is black he is not only the whitest man in the whole d— crowd, but the fastest man on the track. I do not consider it a disgrace to be beaten by him because he always does it fairly and that is more than any of you can do." Then he turned and shook my hand saying, "Major Taylor, I congratulate you on winning this championship race. You're the fastest and squarest man among us."

In this dramatic manner Kimble silenced the whole crooked outfit. They dropped their heads in shame and slunk away. Even Mac-Farland was unable to utter a word of a comeback. Kimble's speech closed the altercation although I heard several of the MacFarland gang threaten under their breath to get even with Kimble. No doubt Kimble was serious at the time and probably meant all the complimentary things he said about me but down in my heart I felt that he simply used that means to bring MacFarland and his crowd to their knees when they cut him to the quick by their insulting language.

One of the Worcester dailies carried the following story relative to that race:

"Major Taylor Rode Like a Whirlwind Last Night. Was Out to Win and Succeeded. Was Cheered by Thousands of Admirers. Major Taylor made good his promises to his Worcester friends by winning the one-mile championship event at the Colosseum last night. People yelled themselves hoarse with satisfaction and jubilation as the dusky champion heat after heat trimmed his opponents. The 'Major' was out to win and did it to a queen's taste.

"His victory over the field was little better received than was the decision by the referee in which Frank Kramer was disqualified from entering the final, and which also caused the big lanky MacFarland to take a quick seat on the bench where he belonged.

"Frank Kramer rode the crooked race in the semi-final with Owen Kimble who started in that heat with the leader. Kimble got the jump and Kramer rode foul in order to secure the pole, crowding Kimble down on the running boards and throwing him off his stride. The crowd saw it and demanded that the referee disqualify Kramer, which he did at once. This gave complete satisfaction although everybody had wished to see Taylor and Kramer come together in the final.

"Owen Kimble took his heat with Iver Lawson second, there being only two men in the heat. Kramer defeated Lester Wilson in his heat, these being the only two in the heat. Willie Fenn, Howard Freeman and Floyd MacFarland were the starters in the third heat. Freeman, who started the jump and got too far ahead of Fenn to be bested, landed first with Fenn second and MacFarland third. Major Taylor won his heat against George Collette and Johnnie Fisher. Major rode a great race. He watched his man who was Fisher, of course, and at the right moment shot out from them and trimmed them nicely.

"Major Taylor took his heat in the semi-final from Fenn, Fisher, and Freeman doing a nice job on them, his wonderful sprint being all to the good. In the grand semi-final Taylor laid in behind

Fisher, trailing him all over the track, and at the proper moment whizzed past him and reached the tape first by all kinds of lengths.

"In the final heat with Major Taylor was Owen Kimble, the Major's old rival. Kimble wanted to win this race very badly for he is a southerner imbued with all of the prejudices of that section. He worked hard to win, resorting to several foxy tactics to induce Taylor to take the lead. He was fair, however, and did not attempt anything foul, but when Major got him in the back stretch in the fifth lap Taylor jumped him, and sprinting furiously around the disk won by several lengths. Major received a great ovation from his many Worcester friends and was obliged to ride a lap of honor while the audience cheered lustily. It was a great race.

"'Nellie' Bly and Charles Porter set up a record for a motor tandem on the disk, negotiating the distance in the fastest time that has yet been made for the saucer track, 1:26 2/5."

Triumphs at Home and Abroad
(1901–02)

While I was gathering fresh laurels in Europe, Frank Kramer was piling up points towards the National Championship at home. I returned to the home tracks in mid-season, and by the end of the last circuit race of 1901 I was twenty points behind behind my chief rival. Kramer was proclaimed Champion.

Friends and eager promoters soon persuaded us to ride a match race that fall in Madison Square Garden to determine who really was the better rider. Floyd MacFarland, Kramer's manager, was so anxious to have his man win that he arranged to have him throw me if he couldn't beat me fairly.

For nine laps of our first heat, Kramer rode according to Hoyle. However, as I started to jump him on the turn just entering the back stretch on the last lap, he bumped me purposely, and bumped me hard. I was prepared for the move though, and instead of me being knocked off my wheel, Kramer was the one to hit the boards as a result of the collision while I managed to stay up.

MacFarland lost no time entering a vigorous protest for Kramer, claiming that I had fouled him. He loudly demanded the race be rerun and I made my way to the referee's stand and volunteered to ride it over again. But the referee informed me that he had seen the collision from his vantage point and added that since I was put on the defensive by Kramer's deliberate foul tactics the heat would not be run over again under any circumstances. The referee further informed me that Kramer had left the black line on the pole and swung up the banking purposely to knock me out of my stride.

No sooner had I crossed the tape in the first heat than a pop bottle thrown by an excited Kramer sympathizer in the gallery narrowly missed hitting me on the head. The missile struck the track a short distance in front of me and scattered the spectators who were gathered inside the railing. Between Kramer's bumping me and the pop bottle incident, I began to think that this was scheduled to be one of my most hectic nights—but luck was with me on both occasions and I felt that was a lucky omen for the next heat of the match race. It turned out to be, for the heat was the final one. I brought Kramer into camp a second time.

In March, 1902, I set out once more on a European tour, during which I successively defeated the Belgian, Danish, German, and French champions. Returning home in late July, I journeyed up to Ottawa for an N.C.A. meet there. My own bicycle went astray in transit, and by the time the races began, on August 3rd, it was still missing. Undismayed, I borrowed a bike from a prominent Canadian amateur rider, and won the Quarter-Mile Championship on that unfamiliar steed.

Royal Welcome to Australia
(1903)

Following in the footsteps of my illustrious predecessor, the first American Sprint Champion, Arthur Augustus Zimmerman of Freeport, New Jersey, I invaded Australia for the season of 1903. Since Zimmerman, who was my boyhood hero, had made a very successful invasion of the land of the kangaroo five years previous to my jaunt there, I bent every effort to duplicate or even exceed his wonderful performances there. Also since I was contemplating retiring from the sport I felt that my career would hardly be completed unless I measured my speed against Australia's best, feeling that this was really the only other world, in a bicycle sense, that I had not conquered.

Frankly, if it were not for the fact that I had previously given my word that I would participate in the 1903 season in Australia I would have permanently retired from the sport with the close of the 1902 season in America. Several factors prompted me to take this step. In the first place I was satisfied that I could never regain my American championship title, which I had won in three consecutive seasons, 1898, 1899, 1900, with the entire field of riders combined against me. On top of that I felt that my seven world's records including the fastest mile ever ridden behind motor pace and also the world's sprint title, to say nothing of my three very successful invasions of Europe, warranted my retirement while I was still at the top of the heap. I also felt that since I had fulfilled and even exceeded the wonderful prophecy of my discoverer, Mr. Louis D. (Birdie) Munger, that I was entitled to the rest that I had so rightly earned, especially since I had won enough honors for any one man on the bicycle track.

However, I had given my word to the bicycle meet promoters in Australia that I would compete for them in the 1903 season and I stood ready, if they gave the word, to go through with that plan. They insisted and within a month of the close of the American season I was *en route* to Australia, via San Francisco. I was accompanied on this long trip by my wife, the voyage being something in the nature of a honeymoon trip.

When I called for my steamship tickets in San Francisco the agent informed me that there was a rigid color line in effect in Australia. This was the first intimation I had had that any such condition prevailed there and I was very much disturbed. It seems that the color line was drawn in Australia to keep out the Japanese and Chinese as it was feared that they might cause labor disturbances there if allowed to enter in large numbers as has since happened in California.

My first thought upon getting this information was to cancel my Australian tour but my dauntless fighting spirit and courage served me in good stead and I decided to go through with the agreement. It was particularly discouraging to me to realize that I would be up against such a proposition in Australia, as I somehow figured that race prejudice flourished only in this country. It certainly was a distressing outlook. Before I had left San Francisco, however, my wife and I were subjected to indignities through the sharp drawing of the color line in that metropolis. Because of it we were unable to get hotel accommodations or food. We breathed a sigh of relief when we got aboard ship the following day but were shortly in throes of severe attacks of seasickness which added to our misery. For the first time in my life I was thoroughly discouraged at the turn affairs had taken. It seemed to me that even nature had taken up the cudgels against us. However, I had faith and eventually the sun burst forth again for us.

Meantime I told my wife I felt the color line tip that I had received relative to Australia could hardly be founded on fact. I did not believe that the promoters would have gone to the expense of taking me away out there unless they knew for a certainty that I would be permitted to land. Furthermore, in order to protect their own interests, I assured her, they would be obliged to see to it that we were treated courteously as we entered the country. I also reasoned that if we could exist in America where race hatred and color prejudice are so rampant we could undoubtedly get by in Australia or in any other country. So pondering on this line of reasoning we took new courage.

I shall never forget the courtesies extended my wife and myself by the purser on the ship. It developed he hailed from Westboro, Massachusetts, which is close to my adopted city, Worcester, Massachusetts. Although he had never seen me ride he was well acquainted with Willie Windle of Millbury, Massachusetts, another of my boyhood heroes, whom he had seen ride a number of times. The purser had followed my racing career carefully and he quoted a number of my records and outstanding achievements without hesitation. Daily he presented a group of fellow passengers to me and we talked for hours about bicycle racing and other sports, thus helping pass the time pleasantly. Gaining his confidence I asked the purser if it was true that there was a color line in Australia. He assured me that it was a fact adding, however, that the step was in the nature of a labor measure rather than as against members of my race as a whole. "You need have no fear, Mr. Taylor," he said, "because anybody with your personality and gentlemanly conduct will command respect over there, or wherever he may go."

With my experiences in San Francisco still fresh in mind I had my doubts about my personality getting me any advantages but I thanked the purser for his kind words, nevertheless. I was satisfied that my personality had secured very little for me in my native land, America, especially as regards fair play, equal rights, political rights and any other number and variety of rights. I vowed to the purser that if they drew the color line against me in Australia I would certainly be a passenger on his return voyage.

Reaching Auckland (New Zealand) I was cordially greeted and interviewed by a group of newspaper men, sport promoters, and prominent cyclists. Naturally I was anxious to ascertain whether or not I should be permitted to land in Australia because of the color line. They assured me that I would have no difficulty passing the immigration regulations and declared my manager had already looked after that detail of my trip. They informed us, however, that Australia did draw the color line, but not as far as I was concerned.

I shall never forget the wonderful sight that greeted us as the steamer rounded the Sydney Heads, the most beautiful natural harbor in the world. To me it was worth the price of the voyage just to sail from the entrance of the harbor to the pier, a distance of seven miles. As I stood drinking in the wonderful scenery the purser came running up to me all excited. Pointing over the rail of the steamer he exclaimed, "Look, look, do you see all those American flags. Do you hear those whistles and horns, now do you think you will be allowed to land in Australia?"

It was a most delightful experience and a very impressive one too, and I shall remember it as long as I live. I could not restrain my tears as I looked over the side of the liner and saw hundreds of boats and all kinds and sorts, both steam and naptha launches, decked out with American flags with their whistles tooting and men and women aboard them with megaphones greeting me with this salutation, "Taylor, Taylor! Welcome Major Taylor!" My friend the purser was as pleased with this royal welcome accorded me as my wife and I were. I told him I felt sure I was going to love Australia and that I would undoubtedly be obliged to delay my trip back to America until the last minute.

Presently the pilot came aboard and with him a number of newspaper men including Messrs. Percy Hunter and Tom Scott under whose management I was to ride. Mr. Hugh MacIntosh, secretary of the League of New South Wales Wheelmen, who later promoted the Johnson-Burns fight in Australia, was also on the welcoming committee. After being cordially welcomed to Australia by that trio I was interviewed by a squad of newspaper men.

As we stepped ashore my wife and I were greeted by thousands of cheering people. We were taken to the Hotel Metripole where a beautiful suite had been reserved for us. At the hotel I was introduced to a number of prominent people and was later escorted to the City Hall where I was formally welcomed by the Lord Mayor of Sydney, city officials, prominent citizens and sporting celebrities. It was a rousing welcome and I shall never forget the flattering compliments the several speakers tendered me in the course of the banquet which followed.

A Sydney newspaper read as follows:

"The cycling champion of the world, Major Taylor, who arrived from America by the R.M.S. *Ventura* on Sunday, was received by the Lord Mayor (Alderman T. Hughes) at the Townhall yesterday. Amongst those present were Messrs. David Walker (general sec. Y.M.C.A.), C. W. Bennett, H. S. Cusack, T. F. Byrne, and a number of prominent officials of the League of New South Wales Wheelmen."

The Lord Mayor's speech was in part as follows: "The Lord Mayor cordially welcomed the visitor as the Champion Cyclist of the World, one who had met and defeated the foremost men in Europe and America, and who now comes to Australia to gain, if possible, fresh victories, and while wishing Major Taylor every success, he sincerely hoped that the Australians would hold their own against him, (applause), although he realized that they had a very difficult task before them.

"They were all pleased to see a man of Major Taylor's standing in the world of sport visit Australia even though he should sweep over the land like a whirlwind, for those who entered into competitions with him were bound to profit by the experience, whether they were successful or not. (Applause.)"

A Sydney newspaper carried the following excerpt of the banquet: "The Lord Mayor proposed the visitor's good health. Mr. Percy Hunter, who supported the toast explained the negotiations which had taken place to secure the visit of Major Taylor, and detailed the difficulties that were encountered before the engagement of the champion was finally settled. He thought that the presence of Major Taylor in Australia would give the sport a new impetus. Major Taylor responded to the toast in a neat speech and expressed the hope that he would be able to come up to the expectations, and that the public would not be disappointed with his performances. Dr. A. M. Gledden proposed prosperity to the League of Wheelmen to which Mr. O'Brien responded, assuring Major Taylor that he would receive a fair field but no favors.

"Mr. J. J. Virgo, General Secretary-elect of the Y.M.C.A. proposed the health of the Lord Mayor. He considered that it was a gracious act on the part of his lordship to receive Major Taylor, who, he was assured, fully appreciated the honor accorded him."

The first place in Sydney that I wanted to visit was, of course, the great battle field—the bicycle track. It was located in Moore Park, being built of concrete, measuring three laps to the mile, about forty feet wide and banked to about thirty or thirty-five degrees. It had a peculiar shape being almost round. The famous Sydney cricket field was located inside the bicycle track which was almost completely surrounded by grandstands.

The Famous Sydney Cricket Ground and Track at Night. At the Start of each Race all Lights are turned off, except those directly over the Track

After spending a few days sight-seeing and shaking off my sea legs I announced I was ready and eager to start my training.

I was much impressed with the hospitality of the Australians from the outset, everyone I met seemed anxious to be of service to my wife and I and we were deluged with invitations to visit or be the dinner guests of hundreds of people whom we met in the course of our stay. However, I knew that I would have to curtail my social activities if I desired to be at my best at my profession, bicycle racing. So I devoted all my spare time to training as I knew my program had been previously arranged for me, since the time allotted for my practice stunts was very limited.

Had I been less serious in my training preparations I could never have gotten in shape for my first race which came only a fortnight after I landed in Sydney. It took me but a few days to lose my sea legs, then I went to work in earnest preparing for my initial race in which Don Walker and Joe Megson, the two best sprinters in Australia, together with the cream of the sprinters in that country, took part. This was scheduled to be held on January 3, 1903. Thousands of people came to the track daily to watch my

training preparations and most of them were impressed at the serious-
ness with which I went about my work. The riders expressed aston-
ishment at my training stunts and the great amount of work I did, all
of which was new to them. Likewise they were surprised when I
went out on the track to work with them as they had an idea that I
preferred to do my training in secret.

My Australian rivals seemed pleased at the frankness that I showed
as they plied me with questions relative to my bicycle, such as the gear,

MAJOR TAYLOR and Trainer Sid Melville at the Sydney Cricket Grounds and
Bicycle Track

length of cranks, height of frame, the pedal reach, etc., and were
again astonished when I gave them the privilege of examining it for
themselves. Most riders regarded these points as vital secrets but I
did not hesitate to give this information to any who desired it. I even
answered questions concerning my tactics in races, and as far as I
know this showing of my hand never reacted against me.

I gradually rounded into shape and things began to look rosy for a
very successful visit in Australia, the greatest sporting country on
earth. I can not emphasize too strongly the pressure off of my mind
upon learning that I would have no worry from the color line while I
was here. This was a tremendous load lifted off my shoulders and
it permitted me to go about my training unhampered. In addition to
this the climate was just to my liking for racing, as it was delightfully
balmy. My manager selected for me as a trainer, Sid Melville, one
of the most faithful and loyal trainers a man could have.

While working out on the Sydney track daily I made a close study of all my new opponents who included the pick of Australasia. In this way I ascertained their strong and weak points and incidentally I discovered that my opponents were not high class sprinters with the possible exception of Don Walker, who was the champion at that time. However, my rivals comprised the greatest aggregation of fast riders as a group of any country I had visited, including even America.

I found also that some of the riders who had the best head for tactics were woefully lacking in heart and courage, while those who had the greatest courage and gameness lacked speed and strength. One of the star riders whom I watched in practice had the head and the gameness but possessed only stamina enough for one heat. After winning one heat this rider could not repeat and for this reason he seldom got into the final, but in that one heat he was a very dangerous contender.

I also found that my superior knowledge and experience in match racing also stood me in good stead. In all of my important races in America and in Europe the big purses were for scratch events and match races, but I found the opposite plan prevailed in Australia where the handicap races take the big purses. Hence the riders of that country were exceptionally strong handicap men and equally as fast and strong in open events, but they were not especially "up" on the fine points of the game, such as tactics and track generalship in match racing. But they were as game a set as I ever competed against and quickly adopted some of my best tactics, forcing me to invent some new and strategic moves.

Just before my first race I was informed that the Quarter-mile Championship of Australia would be the feature attraction on the opening night's program. Mr. Percy Hunter, one of my managers, after watching me work out one day asked me how I felt. I told him I was pleased with my condition and would be sorely disappointed if I failed to win my first start. I also told him I was anxious to be at my very best form to repay the good people of Sydney in my own way for the many courtesies they had extended me. Although I did not tell Mr. Hunter I was still unaccustomed to sprinting for the tape on an almost round track. Naturally this caused me considerable annoyance until I became familiar with it. As a matter of policy, however, I never complained about the track as I felt that would have been giving the other riders an advantage over me in addition to the worry it was causing me.

From long experience I knew that if I could win my first race or even hold my own against the best riders in Australia, after the period of training that I had had, I would have little to fear in my tour of the country. I felt also that I would improve my condition through riding this first race and each time I competed throughout the season. The Australian riders were already at top form, having been racing for two months before I arrived.

Their style of riding handicap races was new to me. A rider never started in a handicap race over there with the idea that he would win on his own, they always worked in combinations of two or three, and sometimes even more, to help pace the contestant whom they had figured stood the best chance of winning. In the event of his winning the race he would split his winnings equally among those who had assisted him.

Another thing that interested me very much was the method adopted by the riders to defeat the scratch man. According to the Australian rules a rider was not obliged to start in a race even after qualifying. The intent of this rule was undoubtedly to spare the riders from being compelled to race with an injury, or after being taken suddenly ill. But in time the riders took advantage of this rule and used it for shady purposes. By taking advantage of it they could remain out of the final intentionally in order to create a gap too great for the scratch man to close up to his nearest competitor unassisted.

For example, if there were ten or twelve men in the final and they were placed out ahead of the scratch man on marks ranging from 10 to 150 yards, the first four or five men nearest the tape would scratch. This would leave as many more riders on the longer marks nearest the limit man, making a gap of 75 or 80 yards for the scratch man to bridge before he really could give them a race. Meantime the long handicap men were alternating the pace, burning the track with speed, while the scratch man was straining every nerve and muscle to overtake them, which in most cases would be physically impossible.

In a combination of this kind, of course, it was understood in advance which rider was to win. Thus the entrants who scratched not only came in for their split of the purse, but could safely bet their last dollar on the result. That's where they made their clean-up. So far as I have been able to learn Zimmerman and I were the only riders who never entered in any such combinations.

A Sensational Championship

(1903)

"The sole topic of conversation yesterday in cycling circles was the forthcoming visit of the world's champion, Major Taylor, to race here in January and February next. The enterprise of the promoters of the big cycling carnivals being held this summer, in securing the presence of the famous negro, met with praise on all sides. The fee which is being paid for Taylor's presence—£1500—is the largest ever given to a racing cyclist in any part of the world, and although this seems an enormous sum to pay any man to come out here and race, the promoters should reap a good reward by securing very large attendances at their meetings to see this wonderful sprinter opposed to the Australian cracks. As Taylor is to appear in sixteen races in all, he will have ample scope to display that lightning sprint which has earned him so much fame and placed him head and shoulders over the rest of the world's crack sprinters.

"When the great A. A. Zimmerman visited Sydney some five years ago he only appeared twice in Sydney, and over 30,000 people attended to see him race each day. Major Taylor is a faster sprinter than Zimmerman ever was, and League authorities here naturally expect that just as many people will attend their next meetings to see the wonderful negro race as attended to see Zimmerman opposed to our best men.

"Major Taylor is recognized all the world over as the world's premier sprinter, as he ought to be, for, after conquering all the champions of his own country, he visited Europe on two occasions—this season and last—and easily defeated the premier riders there. On his return to America this year, after a successful European tour, he had to put up with a great deal from the Americans, who will stop at nothing in order to defeat him. They do not seem to care who wins so long as it is not Taylor, and in nearly every race he was deliberately blocked and 'pocketed' in order that he should not get home first. Whenever he did get a clear run it was Taylor first and the rest anywhere. The American officials must have been prejudiced against the negro wonder too, or else they would not allow such a state of affairs to exist. Taylor can depend on getting a fair deal from the Australian riders during his forthcoming visit. Even should our riders have any intention of resorting to unfair means to defeat the world's champion, the officials would soon put a stop to it. Every athlete that has yet visited Australia, whether black or white, has always received a fair deal from his opponents. This cannot be said of the European

and American riders, who have never given Major Taylor a straight
deal if they could help it.

"The world's champion sprinter was on the Sydney Cricket Ground
track yesterday for the first time since his arrival in Sydney. He only
did a little slow work. He will be on the track twice daily now until
the opening day of the carnival, on January 3, when he hopes to be
in something like proper shape to do himself justice. Taylor has a
nice position on a machine, and is a nattily put together athlete. As he
rides around the track it can be seen at a glance that he is a great rider,
and no doubt he will prove a favorite with the public here. Tremendous interest is being taken in his performances, and it is safe to
say that when he makes his first appearance on the Cricket Ground on
Saturday week there will be a crowd to welcome him quite as large as
that which saw Zimmerman race here on two occasions. Major Taylor
puts in some of his time at the gymnasium of the Y.M.C.A. every
day. Towards the end of the week the champion intends to begin fast
work behind the powerful Massey-Harris motor. He realizes that in
Walker he has a sprinter of the very best class to beat, and consequently
will leave no stone unturned to achieve his true form.

"The largest crowd that had attended any bicycle racing program
in Australia since the great Zimmerman was there in 1895 attended
my first appearance in Sydney on January 3, 1903. There were over
twenty thousand paid admissions to this program, Zimmerman's two
races in Sydney attracting sixty thousand people. Included in the
gathering were practically all of the city's official family, numerous
former cycling stars and enthusiasts and not a few tourists from all
quarters of the globe."

I quote the following article from one of the Sydney dailies:

"The feature race of the program at the Sydney Cricket Grounds
Track yesterday was, of course, the début of Major Taylor, and his
meeting with the Australian Champion, Don Walker. There were
three first-class events on the program in which all of the cracks ap·
peared. They were the Wyalon Half-Mile Handicap, the Quarter-
Mile International Championship Race and the Walker Plate, a five-
mile scratch event.

"All of the racing proved interesting and two or three of the events
aroused a greater pitch of enthusiasm than has ever been witnessed
here before. One of these was the victory of the World's Champion in
the International Championship race in which Major Taylor showed a
flash of one of the sprints for which he became so justly famous.
And again the crowd became wildly excited when Don Walker, the
Australian, defeated Taylor and the big field of first-class men in the
Five-Mile Scratch race which wound up the program.

"The sport provided was entirely to the taste of the huge audience, everyone went away in the best of humor having enjoyed a sporting treat, and fully determined to see more of the meetings between the two champions, the next of which takes place tonight when Taylor and Walker will fight their battle over again.

"When the riders went out to indulge in their preliminary practice Major Taylor was accorded a most flattering reception by the specta-

Don Walker—Australian Champion

tors. He must have been pleased with the welcoming cheer that went up all around the grounds as he pedalled around the track. This welcome was an earnest demonstration of the fair play and consideration that he would receive on the Australian track in his struggles with Australian rivals. The Australian champion, Don Walker, on appearing a few minutes later was as cordially received and it was apparent that if the Australian could prove his superiority over the distinguished visitor the victory would be a most popular one.

"The racing started shortly afterwards with the heats of the Half-Mile Handicap, the first heat being won by Dick Mutton from virtual scratch with a fine burst of speed. The second heat was won by Dan Sheehan from S. Simon, who rode a good race. The third heat brought out Don Walker, who thrice demonstrated that he was in magnificent form. In it he met several other good men in the persons of R. Lewis, J. Chalmers and E. Payne. Walker showed his form by running onto Lewis' wheel at one bound and paced in turn by Payne, Chalmers, and Lewis, this bunch cut out a very hot lap until just leaving the back stretch for the second time, Walker was seen moving around on the outside, getting clear he set sail for the leaders with a great rush amid intense excitement. He cut the front men down in the home stretch and won by a length from Payne, Lewis being a close third. The time from scratch was :57, which was remarkably good.

"The next heat saw Major Taylor on his mark placed five yards behind scratch. This was the first occasion in which a man has ever started behind scratch on a track. The champion was loudly cheered as he took up his position and at the gun fire he jumped like lightning onto Gudgeon, who set sail for the field with Taylor trailing his wheel in fine shape. Some fast men were out front and Gudgeon carried the champion along very fast. When the home turn was reached the riders had a long break and when Taylor settled down for his home run he flew over the last thirty yards at an incredible rate of speed but he was just too late to win, though he was travelling five yards to the winner's one at the finish. He placed third. McLean was first and Drinkwater was second.

"Walker won the final heat, Ben Goodson, the fast and plucky Queenslander, was second, and Boidi, the Italian star, was third, the time being :57 3/5.

"The race next discussed was the Quarter-Mile International Championship. In this event Major Taylor proved victorious, his lightning jump and speedy sprint being too much for Don Walker, who, however, finished with a remarkable burst of speed, making up a lot of ground in the last fifty yards and finishing a good second.

"This event caused the wildest excitement of all and while everyone on the grounds would no doubt have been glad to see the Australian win, no one begrudged the visitor the victory and gold medal, especially in view of the acknowledged fact that he has not yet reached his best form. No discredit attaches to Walker's defeat for he was beaten by the foremost tactician in the world, and it is probably due more to Taylor's better knowledge of tactics than to any superiority in speed over Walker that he will take the Australian medal away with him.

"The pace was slow at the Northern Pavilion, where Lewis on the inside suddenly went with a rush and made a clear break, but Taylor with his marvelous jump got going immediately, and Walker was dropped a couple of lengths. He picked up his sprint quickly and the three made a terrific dash for the tape with Taylor winning by half a length from Walker, who barely beat out Lewis for second. Major

Taylor was accorded a tremendous ovation for his great victory as he rode around the track with the Stars and Stripes fluttering from his hand.

"The final of the Quarter-Mile Championship summary is as follows:—Major Taylor, U. S. A., first; Don Walker, Victoria, second; R. W. Lewis, New South Wales, third, time :32.

"The program wound up with the Walker Plate, a five-mile scratch race. Like a true sportsman, Major Taylor came out for this event

Start of Final Heat of Quarter-mile International Championship Race

although he might well have claimed exemption on the ground that his condition was not good enough to stand the strain. It is all the more to his credit that he rode, though he hardly expected to get through the race, but the fine performance he subsequently put up surprised him considerably.

"The race was fast throughout, but the last three laps were run at a terrific pace, the last quarter being turned in :26, an Australian record. This tearing pace naturally told on Taylor, whose condition is not yet up to the mark, for a race of this distance, but it had absolutely no effect on Walker's strength. After a fine run on the back stretch where he had the good fortune to trail the wheel of Lewis, who is a magnificent judge of position, he swept around Taylor who was trailing Gudgeon and Mutton, who were finishing a terrible lap, and clipped over the tape a clear length to the good.

"The enthusiasm as Walker rode around after his splendid win was wonderful. The people stood on their seats and cheered wildly again and again as the riders re-circled the track. Major Taylor rode along side of the Australian Champion and congratulated him by shaking hands. The crowd burst out cheering anew and the day ended with the honors even and with the good feeling between the two champions unimpaired."

Taylor Winning Final Heat of Quarter-mile International Championship, Sydney, Australia

Don Walker, a Worthy Rival

(1903)

Following our first clash at the opening program Walker and I were interviewed concerning each other's ability under fire.

I was quoted as follows:

"Major Taylor Regards Don Walker, the Australian Champion, As One of the World's Best. I consider, he said, that I have made

Two Great Rivals, TAYLOR and WALKER

wonderful strides while in Sydney in view of the fact that I have only been about ten days on my wheel since I landed. I really did not expect to get in to sprinting form so quickly. The training record I have made while here is far better than any I have previously accomplished in any country. In fact I never before attempted to ride on such a short preparation.

"What do you think of Walker now? Well, my previous high opinion of Walker has not changed by his showing yesterday. It is difficult to compare him with the continental riders as they go in for an entirely different style of training and racing. All of their races are of the short sprint order. Neither Jacquelin or Elleggarde could have stood three minutes of the pace changing, ripping, five miles which Walker defeated me in yesterday.

"The last three laps' pace of that race were corkers and made me absolutely tired, and I finished very slow. But I did not complain at that because I really did not expect to be able to finish at all. I am quite certain there is not an American today that can defeat Don Walker.

"What about the Quarter-Mile Championship? Well, that was a distance that suited my present form better. In that race I had nothing but sprinting to do. I could hold a short sprint like that at my top speed, still it was not easy, as Lewis is another fine sprinter, and gained another good break when he jumped. I touched his rear wheel just as I was about to pass him. It was a narrow escape. This was due, however, to my rear wheel's skidding slightly when I jumped suddenly. I do not think I ever travelled faster than I did over the last sixty yards. Walker came very fast at the finish.

"I received very fair treatment from all the riders and I admire the way they ride, and the pace they can set. They are a much better lot of men than is generally known in other countries, and taking them all around I think they are far better in handicap races than American riders.

"Speaking of his effort in the Half-Mile Handicap, he said, I had a good position throughout the race, but Gudgeon was a bit slow off the mark. I might have won by going out on my own sprint a little earlier, but I thought by so doing I might spoil my chances for the other races. I can plainly see that a scratch man needs a bit of a motor to win in the handicap money in this country."

The following is quoted from Don Walker:

"I think that Major Taylor has nothing more to learn about the racing game, and even after he achieves his form I don't think he will sprint any faster than he did in the Quarter-Mile Championship Race yesterday. The quickness with which he made his famous jump was absolutely a revelation to me.

"I was watching him closely and was all ready for him, and expecting him to jump every moment, but when Bob Lewis got going on the inside, Taylor was gone like a flash of gunpowder. Before I could attempt to hold him he had two lengths on me. We then had less than two hundred yards to go to the tape, and of course, you know what that meant. I buckled and hustled but to get around a man like Taylor in a fresh sprint in 200 yards is a task verging on the impossible.

"A sensational incident occurred just after the three of us started at top speed. Taylor touched Lewis' back wheel just opposite the members' pavilion, I thought Taylor would come down, and eased off speed for a fraction of a second and swerved somewhat up the banking. But the champion made the most remarkable recovery I have ever seen, and seemingly without detracting from any of his speed, and from that point on he travelled faster than I have ever seen anyone sprint. He pulled right clear of Lewis, who is one of the best sprinters in Australia when fresh. I was full of sprint and coming fast. I think I sprinted faster than I ever did before but it was not fast enough to catch Taylor, who seemed to ride the last dozen yards at an increased pace.

"I can see that to have a chance of beating Taylor in that style of race I shall have to get going actually with him, and race every yard of the way. It must not be forgotten, however, that in this kind of racing Taylor has proved absolutely invincible, having beaten every sprinter in the world time and time again. I have hopes of turning the tables on him though before the carnival is over, but I have honestly to acknowledge that in the jump which we had in the final yesterday he was my superior.

"Did his touching Lewis' wheel interfere with your prospects at all? In one way it did, but I cannot blame Taylor for that. It was more for what I fully expected to happen, after he hit Lewis' wheel, than what actually did happen that caused me to run a yard or two up the banking, but Taylor made such an extraordinary recovery that he not only kept up, but he scarcely swerved from his track, so he could not have interfered with me. Of course, on the track one must always be prepared for emergencies. You can't wait. If nothing happens so much the better.

"Do you think you have met your Waterloo in Major Taylor? I won't say that. I don't like to say anything that sounds like a boast. I really believe that I can make the short sprint closer than it was in the Quarter-Mile Race yesterday before the champion leaves us.

"You can beat him in the Walker Plate, how about that? Yes, but I don't count that against him. His ride in that race only increases my admiration for him, for his ability and the pluck with which he goes through his races. Which of us Australian riders could have put up such a sprint in the Quarter-mile Race, and then have gone through a five-mile race in which the last quarter was run in Australian record time, and finish right on the line with the winners after being off the boat only a fortnight after a long sea voyage? No, I take no credit for beating Taylor in the five-mile race. I think his performances yesterday, considering his form, as wonderful, and something that none of us Australians could ever accomplish. I won't consider that we Australian sprinters have defeated him until one of us has beaten him in the short sprints, such as the quarter, third, half and one-mile distances, the recognized championship distances. These are the true tests of speed pure and simple, for all the riders start their sprints absolutely fresh, and the fastest man reaches the tape first."

R. W. Lewis who finished third in the Championship race, and also interviewed said:

"I thought that I was actually winning the quarter-mile championship race, and the pace we were travelling at convinced me that in the short distance that intervened between us and the tape I had a very good chance of remaining in front. Near the members' stand I felt a sensation, as if I had a puncture. It did not, however, interfere with my speed. I realized afterwards that Taylor had hit my rear wheel. Then suddenly something flashed past me. Then I gave up thinking I could win.

"Major Taylor's jump past me was most extraordinary, because I was sprinting at my top speed, and the pace was proven by the manner in which I was able to race Walker. I think Taylor has a wonderful jump, and although I think he will be defeated by some of the Australians when they learn to jump away a bit faster, he will make our racing very interesting. He has wonderful control over his machine, and seems to be a true sportsman. For a great sprinter he has fine endurance. His coming out in the five-miles riding, considering he is not in form, should make him popular with the public. He put up a great race in the five-miles, and that he stuck to the finish proclaims him a great rider, for I don't think I was ever in a faster three laps than those that wound up that race yesterday."

Lewis was one of the fastest sprinters in Australia. He was the first Australian rider to do a mile inside of 2:25, and several years previous to my tour he had reduced the record to 2:08. That he was riding extremely well at the moment was amply proven by his defeating Gudgeon and Mutton, two other Australian stars in the third semi-final heat of the championship race.

A few days later one of the Sydney dailies carried the following self-explanatory article:

"Major Taylor's opinion of Gudgeon, one of the best New South Wales riders, is very high. Gudgeon has come rapidly to the front recently, and made a name for himself by beating all the cracks in Melbourne at the Australian meeting in the International Scratch Race. He hails originally from Cobar and is a big strong rider with quite considerable sprint, and uses a big gear. Taylor first made his acquaintance in the heat of the half-mile handicap in which the world's champion started from five yards behind scratch.

"He was giving Gudgeon twenty yards start, but caught him before the New South Wales rider had got going. When he did begin to move, however, he carried the world's champion in great style. Taylor afterwards expressing the opinion that 'riding behind him is like riding a motor.' Taylor again saw something of Gudgeon in the Walker Plate, in which Gudgeon was very prominent in the final three laps, in which Taylor trailed Gudgeon's wheel throughout the last lap, but Gudgeon dead-heated with Mutton, and beat the champion home.

"It is a pleasing trait in Major Taylor's character that he denies acknowledgment of the capabilities of no rider, and though Mutton and Gudgeon both beat him home, there was no trace of discontent in his reference to them. 'New South Wales,' he said, 'should be proud of having two such fine riders.' They are in his opinion fit to take their place with the best handicap men in the world.

"Some one asked Taylor if he thought Gudgeon was in MacFarland's class. MacFarland is known as the handicap king in America, and he has a wonderful record of wins in this class of racing. Taylor replied, 'MacFarland is not in the same class, but Gudgeon is the best handicap rider I have ever seen, and I believe he will make a champion in time.' "

The newspaper went on further to say, "We have vanquished the world's schulling, held our own in boxing, swimming and other lines of sport, but so far we have failed to produce a world's champion at bicycle racing.

"When Zimmerman was here he had a world's reputation, but he was not so much a world's champion as Major Taylor. We did beat Zimmerman several times, but it is only fair to admit that he was unlucky in the matter of health and scarcely showed at his best. In the same way as Megson, Lewis Payne, Martin, Palmer, Kerr, Beachamp, Goodson and many others who went to England and America, met with varying successes, but owing to climatic conditions and other reasons they never won a championship abroad.

"The recent championship I put by as worthless in comparing the merits of Taylor and Walker, that is, beyond the fact that Major Taylor can use his head, which we knew before, and which he must necessarily do to beat the Jacquelins and Elleggardes at their own game. If it simply becomes a matter of tactics, Major Taylor will always win when well.

"Could it be guaranteed that Taylor will go on improving in form (and it must be remembered that all the conditions were strange to him on his first appearance) in the next fortnight in proportion to what he picked up in a little over a week then there would only be one in it, but I very much doubt if he can. Form is a very elusive thing. You can't hurry over an athlete's preparation. The condition Taylor has may be of the 'mushroom' order, not lasting.

"Taylor certainly made a wonderful recovery after bumping Lewis. As we have said before, Taylor is a master of his machine, and he proved it in this instance. Without detracting from Major

Taylor's victory in the championship we consider that the supremacy between the two men has yet to be settled. Walker said before the final of the championship that he was afraid Taylor, who was an expert in that kind of race, might jump him. Taylor is undoubtedly a great rider, but Walker has few superiors. The American came with a great reputation, and it was not tarnished, but rather brightened by the result.

"Like Zimmerman, almost his first race gave him a championship victory. As a matter of fact if Taylor improves for the next few weeks in the same ratio as he has picked up form in his ten days he would be able to beat all our best men pointless. I am taking his measure by his efforts in the five-mile race. It bordered on the marvelous for a rider, who after three other races, to finish as he did in the long race. Would any of our riders shape up as well under the same circumstances if they went to America?"

A Thrilling Victory
(1903)

Two days after my début on an Australian track, the same being located at Sydney, I appeared for my second program on the same course. Don Walker, the champion, and the cream of the fastest riders in that country were also entered in the various events. The handicap event was a half-mile race and there was a scratch event for the same distance in which Walker and myself were entered.

Winning Half-mile Handicap from 5 Yards behind Scratch and establishing World's Record

The O'Brien Plate, a popular five-mile scratch race, wound up the evening's program.

Concerning my second appearance on the Sydney track one of the local dailies had this to say:

"The Major Taylor Carnival was continued last night and it proved to be a strong attraction. The racing was of the highest order. Major Taylor's heat in the Half-Mile Handicap was a revelation. Starting five yards behind the tape, he flashed along at a terrific pace to victory. He was unpaced throughout the race and finished in :56 1/5, a competitive record.

"In the semi-final heat Major Taylor started from the same mark as Don Walker. They were seen going at top speed and caught the field at the North Pavilion. At this point interest was momentarily taken from Taylor through an accident. There was a crash and a rider flew into the air minus a bicycle, while two others were spread-eagled on the track. Drinkwater had fallen, and Hardy shooting over the prostrate man's machine was hurled against an overhead electric light support breaking the glass. Drinkwater was injured, but Hardy without having any bones broken suffered much pain around his loins and back. Meanwhile, Major Taylor on hearing the crash swerved in and Larry Corbett finished first, equaling the world's record of :56 1/5 which Major Taylor had made in his first heat.

"Taylor's showing in the final heat was wonderfully good. He and Walker caught the field together. Walker got hopelessly blocked and Taylor also looked inextricably so, but Taylor streaked through and won by inches amid thunderous applause. The time, :55 3/5, still further clipping the world's record which was set in the first heat and tied in the semi-final by 3/5 of a second."

Perfect Condition and Correct Position

The "Major Taylor Carnival"
(1903)

The highlight of the third meet of what Sydney newspapers were now calling the "Major Taylor Carnival" occurred in the final heat of a Half-Mile Scratch Race, which I won with a dazzling burst of speed. A local sportswriter described it:

> Don Walker was regarded by the great majority of those present as a certain winner of the final. At the pistol he remained on the pole and kept watching for Taylor, who, however, let him remain in the lead right up to and past the clock, when amid tremendous and excited shouts, "Walker wins, Walker wins, the darkey's beaten, the darkey's beaten," Taylor, crouching very low, flashed out past Walker as if he were anchored, winning by three lengths.

> The spectators were dumbfounded and Major Taylor had ridden almost around the track before his marvelous performance was fully realized. He beat Walker by four lengths in about seventy yards, and that while the Australian was right in the middle of one of his famous sprints.

In succeeding races, I lost out to Billy MacDonald, from Western Australia, in the first heat of the semi-finals for the League Cup, a one-mile scratch event, though it was Don Walker who finally won the Cup.

As a local newspaperman commented,

> Major Taylor, when seen subsequently, said he had no excuse to offer for his defeat. He said he had been fairly beaten. He said he was in good form and he had gotten a fair run. MacDonald has but recently come over from Westralia and was hardly expected to strike form so soon. He had previously expressed the belief that he could beat Taylor, and though his ride was undeniably a fine performance, it must be admitted that he had all the best of the conditions. MacDonald, riding in behind Chalmers, was sheltered to some extent from the northeasterly breeze, which caught the riders in full force. Taylor was riding on the outside, which necessarily exposed him to it more than any of the others.

By this time, the Australians were pretty worked up as they debated the relative merits of the best Australian sprinters and myself.

Out of a Pocket in Record Time

(1903)

In the final meet of the Major Taylor Carnival I won the Centennial Mile (handicap) in 1:57 4/5 thereby establishing a new record for Australia. That this race was hotly contested is indicated by the fact that it attracted seventy-one of the best riders in Australasia and 18,000 spectators.

Concerning this final heat I quote as follows from one of the Sydney newspapers:

"Remarkable Performance by Major Taylor. Sets New Record for Australia. Gudgeon Beats the Cracks. Major Taylor's exhibitions in the heat and final of the Centennial Mile race which was held at the local track last night, were up to his reputation. He made a competitive record for Australia in the final of the mile handicap event, riding from scratch, 1:57 4/5. Taylor's riding was very fine to look at, but we used to see Martin do something like it. Had he not made up his mind to start in this race his share of entertaining the public would have been very small, for his only other appearance was in the heat of the Major Taylor Plate (one-quarter-mile) in which there was no real competition and it was a cake walk for him. Throughout the night he did not meet one of Australia's best.

"I never saw such extraordinary riding among first-class men since the League has been in existence. How badly they are shaping up for want of form or other causes, can be reckoned by Megson's riding. He never rode worse in his life than at this carnival, and yet he beat Gudgeon in the quarter-mile and was only just beaten in turn by Gudgeon in the one-mile. The latter in the night's racing showed himself next to Walker. He will in fact have to race Walker tonight for the honor of meeting Taylor. Fancy Pye beating Jackson in a race of this kind, and Middleton, a tough old battler, who was never in the first fight, downing Morgan, who afterwards won the five-mile scratch race. If this is not a Chinese puzzle to explain, I do not know what is.

"If those who wanted to see Australia's best man chosen at his best, and not the glorification of Major Taylor, nothing could have been worse than the way the Test Mile heats were arranged and the way they resulted. There was, first, disappointment in that Walker should be chosen instead of being made to race in heats like the rest. It was most injudicious that the question of who should meet Taylor was not decided on Monday night. Now Walker and Gudgeon will have to ride a mile race to find out, and they have to then meet Taylor 'fresh' in mile heats, besides that, if it be Walker who wins his way to meet Taylor he has also in the same night to compete in the semi-final and the final of the quarter-mile event.   The Major Taylor Plate (quarter-mile) should have been disposed of on Monday night and the rider definitely chosen to meet Taylor.   As it is now, what hope has anyone that Major Taylor will be beaten?   Most likely Walker will beat Gudgeon and have to meet Taylor, and past experience shows

Winning the Centennial One-mile Handicap, establishing Australian Record

what a poor prospect Walker has of beating Taylor at his own game in mile heats, but should it happen that Gudgeon be the rival, then the only hope would be that his condition would enable him to saddle up well."

Another Sydney daily under the caption of "More Magnificent Racing" commented as follows on the same heat:

"The magnificent finishes witnessed by 18,000 spectators at the Major Taylor Cycling Carnival on the local track last night will undoubtedly sustain the great interest manifested in cycling hereabouts. The racing throughout was excellent and at times became so fast that the crowd could scarcely restrain themselves.

"Another illustration was given the spectators of the marvelous capabilities of the world's champion, Major Taylor.   His defeat on Saturday by MacDonald disappointed some, but his performances last night must amply justify his great reputation.   In the Centennial Mile (handicap—250 yard limit) he put up a new record for the Australian

tracks and he showed such remarkable sprinting in the other events
that the spectators yelled themselves hoarse.

"The racing in the heats of the Centennial Mile was fast and brilliant. The fifth heat in which Major Taylor showed proved one of
the features of the evening. In it he showed some of his splendid skill
by sweeping up his field at terrific speed, then lying in the center of
the bunch until the bell went. He then had the appearance of being
pocketed, but neatly cut himself out, and started to sprint 250 yards
from home, leaving the other five riders who had been in front of him
standing still. With a marvelous jump he got to the front passing the
line six or seven lengths ahead of Orr, amidst tremendous enthusiasm.
His victory, which was accomplished in the very fast time of 2:00 1/5,
was exceedingly popular and the air rang with stirring cheers.

"The final offered Major Taylor another splendid opportunity for
showing off his marvelous powers. Starting off scratch, he caught
Lewis, who started from the 35-yard mark, in half a lap. He hung
on for about a lap, then set out by himself to bridge the big gap. Unpaced, he fairly flew up to the riders and caught them amidst thunderous cheers and applause. At the grandstand he was lying seventh.
Near the score board, he jumped away, taking the lead 250 yards from
home. From this point he cut out a terrific rate of speed, winning by
a length from Orr in 1:57 4/5, a new record for Australia. His performances earned for him a magnificent reception.

"The Major Taylor Plate, a quarter-mile dash from scratch,
brought forth some exceedingly fine racing. Major Taylor, in whose
honor the event was named, won his heat from Dan Sheehan and
Ben Goodson by a length and a half, the champion making his famous
jump when a length behind Goodson on entering the home stretch.

"The preliminary heats to select the rider most qualified to meet
Major Taylor and Don Walker on Wednesday night in the International Test Mile were also run off. Bob Walne defeated Bill Mac-
Donald by half a length in the first heat in 2:07. Arthur Gudgeon
defeated Joe Megson in the second heat by a wheel. Dick Mutton
and Eddie Wilksch rode a dead heat in the third heat. In the first
semi-final Gudgeon defeated Walne by two lengths, Wilksch being
third. Three pace makers assisted the riders and the race was very
fast, time being 2:01 4/5. Gudgeon will meet Don Walker Wednesday night and the winner of this heat will meet Major Taylor on the
same evening in three one-mile heats for a purse of $500, winner take
all.

"With each appearance Major Taylor emphasizes his claim to the
title, World's Champion Cyclist."

Spectacular Wins

(1903)

A crowd of 30,000 attended the final meet of the Major Taylor Carnival equalling the best attendance mark created in the course of Zimmerman's championship tour in 1897. That evening I won the International Championship Match in two straight mile heats and the

Final of One-mile International Match, with Gudgeon leading on the Bell-lap

Major Taylor Plate, quarter-mile scratch race in two heats from the cream of Australia's star riders.

A Sydney daily told the story of those two races, the only ones on the program, in the following paragraphs:

"Major Taylor Shows Superb Form by Winning International Mile Championship Match Race and Quarter Mile Scratch Event. Despite a light rainstorm upwards of 30,000 people were at the Sydney Cricket Grounds bicycle track last night to witness the International Championship Match Race between Major Taylor champion of the world, and Arthur Gudgeon of New South Wales. Never before has the enthusiasm been so prolonged as it was on this occasion, and it is doubtful if the program could have been improved upon. Unfortunately the weather was not of the best, rain falling throughout the evening. In spite of this fact the spectators remained at the track although a very large number could have obtained shelter.

"The first event, in which most interest centered, was the contest between Don Walker and Arthur Gudgeon to decide which of them should meet Major Taylor in the International Championship Match Mile Race. Almost everybody expected Walker to win. But Gudgeon rode around the track after vanquishing the rider who has all along been regarded as the best in Australia. The pace throughout the race was exceedingly fast and although Walker came with a terrific sprint he could not overtake his rival. Thus the question as to who was going to oppose Major Taylor was settled and the spectators were sure that the New South Wales rider was to be the American's opponent.

"Half an hour afterward Taylor and Gudgeon appeared in the first heat of the International Match Race. Two good men, Scheps, and Payne were the pacemakers. Taylor hung onto them while Gudgeon followed, but his ride for the first two laps was not pleasant owing to the way Taylor's machine wobbled. At the score board on the last lap Gudgeon moved up alongside his opponent and remained until the members' stand was reached. Then like a flash of lightning Taylor left Gudgeon, who was, however, bothered by Taylor's wheel swerving. Gudgeon put up a fine finish but suffered defeat by two good lengths. The last 150 yards was covered in the exceptionally fast time of :08 2/5. The American was accorded great ovation.

"The second heat was decided half an hour later. This heat was run on the Continental style of racing, no pace being used. It may be confessed that the method is not a good one, from a spectator's point of view, although the men are called upon to use a good deal of strategy.

"For the first lap Gudgeon led, but the pace was exceedingly slow. When the bell went, however, there was a quickening of pace, and Taylor jumped to the front of Gudgeon unexpectedly. Near the scoring board Gudgeon made an effort to pass the famed rider, but did not succeed, the pair racing in line until the members' stand was approached. Then Taylor left his opponent and won, this time by three lengths. His victory was greeted with the loudest applause, as it was recognized that Taylor had settled all pretensions that any Australian could defeat him in a straight-out, single man, match race. Gudgeon dismounted and shook hands with Taylor at the conclusion of the race and Taylor congratulated Gudgeon for his fine effort. 'You have the strength and speed,' said Taylor to him, 'all you need to know is how to use them.'

"Taylor made two more appearances, the first in the semi-final of the Major Taylor Plate, quarter-mile scratch event, which he won easily. The second and last appearance of Major Taylor in this race came in the final heat in which he opposed Walker and Walne. Taylor led both of them home, although Walker made a good finish with him. An incident happened on this event which showed clearly Major Taylor's good sportsmanship. Owing to the slippery track Bobby Walne, soon after the starting of the semi-final, unfortunately fell. Immediately Major Taylor eased up and returned to the starting place. This action was especially recognized by the spectators.

"Major Taylor is all that he was represented to be. He has put up a phenominal record for the time he was here—beaten only once, in the semi-final of a scratch race, by MacDonald. The feat will stand to MacDonald's credit, as the defeat of Zimmerman stood to that of Walker, Parsons and Pither.

"But I still contend, allowing that Major Taylor is the champion, that our best men rode a good deal below their form, and though they may be unable to beat Taylor, the difference between the American and the Australians is not so great as it appears on the surface."

I was deeply impressed with the treatment accorded me by the sport loving public of Sydney in my first month's racing there. Likewise I was grateful for the fair treatment accorded me twice by the race track officials, the riders and the newspaper men of that metropolis. Incidentally I was pleased with my record on the track in that city, the weather being ideally suited to my training stunts, thereby enabling me to round into top form in an incredibly short space of time. I shall always recall most pleasantly my first stay in Sydney.

Ill, but On to Melbourne
(1903)

After six weeks' stay in Sydney, my schedule called for a series of races in that other great Australian city, Melbourne. I was especially anxious to be at my best when I showed there, but the fates had decreed otherwise. I contracted a bad cold on the last aggravated by the trip on the sleeper en route. The result was that I was confined to my bed for two weeks with an attack of influenza. However, I quickly recovered my form once I started training anew, and eventually made good before the people of Melbourne.

A Melbourne newspaper printed the following article on the after the race:

> Half a lap from home a roar went up, as Walne came with one of his old sprints on the outside. In an instant he was a couple of lengths in front of Chalmers and Pye, the American still being in the "pocket." "Taylor's beat, Taylor's done," the crowd roared. But now they saw the world's champion at his best. One hundred twenty yards from home, a change came over the scene. Taylor eased up, let Pye go on, and in an instant had jumped his machine on the outside of Pye. It looked a hundred to one against his chances of overhauling Walne, but in ten yards he had his machine moving as Victorians had never seen a bicycle travel before.

> The champion fairly flew. He passed Chalmers and Pye in a flash and then set down to take away Walne's two lengths' lead in 30 yards. It looked impossible but Major Taylor made it possible by one of the most marvelous sprints ever seen, for he came like a meteor, and beat Walne over the line by inches.

> Such a finish fairly staggered everyone present. It will be many long years before the American's phenomenal ride is forgotten.

> A week later, Taylor was back in Sydney for a series of matches, which ranged over several weeks. In the course of that series, the Major defeated both Don Walker and George Morgan, "the two fastest men in Australia that season," but wound up his triumphal stay in Sydney in a humiliating tumble.

It came in the final of the Oxford Plate, a special first-class, half-mile handicap. The crash happened just as I had taken the position which would have surely landed me in first money. Wilksch and Sutherland were the riders who figured in the mixup, as I crouched for my jump, and in a twinkling, the entire field was scrambled all over the track, but fortunately, no one was seriously injured.

In commenting on my tumble, one of the daily papers had this to say "Major Taylor's fall at the cycling sports last evening points to the fact that the same gang was determined to bump him regardless of all costs. It would be well to bear in mind that this was Major Taylor's first spill in his racing for the past two years."

One mile International
Championship, Adelaide, 1903

One Mile International
Championship, Adelaide, 1904

One Mile World's Professional
Championship, Montreal, 1899

Quarter Mile International
Championship, Sydney, 1903

Five Mile International
Championship, Melbourne, 1903

Successes in Adelaide

(1903)

Following the race meet on the Sydney Track I went to Adelaide, South Australia, to participate in a three-day meet in that city, under the auspices of the League of South Australian Wheelmen. I was tendered a wonderful reception upon my arrival in Adelaide in which officials of the city, promoters of the bicycle racing, and racers of the country took part.

On the opening day I participated in five events and was beaten only once. That was in the seventh heat of the Walne Stakes (half-mile handicap event) in which I made my début before the Adelaide audience, Thorne, who started from the forty yard mark nipping me at the tape. I won the final of the Walne Stakes and the Sir Edwin T. Smith Stakes, and was first in my heat in the Adelaide Wheel Race, besides winning the fourth heat of the Sir Edwin T. Smith Stakes (one-mile scratch event).

I quote the following account of the first day's racing from an Adelaide daily:

"A hearty round of applause indicated that Major Taylor was on the track to take his place in the last heat of the Walne Stakes, which served to introduce him to the Adelaide public. Taylor quickly picked up Gudgeon's rear wheel and in turn with Hopper they took the champion along in pursuit of the leaders. A hot pace was set by the front men who evidently wished to have something to say at the finish. Major Taylor left his colleagues at the score board and put in a splendid effort. He flashed past King within a few lengths of the tape, but Thorne was not to be overtaken and won by three-quarters of a length in :58 2/5. This was the fastest of the heats and allowed Taylor to start in the final.

"In the final heat Taylor and Walker were on scratch, Walne had ten yards handicap, Shean fifteen, Farley thirty, Mathais thirty-five, Thorne and Payne forty, and Scheps forty-five. Walker was off the mark before Taylor, but the latter soon caught him and took his wheel. Payne led by two lengths at the bell, and Walker was pacing the back men. He gradually overhauled the handicap men and then cut down Scheps and Thorne who had been leading. Walker was in the straight and had not commenced to sprint when Taylor set off at a great rate, and Walker, seeing the futility of chasing him, did not finish as he usually does. Taylor won by several lengths. Thorne was third.

The time was :57 1/5. Major Taylor was loudly applauded as he pedalled around the track afterwards.

"Twenty-seven riders answered the call for the four heats of the Sir Edwin T. Smith Stakes, a Blue Ribbon (half-mile scratch) race. The last heat brought out a representative field. Major Taylor was quickly off his mark, but was content to draw back and allow Forbes and Farley to set the pace, when the bell went Farley was leading

MAJOR TAYLOR, winner of the Sir Edwin Smith Stakes and Blue Ribbon

with Taylor on his wheel. Then came Forbes, Walne and Wilksch, Marshall having retired. Wilksch made his sprint near the score board, but Taylor was quickly in pursuit, making a magnificent sprint and crossing the line half a wheel in front of Wilksch, with Forbes in third place, and Walne trailing.

"The final of this event was by far the most exciting race of the evening. The contestants were Major Taylor, MacDonald, Wilksch, Sheehan, Mutton, Walker, Hopper, and Forbes. This race was notable for the splendid pacing. The field was close together at the bell when Taylor, Walker and MacDonald shot to the front. MacDonald went away with a magnificent sprint with Major Taylor pressing him hard, but he was not easily captured. The pair were on even terms, however, as they raced for the tape, but MacDonald was not able to match the American's final jump and lost the race by over a wheel's length. Meantime Walker had run himself into a pocket and

Wilksch and Morgan finished in front of him. The winner and
MacDonald received an ovation. Lady Smith invested Major Taylor
with the blue ribbon and salvos of cheers rent the air as the distinguished visitor circled the Oval with the coveted ribbon fluttering
in the breeze.

"There were fifty-four starters in the six heats of the Adelaide
Wheel Race, a two-mile handicap. There were eleven men in the
fourth heat, including Major Taylor, Morgan and Mutton, who were
on the back marks. The front markers were overhauled at the end
of the fourth lap with Taylor lying fourth. The American sprinted
at the stand and ran home lengths in front of Mutton, Nalty finishing
third. Major Taylor won his heat in the brilliant manner which
characterizes all of his riding. He declined an invitation to ride into a
pocket, and getting a clear run by the time the straight was reached,
he made hacks of his competitors, and won amid loud cheers.

"The final of the Adelaide Wheel Race was run on the third day
of the meet. The fourteen stars in the final were Major Taylor,
scratch, Forbes, twenty yards, Gudgeon and Mutton, forty,
Chalmers, seventy, Aunger, eighty, Filsell, ninety, Mathais, one hundred thirty, Hunt, one hundred forty, Thorne, one hundred fifty,
Schneider, two hundred ten, McAuliffe, three hundred, King, three
hundred fifty, Madden, three hundred sixty. A handicap of three
hundred yards in a two-mile race is considerable of an advantage, but
as Major Taylor is in splendid form it is thought he will be able to
lead the field home."

In the American Whirl (one-half-mile handicap) I won the third
heat in which I started ten yards behind scratch. I also won the third
heat of the Morgan Stakes (one-mile handicap) starting fifteen yards
behind scratch. I won the final of the Morgan Stakes, but finished
second to Scheps (forty-five yards) in the final of the American
Whirl. In the lap dash (one-third mile handicap) I started five
yards behind scratch and was defeated by Schnider (fifty yards) in the
first heat. The final of the lap dash was scheduled to be held the
closing day of the meet.

An account of the day's racing appeared in one of the Adelaide
newspapers:

"Hearty applause greeted the competitors as they appeared on the
track for their preliminary sprint. The brilliant American champion,
Major Taylor, received a cordial demonstration while he pedalled
around the track. What a master he is on the bicycle! A forceable
illustration of his wonderful sprinting powers was provided in the fact
that for the first time in the history of South Australian cycling, an
Adelaide gathering saw a rider start from behind scratch. Taylor
was heartily cheered as he took up that high position of professional

honor, the penalties inflicted by the handicapper called for magnificent work by the champion.

"In the American Whirl, a half-mile handicap event, Taylor was placed ten yards behind the scratch mark, but with a fine burst of speed he got home from Farley in the third heat. Scheps, the plucky South Australian rider, defeated the crack in the final, and was applauded for his splendid efforts.

"Fifteen yards behind the tape was Major Taylor's position in the Morgan Stakes, a first-class one-mile handicap, which he won by

MAJOR TAYLOR (with white waistband) in a Pocket

magnificent skill. The American was five yards behind scratch in his heat of the lap dash. But notwithstanding the wonderful sprint he made, Schneider, fifty-yard man, was not overtaken by him.

"In the third heat of the Morgan Stakes a splendid field was seen. Taylor riding from fifteen yards behind scratch had to bridge the gap of twenty yards to get on even terms with Don Walker, and one hundred five yards to make up on the limit man. From the start the champion with wonderful judgment and dash plowed his way skillfully through the fast field, and quickly picked up Walker. Gudgeon took the back-mark men up to the leading division, at the end of the first lap, with Taylor on his wheel. An easy pace set by Marshall brought them into the bell, when Champness took charge from Gudgeon, Morgan, Taylor, Mathais, Walker, Corbett, and Wilksch.

"The field opened out at the river end and Taylor promptly jumped into fourth place. At the northeastern turn the pace quickened. Taylor began his sprint rather earlier than usual and ducked his head at the score board. Coming up the stretch with a wonderful sprint he got across the tape comfortably from Morgan and Mathais.

"In that heat there was an attempt to pocket Major Taylor, but the American was on the 'qui vive.' A formidable field was left to battle for first place in the final. Taylor got away from mark smartly and dashed past Morgan and Forbes, and set off in hot pursuit for the leading bunch whom he captured at the southern turn, after a splendid effort. Farley and Aunger were out in front by themselves, while the second division consisting of Chalmers, Rolfe, Filsell, Mathais, and Taylor, now slowed down. Forbes pulled off the track and at the bell Farley and Aunger were well in the lead with

MAJOR TAYLOR winning the Morgan Stakes

Taylor, Rolfe, Mathais, Morgan, and Filsell in the order named. Morgan was unable to stick to the hot pace and retired from the race.

"Quickly Taylor shot out at the turn just entering the back stretch with Rolfe sticking to his rear wheel. The American flew past Chalmers and with a magnificent sprint crossed the tape six lengths ahead of Farley. Rolfe was third, Mathais and Aunger next. Major Taylor, the winner, rode a splendid race showing both superior speed and tactics, and was loudly cheered by the vast throng. The time was 2:04 4/5.

"Lap dashes always spell excitement and yesterday's events were no exception to the rule. In the first heat Major Taylor was placed five yards behind scratch, and he failed to catch Schneider, who started from the fifty yard mark. Taylor caught MacDonald and Burton and took them along at a merry clip, but he could not overtake Schneider. The American got a bad start, being a length behind with Burton, MacDonald, and Nalty in his wake. The final in this event will be decided on Saturday, Major Taylor's second place allowing him to enter that heat."

On the third and final day of the Carnival at Adelaide I won the lap dash final, starting five yards back of scratch, by two lengths from Hopper (twenty yards) with Walker (scratch) third, and King (80) fourth. I won my heat in the one-mile International Championship event and won the final with Don Walker and Chalmers finishing in that order, the time being 2:02 2/5. Then I won the final of the Adelaide Wheel Race in 4:09, the fastest time ever made in this race from scratch, and the final of the Walker Stakes, a mile and a half handicap.

Record breaking crowds attended the first two day's meeting at the Adelaide Track and the third and final day saw a gathering far in excess of the opening day's, there being twenty-two thousand present on this occasion. The Adelaide Wheel Race was the feature of the program. In this event, a two-mile handicap race, I had to concede the limit man three hundred sixty yards. There were fourteen riders in the event including the cream of Australia. There were forty starters in the Walker Stakes in which I started twenty yards behind scratch, the limit man having a handicap of two hundred fifty-five yards. In the International One-mile Championship event there were forty-four starters including Hopper, and all the Australian stars.

One of the Adelaide newspapers carried the following article relative to the final day's racing of the Carnival in that city:

"In addition to the two International victors, Major Taylor, the world's champion cyclist, and N. C. Hopper, the other American representative, who was formerly amateur champion of that country, were all the first class riders from every state in the Commonwealth and New Zealand.

"The final of the Lap Dash gave the spectators a treat, Major Taylor giving his most magnificent exhibition of sprinting to win the laurels. Only a rider of Taylor's caliber could have conceded eighty yards to such a strong handicap man as King, the race covering only one-third of a mile.

"Don Walker got away to a good start, and set a pace that took Taylor along for half the distance. Then the American ran high up on the bank and with a wonderful burst of speed jumped into the leading position and crossed the tape two lengths in front of Hopper with Walker and King following in that order.

"There was some excellent racing in the One-Mile International Championship Event. Major Taylor's success in the second heat was a foregone conclusion, and at no period of the race was he pressed for victory. In the final of this event Farley and Marshall furnished the pace right up to the bell. Major Taylor then took charge from Walker, Chalmers, Hopper, Burton, MacDonald, Payne and Morgan. Burton went out and Taylor trailed him. Gudgeon took Mac-

Donald up on the outside, but in the race for positions, these two faded away. Taylor settled down for his terrible sprint for the tape in the meantime, and won handily from Don Walker and Chalmers in the fast time of 2:02 2/5 amid tremendous cheering.

"The great Adelaide Wheel Race proved to be a magnificent test. Major Taylor had twenty yards to make up before catching Forbes, Gudgeon and Mutton, but he was up with them on the first lap. The

Final of the One-mile International Championship
Taylor   Walker   Chalmers
American   Australian   New Zealand

leaders, McAuliffe, King and Mutton assisted each other with clock-like regularity.

"Passing the judges for the first time around Taylor put in a magnificent sprint and caught the middle division at the first turn. This splendid effort practically decided the race, for the three leaders were within reach with three laps to go. On entering the home stretch preparatory to the final lap Madden had command, leading McAuliffe, King, Hunt and Aunger until Chalmers shot forward with Taylor lying on the outside. The success of the American was now assured, which was further demonstrated when he leaped to the lead followed by Gudgeon, Chalmers and Aunger. He jumped for the tape in front of Aunger, who was too smart for Chalmers, Schneider finishing fourth.

"Taylor was greeted with rounds of applause as he pedalled around the track. In the history of the Adelaide Wheel Race which was introduced as the premier event of the South Australian League in 1895, being contested annually ever since, only once previous to yesterday has it been won from scratch, Walne turning the trick in 1898. Incidentally up to yesterday's win by Major Taylor the Adelaide Wheel Race has always been won by an Australian rider, although contest-

Start of the Adelaide Wheel Race

ants have included international champions. Major Taylor's time, 4:09, is the fastest time ever made in this race from scratch, clipping :07 1/5 off the previous record which was made by Walne, when he won in 1898.

"Major Taylor stands head and shoulders above all the other competitors at the meeting just closed on the Adelaide track. He started in fourteen races, scoring eleven first's and three second's. The next best scorer was Don Walker with four first's, three second's, and two third's. Major Taylor's riding was a revelation in these three programs and nobody begrudges the brilliant sprinter the $1,250 in prize money he is taking away from this state. His superior judgment and faultless tactics were delightful to witness, and his sprints for the tape which he accomplished with a phenomenal burst of speed were far and away the finest efforts ever seen on an Adelaide track.

"The enterprise of the promoters in securing this hero of the world's cycle tracks was substantially rewarded, a credit balance of $2,350 resulting. Excluding the appearance money of $750, Major Taylor has won nearly $500 in prizes. His chief victories were the Walne Stakes, Morgan Stakes, Sir Edwin T. Smith Stakes, the Adelaide Wheel Race, the Lap Dash (1/3 mile), and the One-mile International Championship Event.

First Place, Old
Timers' Race, September, 1917

Half Mile International
Championship, Melbourne, 1904

Grand Circuit Champion, also Quarter, Half,
Third, and Two Mile Championships, 1900

European Racing Tour
April, May, June, 1901

Ten Mile International
Championship, Melbourne, 1904

Riding for a Fall
(1903–04)

From Australia, I sailed for France, a trip of a month. I raced in a meet in Paris the day after arrival, and naturally, being out of condition, I failed to win. But in the course of that third European tour, in the spring and summer of 1903, I won thirty two first places, twenty two seconds, nine third places, and two fourths.

As soon as I got home from Europe, an offer came to entice me into making another Australian tour, this time to include New Zealand.

The tour began in the late fall of 1903 and ran through the first months of 1904. I failed to win a majority of my races in New Zealand, for the first time in a foreign country, but did very well in Australia. However, I had long been pushing myself too hard. The pace of this tour was gruelling, and before it was over, I was becoming increasingly nervous and was nearing the edge of exhaustion.

My principal rivals were MacFarland and Iver Lawson. The latter was responsible for causing me to take the worst fall of my career, in a special match at Sydney. I was warned just before the last heat to be on the lookout for dirty work.

Being thus forewarned, and on my guard, I intended to go on the front coming up to the bell lap, in order to have the lead in the last lap. He would then have no chance of cutting in on me when he attempted to pass. No pacemakers being employed, I took the position on his rear wheel at the start, as a matter of tactics, which I held until just entering the back stretch of the last lap. Lawson was holding the inside, and in order to avoid any possible chance of interference or collision, in making my jump I gave him a wide berth in passing by, pulling to the center of the track. But before I could get quite past, he deliberately swung to the center of the track and dashed into me, bringing me down with a terrible crash. It looked like murder, but fortunately it was not, and although no bones were broken, I suffered the worst fall I ever had and was unable to ride for the next fortnight.

The two track officials who helped gather me up were horrified. One of them said that it was one of the most treacherous things he had ever seen.

The spot where I hit the track was examined by officials, trainers, riders, and the public, and the heavy marks left for a distance of fifteen feet or more were mute evidence against Lawson.

Home to Prejudice
(1904)

Leaving Australia for my home in Worcester, Massachusetts, I was accompanied by Don Walker, the Australian Champion. He had decided to compete for the World's Championship at London, England, in the fall.

Upon our arrival in San Francisco we decided to rest up for a few days before starting the long trip to my home town. However, we encountered a new epidemic of Colorphobia which made me completely revamp my plans and leave California at the earliest possible moment. Don Walker was completely nonplussed as he observed the treatment accorded to Mrs. Taylor and myself and our infant baby. We found it impossible to dine in the restaurants because the management drew the color line, and the same condition confronted us at the hotels.

We made the rounds of the city, only to be refused shelter and in many cases to be actually insulted. After having been refused service in one of the largest cafés in the city we drove vainly for hours to the different restaurants, and it was late in the afternoon before we could get any lunch. Walker was still game, however, ("as only bicycle riders can be,") and positively refused to eat unless we could all dine together.

As a last resort, I suggested a plan whereby we might be served. We drove to one of the big restaurants where we had been denied earlier in the day. My wife and baby and I remained in the carriage outside. Walker went inside, seated himself, and ordered lunch for three, saying that the others would be along shortly. When it was served he paid the check, stepped out, and brought us in. The waitresses were shocked, the manager was nonplussed; but he did not molest us. So we did have at least one square meal in San Francisco, but we left for the east on the midnight sleeper.

This was our greeting upon our arrival in America after the rousing send-off three weeks before in Australia. I could hardly blame Walker when he broke out indignantly in this fashion after seeing the treatment of Negroes as practiced in this country:—"So this is America about which you have been boasting in Australia. From what I have seen of it in the past few days, I cannot understand why you were in such a hurry to get back home here. Do you prefer to live in a country where you are treated like this than to live in my country where you are so well thought of, and where you are treated like a white man, and where many inducements were made you to return to live? I can't understand this kind of a thing." I was unable to explain conditions satisfactorily to him, the more I tried to smooth matters over the more incensed he became.

Floyd MacFarland's attitude toward me, both on and off the track, was one of genuine hatred and bitter prejudice. I found that he reflected the attitude of the people of California, his native state, whom I encountered. While I thought of a time a few years later when the opportunity presented itself for my wife and me to contribute our bit toward a fund for the suffering people of San Francisco following the dreadful earthquake and fire there. When the city lay in waste and ruins, and thousands of souls were suffering, our hearts were touched and we gave liberally to that same city where we were actually denied the privilege to buy and pay for food and hotel accommodations. The contrast was indeed great.

Notwithstanding these indignities, however, I bear no animosity toward the people of that state, nor toward Floyd MacFarland a native son, Orlando Stevens, Hardy Downing or any rider from that State or elsewhere. In fact I have never hated any rider that I ever competed against. As the late Booker T. Washington, the great Negro educator, so beautifully expressed it, "I shall allow no man to narrow my soul and drag me down, by making me hate him." In these well-chosen words, he voiced the true sentiment of the entire Negro race. We Negroes have our likes and dislikes, of course, but literally speaking, Negroes as a race do not hate white people or others, but white people as a race do hate Negroes because of color.

I am a Negro in every sense of the word and I am not sorry that I am. Personally, however, I have no great admiration for white people as a whole, because I am satisfied that they have no great admiration for me or my group as a whole.

We do have numerous white friends and sympathizers, however, such sterling characters as the world famed Rev. Dr. S. Parkes Cadman of Brooklyn, N. Y., and Mr. Julius Rosenwald of Chicago, Illinois, who have sacrificed everything for Negroes, and who are still doing all in their power to bring about a new era with regard to equal rights and the brotherhood of all mankind regardless of creed, race or color.

There are still thousands of white friends who have the utmost admiration and affection for certain colored people and who have laid the foundation stones for many successful and prosperous Negroes just as my friend Mr. Munger did for me. Without such sympathy and support America would be a far worse place for Negroes to live in than it is at the present time.

Mr. Munger by the way would never accept one single dollar of my prize winnings.

Not long after I reached my home in Worcester I suffered a collapse and narrowly averted a nervous breakdown. This was caused by my recent strenuous campaign in Australia augmented by the incidental worries of life. Upon the advice of my physician I cancelled my European engagement and sent word by Don Walker to my friends whom I felt he would meet on his trip to London, that I hoped to be back racing with them. Later I confirmed my cable to my agents on the Continent relative to the cancellation of my tour with a letter which contained my doctor's certificate, explaining my physical condition.

However, they insisted that I fulfill my contract with them, and interested the N. C. A. of this country in my case. Since I had been at odds with the last named organization on several occasions it naturally welcomed a chance to get back at me. Not many days elapsed before the N. C. A. had brought my suspension for failure to fulfill my agreement to ride in Europe.

Noting my indifference to the suspension the Continental promoters, who had arranged another racing tour for me, brought suit against me for breach of contract in the sum of $10,000. This action dragged through the courts for three years. Then Mr. Robert Coquelle, the French promoter, came over to see me personally. We got together settling the dispute in short order. It was a compromise arrangement, my part in it calling for my participating in a stipulated number of races on the Continent. The agreement was entirely satisfactory to me with one exception—Mr. Coquelle insisted that I break my hard fast rule by riding on Sundays on this tour. Feeling that had I not consented to ride on Sundays the suit against me would have been continued through court action as previously, I reluctantly and sorrowfully too, I confess, was obliged to break my rule "never to ride on the Sabbath." However, like many other men I felt I was caught in a "jam." I wanted the worry of the suit ended, and to be free from the chance of losing such a sum of money. It would be a big slice of my savings and when I thought of my wife and child I weakened, as better men have done, and signed the agreement that demanded my racing on Sunday.

My Great Comeback
(1908)

Following a three-year lay-off I resumed riding on the European tracks in 1908, staging a great comeback, and establishing two world's records which still stand.

I was accompanied on this trip by Mrs. Taylor and little Sydney who was now about four years old. Following my three-year lay-off

Serious Faithful Training Brought Perfect Results

after my collapse upon my return to my home in Worcester, Massachusetts, due to my strenuous 1904 tour of Australia, I resumed racing in Europe. In that space of time I had acquired thirty pounds, tipping the scales at exactly 198. For six weeks after my arrival in Paris I followed a systematic course of training which brought my weight down to my former sprinting figure. I felt I was in fairly good shape but later developments proved that I had taken weight off too quickly. The result was I rode poorly in my first six races, failing to win one.

Undismayed, however, at my failure to regain my wanted form, I continued my serious training routine, and in the last race of my first series I was moving along in fine style. In fact I was so pleased with my condition that I signed up for another series of races. I told my wife that I had fulfilled my obligation to the race promoters and would return to Worcester any time she said the word. However, I informed her also that I was just striking my winning form and felt if she would remain a while longer I would sign up for more races.

Physically Fit and "Rearing to Go"

I did not want to leave Europe until I had made a creditable showing against the new field of riders over there.

Time proved that I had sized my condition up accurately. After the talk with my wife I signed up for a half dozen more races winning all but one of them. Among those whom I turned back after I arrived at my best form on this tour, which was my fourth to the Continent, were Elleggarde, Jacquelin, Poulain, Friol, Dupre, Verri and Van den Born, all top-notchers, in fact I defeated several of them on a number of occasions.

In the meantime, I established two world's records on the Vele-

drome Buffalo Track, Paris, which have withstood the assault of
crack riders of the world in the intervening score of years. One of
them was :25 2/5 for the quarter mile, while the second was :42 1/5

Winning International Scratch Race, Paris

Winning the Race of Nations
Taylor   Dupre   Schilling
America   France   Holland

for the half mile. In both of these events I rode from a standing
start.

On this same track I won the "Race of Nations," one lap of the
track, establishing a record of 18, the fastest ever ridden on that
track. Others entered in that race were Rutt, Dupre, Jacquelin, Schilling and Friol. I also won a three-cornered match race with Friol
and Elleggarde here.

I recall a three-cornered match race between Elleggarde, Verri and
I at Marsailles which was perhaps the greatest three-cornered match

race that I ever won. In this race I won in straight heats, my margin
of victory varying from three to four lengths on each occasion. In
them I shook off my opponents in the last 200 yards, Elleggarde ad-
mitting later that in all our great match races he had never seen me
display the form I showed in this event.

In a match race with Verri, who at the time was champion of Italy,
I was at top form when we were called to the scratch for this feature

THE TAYLORS

number in a carnival in Milan. Although an excellent rider I managed to defeat him in the first heat by a full length before a tremendous
gathering. I was given a splendid ovation when we came out for the
second heat. I allowed Verri to lead until the bell lap, and did not
attempt to pass him until we were entering the back stretch. As I
started to jump past him, Verri deliberately brought me down with a
crash. I had to be carried to my dressing-room, and while I escaped
serious injury I was badly bruised and cut by the malicious act. The
track officials immediately disqualified Verri for one year.

Still another of my come-back races that season was with Friol, who
was then champion of France. The match took place on the famous
Parc des Princess track in Paris and I won in two straight heats. This
proved to be a great race. I found Friol a thorough sportsman with a
charming personality both on and off the track. Despite the fact that
I defeated him a number of times we remained the best of friends.

My last race of the season was the match with Poulain which I won. The next week Mrs. Taylor and myself and little daughter, Sydney, sailed for home.

As we pulled out of Cherbourg I could not help but reflect on the

SYDNEY on her Peugot, French Bike

great comeback I had staged on this trip after my enforced lay-off of three years. Most riders would have been discouraged and withdrawn from racing had they encountered the set backs that met my first half dozen efforts on this trip. However, I refused to be disheartened and kept on my serious training stunts until I showed a complete recovery of form before my schedule was completed.

Before I hit my stride on this trip the French sporting papers berated the promoters of the races which featured me, saying the public had rather remember me as I was in 1903 instead of the slowed-up rider I appeared in my first few starts this year. However, my managers had the last laugh when I finally arrived at my best form, and the newspapers were profuse in their apologies for rushing at their hasty conclusions.

On this, my last European tour, I won thirty-two first places, thirty second places, four third places and four fourth places in my four months' racing there.

I Retire at Thirty-Two

(1910)

After the season of 1910 I hung up my racing equipment. I felt that in my sixteen years of riding I had given my very best in every race that I started and that I was, therefore, entitled to a rest. I made this step despite the fact that in the closing days of that season I felt I was riding as fast as I ever had before. Recalling the great Zimmerman's advice to me as quoted in the preceding chapter, however, I decided to quit racing before second and third raters started to defeat me. During my heyday I defeated more than once every bicycle rider in this country in match races who was game enough to take me on including Butler, Bedell, Clark, Cooper, Elks, Eaton, Fenn, Fogler, Freeman, Lawson, Kimble and Kramer. Bald, Gardiner and Kiser drew the "color line."

I have been asked many times why I quit racing so early. Many of my friends criticized me for taking this step. Many of them felt that I should have remained in the sport until forced out, after the second and third raters had led me home time and again. They could not understand why I should retire from racing as physically fit as when I started.

Little did they realize the great physical strain I labored under while I was competing in these sixteen years of trying campaigns. Nor did they seem to realize the great mental strain that beset me in those races, and the utter exhaustion which I felt on the many occasions after I had battled under bitter odds against the monster prejudice, both on and off the track. In most of my races I not only struggled for victory, but also for my very life and limb. Only my dauntless courage and the indomitable fighting spirit I possessed allowed me to carry on in the face of tremendous odds. My trying experience on the tracks had exacted their toll from me, and I was certain the day had come for me to step out of the sporting limelight. Father Time was gaining on me.

I felt I had my day, and a wonderful day it was too. As I think back over those old days I have no retrospective regrets. Many of my good friends ask me if I would like to live the old days again. My answer in each case is "positively no." I have often wondered how long some of these friends would have carried on had they been in my place.

I was thirty-two years old when I retired having at that time spent more than half my life battling on the bicycle tracks. I cannot help but recall the many narrow escapes I had in my races, and shudder as I think of the many brave and outstanding riders who were killed or maimed for life in the pursuit of success on the track. I am grateful for having escaped serious injury in my races, and that I was able to leave the track in perfect physical condition.

I recollect that my good friend and team-mate, Harry D. Elkes of Little Falls, New York, as fine a motor paced rider as ever sat in a saddle, and the king of them all in his day, was instantly killed during a race on the Charles River Track, Cambridge, Massachusetts. Among other brave riders who lost their lives on the track were Joe Greibler, Myles, Aronson, Stafford, Nelson, McEchren, Leander, McLean, Mettling and the great Jimmie Michaels.

Floyd MacFarland was instantly killed in a quarrel over some trifling matter at the Vailesburg track where he had become manager after retiring from racing.

These athletes were killed on American tracks and I could recount a number of others who met a similar fate overseas. And still my friends wonder why I quit the game when I did!

Anybody that has followed bicycle racing knows that it is a hazardous pastime even when played fair. In my day I saw chances for fatal accidents, especially among followers of motor pacing, materially reduced through changes in the racing rules. One of the most notable of these common sense changes in the code book was the placing of the rollers on the motors back farther from the rear tire of motor pacing machines. This idea was adopted in order to place the rider so far back from the machine that he would have to combat greater wind resistance. Thus while he would be compelled to ride harder behind pace, his speed would also be retarded. Before the rollers were pushed back it was not an uncommon thing for a rider to be up so close to the motor that his head touched the back of the pacemaker. In another day I saw many other bad smash-ups on the track caused by the high speed of a rider. Friction caused the air in the tire to expand to such an extent that it burst, throwing the rider to serious injury or even death.

Upon being introduced to the late ex-President Roosevelt several years ago he grasped my hand with a hearty grip as he said:

"Major Taylor, I am always delighted to shake the hand of any man who has accomplished something worth while in life, and particularly a champion. I know you have done big things in your profession because I have followed your racing through the press for years with great pleasure. I was especially pleased and interested while you were racing abroad, defeating all the foreign champions, and carrying the Stars and Stripes to victory. Taking into consideration all the millions of human beings on the face of the earth, whenever I run across an individual who stands out as peer over all others in any profession or vocation, it is indeed a wonderful distinction, and

honor and pleasure enough for me." It certainly was a distinction and
a pleasure for me to hear such words from the great Colonel Roosevelt himself.

Notwithstanding the bitterness and cruel practices of the white bicycle riders, their friends and sympathizers, against me I hold no animosity toward any man.   This includes those who so bitterly opposed
me and did everything possible to injure me and prevent my success.
Many of them have died and when I am called home I shall rest easy,
knowing that I always played the game fairly and tried my hardest,
although I was not always given a square deal or anything like it.
When I am finally run off my feet and flattened by that mighty champion Father Time, the last thought to remain in my mind will be that
throughout life's great race I always gave the best that was in me.
Life is too short for a man to hold bitterness in his heart, and that is
why I have no feeling against anybody.

Concerning my retirement from the track a New York newspaper
printed the following paragraphs among others:

"A Picturesque Champion.   Peculiar Traits and Career of Major
Taylor Who Quits a Winner.   The retirement of Marshall W. Taylor, better known as 'Major' Taylor, from cycle racing, removes one
of the most striking and picturesque figures from that field of sport.
Taylor who announced his retirement last week after his return from
Europe, is the only Negro champion that cycle-racing has ever had, in
spite of the fact that there have been many colored riders.   But Major
Taylor is a true champion and has proven himself on the track to be
the peer, if not the master, of every white rider in the world.

"In 1897 Taylor, who was a professional at the outset, raced occasionally and gained some distinction.   He was rounding into form,
but on July 16 the following year, he shot to the fore in front of all
the big racing men, by winning the One-Mile National Championship
event at Philadelphia, defeating the great Eddie Bald, who was champion at the time, also Tom Cooper, who stood second to Bald, and the
whole field of professional cracks, the best in America.   Ever since he
has been quite conspicuous.

"He won the championship of America for the first time in 1898.
In 1899 he took the pace-following and proved himself as great at
middle distances as in sprinting.   He also won the sprint championship
again that season and again in 1900. His ability to win at long or short
distances is the one great distinguishing trait of Taylor's prowess.   It
is unusual and stamps him an exceptional rider.

"His physique from the points of symmetry and muscular development is one of the very best.   Perfectly proportioned, he has a figure
that excites unfailing admiration, though his skin is as black as ebony.
In 1901 Major Taylor was beaten for the championship title by Frank

Kramer, but there was much complaint of unfair treatment that he received on the track, as all the other men being opposed to him were practically combined against him in every race.

"Last year Taylor returned late from abroad and entered the championships on the circuit when Frank Kramer had a lead of 31 points to his credit.   Taylor scored a number of victories over him, but his unpopularity with the other riders was such that he lost heart and fre-

Bell Lap, Old Timers' Race—Won by Major Taylor, Vailesburg, 1917

quently failed to compete, and finally resolved to compete for the title no more.   He went abroad last fall and remained in Australia all winter proving himself the best of all there.   He went to Europe again in the spring where he again defeated all the best riders in Europe including Elleggarde, the great Danish rider, who held the World's Championship title.   A couple of years ago Major Taylor held many American records, and his mile record of 1:19 stood for several years, but the figures have all been changed since he quit riding in this country."

The sporting editor of a newspaper in Sydney, Australia, published the following article relative to my retirement:

"Great Praise for Major Taylor.   Sydney, New South Wales Paper Credits Him With Being Wonder of the World.

"Major Taylor recently received a copy of the 'Referee,' a Sydney, Australia paper which gives the former World's champion a measure of praise not often dealt out to an athlete. The 'Referee' in speaking of Taylor's retirement says:

" 'The retirement of Major Taylor is quite an event in the cycling world, that is, presuming the report is correct, for it is no uncommon thing for a star to be retiring annually.

" 'But in Major Taylor's case the probabilities are that he has really had enough of the racing game. No doubt he could keep on successfully for another year or two longer but his retirement would be compulsory in the near future, and as he had made considerable money, and has had the good sense to take care of it, he can well afford to leave the dangerous game of racing alone.

" 'It is not likely, however, that we shall look on his like again for some time. In my opinion he was the greatest racing cyclist the world has ever seen, and, as I pointed out only recently, that his wonderful record was gained under very often the most adverse conditions; for he was hustled and hated as only a colored person can be by the superior men in God's country; and he did not always receive fair play on the Continent, or even here in Australia.

" 'Had he not been a marvel of pluck, speed, and skill, he would not only have been the world's very best, but he would have either been killed outright or disabled years ago. Cycle-racing is a very dangerous game, even under ordinary conditions, but when deliberate fouling is introduced, it is then too risky for even the most daring, yet Major Taylor often had to chance it.

" 'Like all other mortals, however, he had his failings, but he was one of the straightest athletes that ever entered the arena. Although his absence will be a great loss to the sport, all admirers of a great cyclist and an honorable one will wish him the very best of luck for the future.' "

The Value of Good Habits
and Clean Living

In closing I wish to say that while I was sorely beset by a number of white riders in my racing days, I have also enjoyed the friendship of countless thousands of white men whom I class as among my closest friends. I made them in this country and all the foreign countries in which I competed. My personal observation and experiences indicate to me that while the majority of white people are considerate of my people, the minority are so bitter in their race prejudice that they actually overshadow the goodwill entertained for us by the majority.

Now a few words of advice to boys, and especially to those of my own race, my heart goes out to them as they face life's struggles. I can hardly express in words my deep feeling and sympathy for them, knowing as I do, the many serious handicaps and obstacles that will confront them in almost every walk of life. However, I pray they will carry on in spite of that dreadful monster prejudice, and with patience, courage, fortitude and perseverance achieve success for themselves. I trust they will use that terrible prejudice as an inspiration to struggle on to the heights in their chosen vocations. There will always be that dreadful monster prejudice to do extra battle against because of their color.

It is my thought to present the facts to the rising generation of my people without coloring or shading them in the least. In a word I do not want to make their futures appear more rosy than they will be, nor do I wish to discourage them in the slightest degree as they face life and its vicissitudes. My idea in giving this word to the boys and girls of my race is that they may be better prepared than I was to overcome these sinister conditions.

I might go on discussing this subject at great length, but after all is said, done, and written, my own book of experiences will best show what these obstacles are, and how I managed to overcome them to some extent. I would advise all youths aspiring to athletic fame or a professional career to practice clean living, fair play and good sportsmanship. These rules may seem simple enough, but it will require great morale and physical courage to adhere to them. But if carried out in the strict sense of the word it will surely lead to a greater success than could otherwise be attained. Any boy can do so who has will power and force of character, even as I did, despite the fact that no one of my color was able to offer me advice gained through experience as I started up the ladder to success. In a word I was a pioneer, and therefore had to blaze my own trail.

I would like to cite an instance which proves the efficacy of clean living on the part of an athlete coupled with the inspiration received from a champion which go a long way to making a champion. Realizing full well that fine condition and confidence will not in themselves make a champion, it is my belief, however, that they are essential factors. Of course an athlete must have ability to reach the top, but many who have ability and who do not live clean lives never have and never will be champions for obvious reasons.

I recall that on my first trip to Europe in 1901 I saw a French youth, whose name was Poulain, ride in an amateur event at Nantes, France. He was very awkward as he rode about the track, but something about him caught my eye, and I became interested in him at once. At the close of the race I made several suggestions to him, adjusting his pedals, and handle bars, and giving him some advice on how to train. I stressed clean living upon him, and told him in conclusion that if he trained carefully and lived a clean life, I would predict that some day he would beat all the amateurs of Europe and the professionals as well.

When I returned to France in 1908 this same Poulain, who in the meantime had won the amateur and professional championships of France, defeated me in a special match race. Imagine my surprise at the conclusion of this event when my conqueror told me who he was. The laugh certainly was on me. I did manage to bring him into camp, however, after I reached my best form.

I know that a good many champions have entertained the thought that the more they discourage youngsters, the longer they would reign. However, this theory never impressed me, and I always made it a point to give youths the benefit of my experience in bicycle racing. I do this for a two-fold reason. First of all it was through the kindness of Louis D. (Birdie) Munger, now of Springfield, Massachusetts, that I became inspired and rode to American and world's championships. Secondly I always felt that good sportsmanship demanded that a champion in any line of sport should always be willing to give a helping hand to all worthy boys who aspire to succeed him.

When I was enjoying my heyday on the track I received hundreds of letters from youths asking for suggestions as to how to become a bicycle champion. As far as was practical I answered them personally, but as I was campaigning at the time it was physically impossible for me to pen notes to all of them. Naturally this procedure took considerable of my spare time, but I willingly did it as I realized and appreciated the kindness extended to me by Mr. Munger and many other good friends, which made it possible for me to lay the foundation for my remarkable career covering sixteen years on the track.

Modesty should be typical of the success of a champion. It always seemed to me that a real champion while possessing self-confidence on the eve 'of a race never became conceited. On the other hand I have seen mediocre riders who fairly breathed conceit in advance of the race in which they were entered. I have also noticed that when a rider who had confidence in his ability was defeated, after doing his level best to win, always received an ovation from the gathering. The reverse was true in regard to the conceited rider, regardless of how hard he tried in a race. The public has long since drawn a fine line between self-confidence and conceit. Sport lovers know that when they see a real champion he is going about his work in a businesslike manner. He does not have time nor the inclination to scorn his competitors, but rides against everyone of them as though he were his superior, with the result that the public is sure to witness a fine performance every time he starts.

Countless athletes have written articles relative to physical training which they deem essential to championship form. Many of them have dealt with the subject in a scientific manner, some foisted pet theories on their readers, while others advocated practical methods. I do not believe there is any royal road to success as an athlete any more than there is to others in everyday life. It is my thought that clean living and a strict observance of the golden rule of true sportsmanship are foundation stones without which a championship structure cannot be built. In a word I believe physical fitness the keynote of success in all athletic undertakings. Fair play comes second only to that factor, and I believe it should be impressed upon all boys from their marble-playing days.

Last, but not least, I would urge all boys aspiring to an athletic career to strictly observe the rules of the game, to practice good sportsmanship and fair-play, and also to be able to abide by an unfavorable decision with the same grace that they accept a victory. To these ideals which were instilled in me when I was a youth, I attribute in a large degree the success that was mine on the bicycle tracks of the world.

The moral turpitude of the boys of today appears to center in their failure to concentrate on any particular objective long enough to obtain their maximum results.

Clean living is the cardinal principle in the lives of the world's greatest athletes, as the phenomenal performances of these outstanding characters will obviously show.

In marathon running the marvelous Clarence Demar is a model in this respect. As a jockey the famous Earl Sande is another, in tennis the redoubtable William ("Bill") Tilden and the brilliant Helen Wills excel; while in golf Bobby Jones, the greatest golfer of all time, and the invincible Glenna Collette, the peer of women golfers, are exemplary; in wrestling the mighty Zybesco, Joe Stecher, and Ed. Lewis, the present champion, rule.

In baseball the late Christy Mathewson, Walter Johnson, Tyrus Cobb, and the "King of Swat" Babe Ruth, are splendid examples, and in prize fighting the late champion "Tiger" Flowers, Benny Leonard, the erstwhile champion Jack Dempsey, and the present champion Gene Tunney are exponents. In bicycle racing the former champion Frank Kramer, and Willie Spencer, the present title holder, lead all others. As an aviator the celebrated Col. Charles Lindberg is the shining example.

As a reward of their clean living and good habits these great stars have been able to withstand the rigorous test of stamina and physical exertion and have thus successfully extended their most remarkable careers over a period of many strenuous years.

Notwithstanding these facts, however, they must some day fade out of the picture altogether, even as I. They must some day bow to that perennial old champion, Father Time, even as I, for *Time* eventually wins.

A DOZEN DON'TS

Don't try to "gyp."
Don't be a pie biter.
Don't keep late hours.
Don't use intoxicants.
Don't be a big bluffer.
Don't eat cheap candies.
Don't get a swelled head.
Don't use tobacco in any form.
Don't fail to live a clean life.
Don't forget to play the game fair.
Don't take an unfair advantage of an opponent.
Don't forget the practice of good sportsmanship.

FINIS

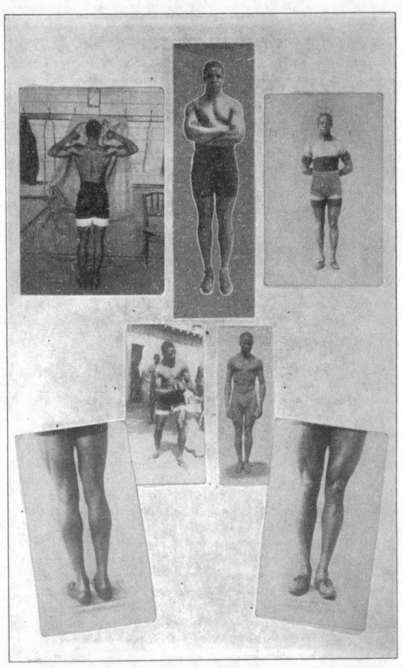

Clean Living and Serious Training are necessary for the Perfect Condition shown
Above. It has often been said by Leading Sports Writers that Major
Taylor's Legs were the best ever developed for Bicycle Riding